C0-ASR-458

JAPAN'S WAR ECONOMY

Japan's economic growth in the wake of the Second World War was extraordinarily rapid. The August 1945 surrender is often taken as the starting point for studies of this growth, but it is now accepted that a continuous line of economic development may be traced from the pre- to postwar periods. *Japan's War Economy* explores the substantial and dynamic innovations of the wartime era, identifying this period as the most influential for the country's postwar economic structure.

Erich Pauer and a team of leading Japanese and German scholars discuss important aspects of the Japanese wartime economy, including:

- ideological background
- the Japanese 'planned economy'
- technical mobilization
- women and the war economy
- socio-economic change
- food shortages, the black market and economic crime
- national policy companies
- financial reforms

This fascinating work clearly reveals the influence of the German quest for *Lebensraum* and the stunning success of subjecting the economy to national goals. *Japan's War Economy* will prove essential reading for economists, historians and political scientists working in this growing area of research.

Erich Pauer is Professor of Japanese society and Japanese History at the Philipps University of Marburg, Germany. He has published on Japanese economic history, history of technology in Japan and German–Japanese technology transfer.

ROUTLEDGE STUDIES IN THE GROWTH ECONOMIES OF ASIA

1 THE CHANGING CAPITAL MARKETS OF EAST ASIA
Edited by Ky Cao

2 FINANCIAL REFORM IN CHINA
Edited by On Kit Tam

3 WOMEN AND INDUSTRIALIZATION IN ASIA
Edited by Susan Horton

4 JAPAN'S TRADE POLICY
Action or reaction?
Yumiko Mikanagi

5 THE JAPANESE ELECTION SYSTEM
Three analaytical perspectives
Junichiro Wada

6 THE ECONOMICS OF THE LATECOMERS
Catching-up, technology transfer and institutions in Germany, Japan and South Korea
Jang-Sup Shin

7 INDUSTRIALIZATION IN MALAYSIA
Import substitution and infant industry performance
Rokiah Alavi

8 ECONOMIC DEVELOPMENT IN TWENTIETH CENTURY EAST ASIA
The international context
Edited by Aiko Ikeo

9 THE POLITICS OF ECONOMIC DEVELOPMENT IN INDONESIA
Contending perspectives
Edited by Ian Chalmers and Vedi Hadiz

10 STUDIES IN THE ECONOMIC HISTORY OF THE PACIFIC RIM
Edited by Sally M. Miller, A. J. H. Latham and Dennis O. Flynn

11 WORKERS AND THE STATE IN NEW ORDER INDONESIA
Vedi R. Hadiz

12 THE JAPANESE FOREIGN EXCHANGE MARKET
Beate Reszat

13 EXCHANGE RATE POLICIES IN EMERGING ASIAN COUNTRIES
Edited by Stefan Collignon, Jean Pisani-Ferry and Yung Chul Park

14 CHINESE FIRMS AND TECHNOLOGY IN THE REFORM ERA
Yizheng Shi

15 JAPANESE VIEWS ON ECONOMIC DEVELOPMENT
Diverse paths to the market
Kenichi Ohno and Izumi Ohno

16 TECHNOLOGICAL CAPABILITIES AND EXPORT SUCCESS IN ASIA
Edited by Dieter Ernst, Tom Ganiatsos and Lynn Mytelka

17 TRADE AND INVESTMENT IN CHINA
The European experience
Edited by Roger Strange, Jim Slater and Limin Wang

18 TECHNOLOGY AND INNOVATION IN JAPAN
Policy and Management for the 21st Century
Edited by Martin Hemmert and Christian Oberländer

19 TRADE POLICY ISSUES IN ASIAN DEVELOPMENT
Prema-chandra Athukorala

20 ECONOMIC INTEGRATION IN THE ASIA PACIFIC REGION
Ippei Yamazawa

21 JAPAN'S WAR ECONOMY
Edited by Erich Pauer

22. INDUSTRIAL TECHNOLOGY DEVELOPMENT IN MALAYSIA
Industry and Firm Studies
Edited by K. S. Jomo, Greg Felber and Rajah Rasiah

23. TECHNOLOGY, COMPETITIVENESS AND THE STATE
Malaysia's Industrial Technology Policies
Edited by K. S. Jomo and Greg Felber

24. CORPORATION AND KOREAN CAPITALISM
Edited by Dennis L. McNamara

JAPAN'S WAR ECONOMY

Edited by Erich Pauer

London and New York

First published 1999
by Routledge
11 New Fetter Lane, London EC4P 4EE

Simultaneously published in the USA and Canada
by Routledge
29 West 35th Street, New York, NY 10001

Typeset in Garamond by
The Florence Group, Stoodleigh, Devon
Printed and bound in Great Britain by
Biddles Ltd, Guildford and King's Lynn

British Library Cataloguing in Publication Data
A catalogue record for this book is available
from the British Library

Library of Congress Cataloguing in Publication Data
Japan's War Economy / edited by Erich Pauer.
Includes bibliographical references and index.
1. Japan–Economic policy. 2. World War 1939–1945 – Economic aspects – Japan. 3. Economic history – 1918–1945. I. Pauer, Erich,
HC462.8.J379 1999

330.952′033–dc21 98–4048

ISBN 0–415–15472–3

CONTENTS

FIGURES

TABLES

CONTRIBUTORS

Itō Osamu, born in 1956, is a Professor at Kanagawa University, Faculty of Economics, Yokohama, Japan. His most recent publication is *Nihon-gata kinyū no rekishi-teki kōzō* (The historical structures of the Japanese financial system) (University of Tōkyō Press, 1995).

Ortrud Kerde is Junior Lecturer of Japanese Politics at the Center for Japanese Studies, Philipps-University of Marburg, Germany and is currently completing a study on corruption and reform in Japanese politics (Ph.D. thesis). She is also doing research on Japanese party politics and party finance.

Regine Mathias is Professor of Japanese History, Faculty of East Asian Studies, Ruhr-University, Bochum, Germany. She has published on labour in Japanese coal mines, German–Japanese relations and on *shokugyō fujin* (female employees). She is currently doing research into the development of the new middle class and modern life styles in prewar Japan.

Nakamura Takafusa, born in 1925, Professor Emeritus of the University of Tōkyō, has also served as Director-General of the Economic Research Institute in Japan's Planning Agency (1977–9), has also taught at Ochanomizu University and is currently professor at *Tōkyō Eiwa Joshi Gakuin* (Tōkyō Eiwa Women's University), Tōkyō, Japan. He has published numerous books and articles in Japanese and English on various aspects of the Japanese economy and economic history.

Okazaki Tetsuji is a Professor at Tōkyō University, Faculty of Economics, Tōkyō, Japan. He has published on various aspects of the structure and working of the planned economy in wartime Japan. His current interests include the development of the Japanese economic system from the historical perspective. He is the co-author of *Gendai Nihon keizai shisutemu no genryū* (Historical origins of the contemporary Japanese economic system) (Nihon Keizai Shinbun-sha, 1993).

Silke-Susann Otto works as a Junior Lecturer of Japanese Economy and Business at the Center for Japanese Studies, WHU Koblenz, Otto Beisheim Graduate School of Management (Germany). Her main fields of research are Japanese accounting and auditing, controllership and corporate governance in Japan. She is currently completing a study on controllership functions and their organization in Japanese corporations (Ph.D. thesis).

Erich Pauer, born in 1943, is Professor of Japanese Society and Japanese History, Center for Japanese Studies, Philipps-University of Marburg, Germany. He has published on Japanese economic history, history of technology in Japan and German–Japanese technology transfer. He is the editor of *Papers on the History of Industry and Technology in Japan* (3 vols, Marburg 1995).

Anke Scherer is a Junior Lecturer at the Japanese History Section, Faculty of East Asian Studies, Ruhr-University, Bochum, Germany. Her interests include modern social history and historical anthropology. She is currently researching the impact of tourism on the development of Japanese resorts.

PREFACE

Until the beginning of the 1980s, studies on the Japanese social and economic situation during the Second World War were rather scarce, even in Japan itself. Academic research was to some extent hampered by the lack of adequate sources. Researchers interested in this period therefore collected prewar and wartime materials, and published them in several large series (for this see the short bibliographical notes at the end of this volume). Despite this situation, a few economic historians, including Nakamura Takafusa and Hara Akira, wrote extensively on the Japanese war economy, thereby influencing younger scholars. As a result, the situation changed rapidly during the 1980s and even faster in the 1990s. Japan's wartime economy and its impact on postwar economic development became topics of growing interest to scholars in Japan. Nowadays a large number of books and articles on the war economy and related subjects are available in Japan. Several recent publications have also dealt with the impact of the war economy on Japan's postwar economic development.

Outside Japan, problems of Japanese wartime economic development were rarely taken up by economic historians or scholars of Japanese Studies. Few researchers were interested in this subject and in the results of Japanese research. Even the question of how prewar and wartime developments had influenced Japanese economic development after the war remained almost undiscussed in Western scientific circles. There, many upheld the view that Japanese postwar development started from scratch after the surrender in August 1945. Consequently nearly all studies either end or start with this year, and a clear line is drawn between the pre- and postwar periods – even though this made it difficult to explain postwar Japan's stunningly rapid economic growth.

The reader must therefore understand that Japan's surrender did not bring Japan's economy to a complete standstill. Even though Japan surrendered in 1945, there was still a Japanese government headed by a prime minister, the whole administration network remained almost unchanged for a while, and the whole basket of laws and ordinances governing the planned economy changed only slowly. Despite massive destruction, especially in manufacturing industries, the economic structure was damaged only to a certain degree, and industrial work soon restarted. The Ministry of Munitions managed to reorganize itself immediately after the surrender, again becoming the Ministry of Commerce and Industry before the official arrival of the occupation forces (Johnson 1982: 172). In various areas the transition from wartime to the postwar period thus went quite smoothly, and ensuing economic developments incorporated many features originating in wartime. Economic life continued beyond the end of the war, and a closer look into wartime and prewar economic structures can provide a better understanding of Japan's postwar recovery and present-day economic system.

As the Japanese language still poses an obstacle, Japanese research often remains unknown outside Japan, or it becomes known only belatedly and in a very selective way. This may be one reason that comparative studies by Western scholars often ignore the Japanese example. To close this gap is not an easy task, and it surely will take the efforts of many scholars to reach a level where a broader knowledge about Japanese history is a matter of course.

The articles in this volume cannot provide a comprehensive view of the now-common understanding of prewar and wartime economic structures in Japan and their implications for postwar developments. But they can give an insight into a changing view of the period, which draws a line of continuous development from the prewar to postwar era, and regards wartime changes as most influential for the postwar structures.

Most of the articles (by Nakamura, Kerde, Itō, Mathias, Otto, Pauer) in this volume are based on papers given in a section on Japan's War Economy at the Eleventh International Economic History Congress in Milan in September 1994. The papers have all since been rewritten or revised and enlarged. The article by Okazaki has been translated especially for this book from the Japanese original, *Dai-ni sekai taisen-ki no kinyū-seido kaikaku to kinyū shisutemu no henka* in *Discussion Paper Series* 94–J–21 of the Research Institute for the Japanese Economy, Faculty of Economics, University of Tōkyō, November 1994. Pauer's article on 'A New Order for Japanese Society' is a rewritten and enlarged version of an article on 'Neighbourhood Associations and Food Distribution in Japanese Cities in World War II', in Bernd Martin and Alan S. Milward (eds), *Agriculture and Food Supply in the Second World War*, Ostfildern: Scripta Mercaturae Verlag, 1985. The article by Scherer has been especially written for this book.

Even though the articles in this volume deal with topics rarely addressed in Western languages, there still remain many open questions on Japan's war economy. To mention just a few: there is a lack of comprehensive studies on the social implications of the war economy, and the overseas dimension of economic policy in the Greater East Asia Co-Prosperity Sphere. Wartime economy and raw material supply is another topic to be taken up, especially with regard to the 'usefulness' to Japan of the colonies and the puppet state of Manchukuo. And last but not least, the question of conversion from civilian to armament industries during the war, and the (re-)conversion from armament to civilian industries after the war has hardly been tackled at all. It is hoped that this volume will help to stimulate the debate about this crucial period of Japanese economic and social development, and bring it from one small group at the Milan congress to a wider public.

Erich Pauer
Marburg, December 1997

ACKNOWLEDGEMENTS

I am very grateful to Paul Mundy Ph.D. for numerous comments on the manuscripts and for editing the English language.

NOTE

Japanese words are transcribed according to the standard Hepburn romanization. Japanese names are given in the normal Japanese order, i.e., family name first followed by the given name.

INTRODUCTION

Erich Pauer

The Japanese economy reached a state of maturity during the First World War. Because of the war, the European powers had to withdraw from their East and Southeast Asian markets, thereby leaving room for Japanese trade. Improving foreign trade boosted Japanese manufacturing industries, and by 1920, Japan could be called an industrialized state.

But the wartime boom ended in 1920. Economic problems led to a financial crisis, with bankruptcies in the banking sector. Consolidation of the economy was hampered by the great Kantō earthquake in 1923, which destroyed a number of company headquarters in the Tōkyō–Yokohama region. Further blows came with the financial crisis of 1927 and the world economic depression in 1929.

Difficulties arose within the Japanese economy not only in the manufacturing sector but also in agriculture. Landlord–tenant disputes became common in several regions in the 1920s. In the current widely accepted ideological environment, these problems were seen as 'contradictions' in Japanese economic development. They fuelled discussion within Japanese intellectual circles (influenced by Marxian ideas) on the nature of Japanese capitalism. As a result, in the 1930s they supported the development of economic tools such as 'planning', which was seen as a way to overcome the contradictions (see the chapter by Nakamura in this volume).

A debate about the reasons of an apparent 'backwardness' of Japanese capitalism, in comparison to the Marxist model of capitalist development, emerged in the 1920s. This was a decade when intellectuals were heavily influenced by the Russian Revolution and by social tensions in Japan, with class antagonism reaching a peak during the Great Depression in 1929. The discussants were divided fundamentally into two 'factions', the *Rōnō-ha* (Labour and Farmer Faction), and the *Kōza-ha* (Lectures Faction). The factions differed in their view and interpretation of social change and economic development in Japan. The 'Labour and Farmers Faction' assumed that the bourgeois revolution had already taken place; it regarded the Meiji Restoration in 1868 as the end of feudalism in Japan (therefore calling it the 'Meiji revolution') and as the start of fully fledged capitalist development. The 'Lectures Faction', on the other hand, believed that the Meiji Restoration simply developed a feudal land system under an absolutist monarchy, that a bourgeois revolution was still ahead and was necessary for Japan, and that feudal (or at least semi-feudal) relations within society prevented Japan from developing.

Although most of these discussions were confined to academic circles, some of the ideas spread outside. The Russian Revolution was viewed with sympathy by intellectuals not only in Western countries but also in Japan. As neither Marx nor Engels wrote in detail about the economic system that was to follow the proletarian revolution, people were interested in the newly installed economic mechanisms in the Soviet Union. Planning the economy promised to meet the people's wishes, but a 'planned economy' was not yet synonymous with a 'socialist economy'.

In Japan, other developments coincided with the spread of ideas for overcoming the capitalist economy. Military circles centring around Ishiwara Kanji[1] discussed ideas that global antagonisms ultimately would lead to a big 'Final War' (*sekai saishū sensō*) between Japan and the United States. Ishiwara argued that Japan therefore had to prepare itself, especially by taking economic measures for 'planning' for such a war. The Japanese army had the opportunity to try out its ideas of a 'planned economy' after 1931, when the Manchurian incident led to the occupation of Manchuria and northern China, providing the army with a big playground for their economic development ideas. For 'planning' the military also looked with some sympathy at the neighbouring Soviet Union. While military planners were heavily influenced by Soviet planning, government planners also favoured such methods (Okazaki 1993: 184).

'Planning' and a 'planned economy' (*keikaku keizai*) became more and more a focus of discussion in the late 1920s and early 1930s, in both military circles and in politics. The crisis after the worldwide depression led even liberal thinkers such as Minobe Tatsukichi[2] to a harsh critique of political parties and politicians. As party politicians – in his opinion – lacked the knowledge to solve the enormous political and economic difficulties Japan was facing, specialists were necessary. Difficult decisions could obviously not be left to politicians sitting in the Diet, so Minobe also questioned the role of the parliament in such difficult times. As most of the laws already had been made by specialists – mostly bureaucrats – he saw the parliament as degenerating into a mere voting machine without deeper insights. And because parliament had lost its decision-making power, specialists were further discouraged from entering politics.

Minobe's criticism shows why decision-making went to other bodies – to the ministries and their bureaucrats – who implemented policies and built up structures according to their own ideas. The campaign to establish a network of small, local manufacturers, bound together in so-called 'production unions' (*sangyō kumiai*), is an example of how Ministry of

Agriculture bureaucrats attempted to implement their ideas through non-parliamentary means. Therefore the militarization of life in the early 1930s and the growing influence of ideas favoured by military planners were not least caused by the vacuum left by the politicians. Furthermore, bureaucrats in the 1930s also showed a strong willingness to influence economic development through planning.

So, it is no wonder that the idea of the 'national defence state' (*kokubō kokka*), which was developed by military planners in the 1930s, also found strong support among civil servants in various ministries and government bodies, and came to play an important role in the 1930s. In principle, such a 'national defence state' required state control over the economy.

The basic points of an overall national reform as conceived by Ishiwara Kanji and formulated by Miyazaki Masayoshi (the 'brain' of economic planning in Manchuria; for details see Kobayashi 1995) were the substitution of the Cabinet by a national leadership body (named *kokumu-in*), the nationalization of key industries, the establishment of a new political mass organization, and the assumption of government leadership by the military. The plans aimed at self-sufficiency of Japan within an economic bloc in East Asia (paralleling ideas of the *Großraumwirtschaft* advocated in Germany and – though in different terms – by other Western nations). Although such plans went too far even for the 'reformist bureaucrats', these bureaucrats nevertheless followed the military planners' ideas in much of what they did.

Nakamura Takafusa (in the first chapter in this volume) discusses the topics of ideology and reality of 'planning' as well as of continuity and discontinuity between the wartime and postwar periods. He points out that the ideas of a centrally planned economy were brought into existence in the 1930s and were based on Soviet ideas. This can be shown by writings of the military personnel mentioned above, and of members of the Shōwa Research Association (*Shōwa kenkyū-kai*, the brains trust of Prime Minister Konoe Fumimaro in the late 1930s).

Another point has so far been almost completely neglected in discussions on Japan's 'planning': the political rapprochement between Germany and Japan after 1936 paved the way for the ideas of economists who influenced the Nazi economic model. These ideas were taken up by government ('reformist') bureaucrats, one of their main representatives being Mōri Hideoto, a Ministry of Finance official (see the chapter by Ortrud Kerde on the ideological background of the war economy in this volume). In other fields, too, such as the state control of labour, Japanese civil servants became fascinated by Nazi ideas, and designed a new system for Japan according to the German model they admired (for details see Garon 1987: 213–18).

Eventually, military developments (the outbreak of the Sino–Japanese War in 1937) and the demand for armaments resulted in stricter state control of the economy. The economic order brought about after Prime

Minister Konoe introduced his 'New Order' in various political and economic (and even technical and scientific) policies in 1940, is frequently referred to as the 'controlled economy' (*tōsei keizai*). The ideas chosen to justify growing government intervention in the economy differed depending on the background of the respective decision-makers (as shown in the contributions by Nakamura and Kerde in this volume). Thus it should not be considered contradictory that part of the Shōwa Research Association and the military frequently referred to Soviet ideas of a planned economy, whereas the 'reformist bureaucrats' were predominantly influenced by the German 'historical school' of the nineteenth century and Nazi economic doctrines. Various ideologies and economic ideas existed simultaneously in Japan and were sometimes even combined in order to rationalize the restructuring of the economy.

A growing government intervention in the free market economy is a common feature of different countries in wartime. This happened in the United States (as illustrated by the New Deal), Britain, in Germany and Italy of course, and nearly all other combatants in the Second World War. Japan, too, is no exception. But two points have to be stressed in Japan's case:

- Government intervention – or 'control' (*tōsei*) as it was officially called, because 'planning' was connected with Soviet communist ideas, which at the end of the 1930s were looked at with suspicion – did not start at the eve of the war.
- 'Planning' and 'control' not only led to ideas for government intervention in the free-market economy, but also induced steps aimed at overcoming the Japanese capitalist economic system as a whole.

The first move for possible government intervention was made in 1918, when the Japanese government – drawing on the knowledge of Germany's experiences during the First World War – passed a law giving it the authority to intervene during an emergency. A further step to strengthen government control can be seen in the Major Industries Control Law (*Jūyō sangyō tōsei-hō*), enacted in 1931 and based on the German cartel law. Aiming at legalizing cartels and giving industries a means of 'self-control', it became a tool for strengthening government influence over industry. In the ensuing period of a 'quasi-war economy' (*jun senji keizai*) from 1931 to 1937, several laws permitted government control over most industry and manufacturing branches (as described by Nakamura in the first chapter in this volume). Similar controls were applied in agriculture and on the supply of rice and other cereals between 1921 and the Second World War.

The economic crisis in the early 1930s was clearly visible to everyone, and especially to the rising number of unemployed. The obvious inability of the politicians to find a solution to the crisis was the starting point of more widespread criticism of the capitalist system – criticism which had previously been confined to intellectual circles. Theoretical considerations and practical experience thus both became the basis for ideas for a new economic system. Ideas for a 'soviet of technicians' show the influence of the Soviet model, but also indicate the type of governmental body favoured by the Japanese technocrats. Other voices called for an 'industry-oriented state', with science and technology as leading forces in decision-making. Erich Pauer's chapter on technical mobilization in this volume shows that the technocrats aimed to create such a new society. While most of the technocrats remained within the boundaries of the political system, others aimed at a wholly different order – which would require the overthrow of the existing system.

These various ideas were formulated and propagated by many people in all kinds of publications. Putting together the scattered parts, we can discern certain underlying ideas which, although somewhat naive and often untried, shaped the perception of the necessity to change the system. These basic ideas can be summarized as follows: in a capitalist society (one based on liberalism and with free, competitive trade) as then experienced in Japan, industrialists compete against one other. None of the competitors is able to gain enough influence on supply and demand. Competition leads to a downward pressure of prices. The industrialists' response is to increase production. They introduce mass production by importing new technology. If profits are still not sufficient, they will cut production costs further by reducing pay or extending working hours without raising pay. This will raise production, but as workers' pay will not rise, the number of consumers will not grow. This will result in overproduction, thus disturbing the equilibrium between supply and demand. A capitalist society will not survive long in these conditions, so self-control (through cartels) or government control seems necessary to restore equilibrium between industrial production capacity and consumers' buying capacity. It is argued that only state control could lead to such an equilibrium between supply and demand. If demand is higher than production capacity, production priorities and capacity should be determined by the state. But the distribution of production on one side also needs planning on the demand side. Therefore a coordinated plan for the economy must be established.

A planned economy based on such ideas does not reject profits, because such a move would hamper production increases. But speculative and monopolistic profits are rejected, because they would interfere with a coordinated economic plan. Moreover, it becomes clear that planning and control of production alone will not be enough. Therefore profits as well as payments must also be checked, as they also influence production costs. Furthermore, investment has to be planned, as well as the course of manufacturing and, in a further step, rationalization moves. And finally, work and the workforce, too, have to come under control.

Many authors striving to establish an economic framework based upon such ideas assumed that in such a new economy, not state control, but a new economic morality – induced by the new economy – would become the driving force of economic progress. A foundation for such a new morality can be found in the term '*kyōdō-shugi*'. This meant a kind of 'cooperatism', under which not a self-seeking egoism or individualism, but a sense of solidarity with the community and the nation as a whole would become the basis of economic action.

The framework of this new concept is only vaguely described by terms like 'spirit of (Japanese) cooperatism', a 'new morality', a 'new state', and a 'community-based working of all people'. The only implicitly stated goal was a kind of a national cooperative and community-based state. To establish such a new state, political and economic reorganization seemed unavoidable. Such thinking became the driving force for the New Order in the area of politics, economics, finance, technology and other fields, as later proclaimed by Prime Minister Konoe Fumimaro.

Based on this rather simplistic analysis of the situation, planning began. As most big industrialists opposed any state control, the government began where resistance could not be too strong: on the consumer side.

Starting shortly after the outbreak of the Sino–Japanese War in 1937, the process of changing distribution systems began. In the years up to 1945 the distribution sector was reorganized (as described in Pauer's chapter on a New Order for Japanese society). This aimed to substitute neighbourhood associations for individual consumers as units of consumption, and to replace small retailers with big distribution stations.

Most of the arguments leading to the replacement of the familiar units (consumers, retail shops) were based on ideas of an economy in a state of equilibrium: the amount of supply should be distributed according to the reported (and expected) demand. Therefore no overproduction was to be expected, and no goods or commodities (being in short supply anyway) would be wasted, as often occurred in existing retailers.

Planning distribution has always held a fascination for planning economists, but history has shown that planning usually fails and leads to unanticipated contradictions. The Japanese example is no exception. The chapter by Anke Scherer on the drawbacks of wartime controls shows that food shortages and the rise of a black market closely followed the establishment of the controlled distribution system.

The changes in the distribution sector reveal another feature with far-reaching implications. If fully enforced throughout the country, the reforms would eventually have replaced the existing system. They would have made tangible the goal of a new economic system. Although such a goal was never described in detail, the catch phrase of a 'New Order' provided the foundations for incremental progress in various fields. This progress reflects the traditional Japanese approach to decision-making, which emphasizes a process of change influenced by shifting conditions and interests, and where goals are formulated in a global, general fashion, and are open to a multiplicity of interpretations (for details of this way of thinking see Pauer 1996). Only a very vague and diffuse picture of the New Order was given, and this also changed along with external conditions.

Such long-term goal-setting was applied not only to distribution, but in other fields as well. The chapter by Regine Mathias on women's labour shows that open, vague 'visions' of a 'new productive society' based on the ideal of 'productive persons' were discussed in magazines, but left open questions as to the possible paths to achieve this goal. 'Joint establishments' were to become the centre of people's life, and people would concentrate on 'work' for the whole society. The idea of cooperatism (*kyōdō-shugi*) within such a society can once more be found as a basic feature. But the magazine articles give few details of the aspired-for 'fundamental social change', or what such a changed society would look like.

What kind of firms should be in the centre of the new economy? Laws on economic matters, introduced from the late 1930s onwards, did not respond merely to the changed needs due to wartime circumstances. Such a view is too simplistic, and does not match the true goal. Rather, these laws represent a new category within the Japanese law system, based not on principles derived from (European) liberalism or ideas of an individualism, but on the idea of community-based cooperatism. With the introduction of 'economic laws' (*keizai-hō*), a new (economic) state order was to be enforced. Its basic features were to change from that of a free-market economy, to one where state intervention is legally allowed and indeed seen as necessary. This would replace the basic Civil Code (*minpō*) and form the basis of a new system. The newly established National Policy Companies were looked upon as 'juridical persons according to the new economic law' (*keizai hōjin*), whereas traditional companies were referred as 'juridical persons according to company law' (*kaisha hōjin*) – the 'company law' being part of the Civil Code. The government designated many existing companies as National Policy Companies, thereby gaining ground for state intervention. Such moves can be seen as the first steps in changing the character of free-market firms into bodies striving for mutual, cooperative interest. Silke-Susann Otto's chapter in this volume on National Policy Companies concentrates on the inner workings of these companies; she describes their differences with 'ordinary' firms, and shows how the government developed policies and instruments to intervene in each company. However, lacking management skills and technical know-how, many of these companies were outmanoeuvred by similar 'ordinary' companies. Nevertheless, because of the National Policy Companies' numerous subsidiaries and extensive investments, the state's influence was larger than the mere number of such companies might suggest.

Financing a war is a topic that is as interesting as difficult to research. The chapter by Okazaki Tetsuji provides insights into the 'New Financial

Order', which was to provide wartime industries with enough capital to fulfil the state's goal. The role of the government itself in the process of changing the financial system is one of the main points in this chapter. Instruments developed by the banks during the war (mediation, financial monitoring) became helpful for the economic recovery in the postwar era.

In the last chapter, Itō Osamu discusses the economic changes that took place during the war. By analysing important fields and relationships among institutions before, during and after the war, he shows that Japan's wartime economy, sometimes called the '1940 system' (see the title of a book by Noguchi [1996]), was a turning point for Japan. These changes surely became the basis for the reforms in the postwar period.

NOTES

1 Ishiwara Kanji was an army officer and nationalist writer. He lectured in military history at the War College from 1925 to 1928, and later became Guandong Army Senior Staff Officer in Manchuria and occupied other high positions in the General Staff in Tōkyō.
2 Minobe Tatsukichi was professor at Tōkyō University for administrative law, history of the Japanese legal system, and later, constitutional law. He was also a member of the house of peers from 1932 to 1935.

REFERENCES

Garon, Sheldon M. (1987) *The State and Labor in Modern Japan*, Berkeley/Los Angeles/London: University of California Press.

Kobayashi Hideo (1995) *'Nihon kabushiki kaisha' o tsukutta otoko* (The man who built 'Japan Inc.'), Tōkyō: Shogakkan.

Noguchi Yukio (1996) *1940nen taisei – saraba 'senji keizai'* (The 1940 system – The case of 'war economy'), Tōkyō: Tōyō Keizai Shinpō-sha (first publ. 1995).

Okazaki Tetsuji (1993) 'The Japanese firm under the wartime planned economy', *Journal of the Japanese and International Economy* 7, pp. 175–203.

Pauer, Erich (1996) 'Rules, goals, information – a key to the question of continuity and change in Japan', in Sarah Metzger-Court and Werner Pascha (eds), *Japan's Socio-economic Evolution: Continuity and Change*, Sandgate, Folkestone: Japan Library.

1

THE JAPANESE WAR ECONOMY AS A 'PLANNED ECONOMY'

Nakamura Takafusa

THE IDEALIZATION OF SOCIALIST SOCIETY

In the 1930s, many people were disillusioned with capitalist society and instead they idealized socialism. Britain and the United States had long been reluctant to accept Marxism, although the best minds of the 1930s finally broke away from this constraint. At Harvard University in the United States, there were two prominent Marxist economists: Paul Sweezy and Paul Baran. Maurice Dobb at Cambridge, England, also studied Marxist economics in earnest.

In both countries, Marxism appealed to some intellectuals, but never gained the support of the working classes. As a result, communist parties in both countries were unable to wield influence or political power, and they remained minor opposition parties.

In France and Germany, on the other hand, Marxist-inspired leftist parties, such as the Communist Party and the Social Democratic Party, were formidable. Many intellectuals took a political stand in favour of Marxism, whether or not they joined the Communist Party.

Lenin reasoned in his *Imperialism as the Highest Stage of Capitalism* (publ. 1916) that capitalist states would fight for overseas markets and would inevitably rush into imperialistic wars, while strengthening their monopolies and exploiting the working class at home. The First World War clearly illustrated this. While the United States profited from the war, the European powers were exhausted by it and lost the prosperity that they had once enjoyed. Then the worldwide depression began. The United States, Europe and Japan all faced an economic crisis, and all seemed to be on the verge of revolution and the fast-approaching transition to socialism. It seemed obvious that the capitalist system had lost all momentum for future development.

The Soviet Union, established as a result of the 1917 Revolution, went through great difficulties in the War–Communism period. This led Lenin to initiate the New Economic Policy (NEP), which allowed a temporary revival of capitalism. In 1928, Stalin launched the First Five-Year Plan to construct one-state socialism. Collectivization of agriculture and the construction of electric power stations effected a great leap forward for heavy industry. Despite the Great Depression, the Five-Year Plan achieved its targets one year earlier than expected, and was followed by the Second Five-Year Plan in 1932. The intellectuals believed that these achievements were tangible proof of socialism's superiority over the capitalist system. In addition, there was little coverage of the dark side of Soviet socialism, including imposed *kolkhoz* formation, the large number of farmers sent to labour camps, and forced labour. Consequently, numerous intellectuals praised the Soviet system, including Sidney and Beatrice Webb (the former a socialist economist and co-founder of the London School of Economics), and the French writer André Gide.

Italian Fascists led by Mussolini, as well as the German Nazis, criticized the capitalist system and advocated centralized planning of the economy, at least in principle. This carried over to Japan in the form of criticism of capitalism and the free-market economy, coupled with an adoration of a planned economy among nationalists, military personnel and bureaucrats – even among those who opposed Marxism.

In Asia, young intellectuals, students and workers had leaned towards Marxism since the 1920s. Many university students were deeply moved by Marxist thought and read the complete works of Marx and Engels, though not all joined the Communist Party or were active in political or labour movements.

In the 1930s, Japan became the first country to publish translations of the complete works of Marx and Engels. Many Japanese students who had accepted Marxism in their college days went on to become government officials or regular salaried workers, and were absorbed into the political and economic system. Nevertheless, their Marxist sympathies remained quietly buried in their hearts. Social scientists studied Japanese capitalism using a Marxist analytical framework and presented their papers openly or in periphrastic terms. The most outstanding example was the debate on Japanese capitalism in the 1920s and 1930s between the Lectures Faction, which took the line of the Japanese Communist Party, and the Labour and Farmers' Faction, which kept its distance from the Party.

This debate also influenced American thinking: a provisional English translation of the Lectures Faction's theoretical guide, Yamada Moritarō's *Nihon shihon-shugi bunseki* (An analysis of Japanese capitalism) (publ. 1934) is said to have been read by history students at Harvard, and this faction heavily influenced the writing of E. Herbert Norman (1940), a Canadian scholar and Harvard graduate (well-known for his book *Japan's Emergence as a Modern State*).

Adam Smith, and before him Mandeville, argued that the price mechanism brought about the optimum allocation of resources, and this view has prevailed ever since. But despite this, more and more people (and not just Marxists) became critical of the capitalist economic system and believed some form of socialist planned economy to be superior. Some of them were even in a position to influence government decision-making. Among those in Japan who criticized the capitalist system and argued for economic controls and planning were – to give three examples from different groups (for details see Nakamura 1993: 167–84) – Nakano Seigō, a nationalist politician, Kawai Yoshinari, a successful businessman and former bureaucrat, and Matsui Haruo, a government official.

One of Nakano's major works advocating his idealistic populism and individualism is entitled *Kokka kaizō keikaku kōryō* (General principles for a national reconstruction plan) (Nakano 1933). His ideology and policies were based on Kita Ikki's *Nihon kaizō hōan taikō* (Outline plan for the reorganization of Japan) (Kita 1923). Kita (1883–1937) advocated revolutionary national socialistic reconstruction and the expansion of Japanese territory by military power. His book was admired as a bible among young nationalist groups in the 1920s and 1930s.

Kawai Yoshinari (born 1886) started his career in the Ministry of Agriculture and Commerce, and later became director of various companies. He published his ideas in a book entitled *Kokka kaizō no genri oyobi sono jikkō* (Principles of national reconstruction and their implementation) (Kawai 1934).

Matsui Haruo, an official in the government National Resources Bureau (*Shigen kyoku*), wrote an influential book entitled *Keizai sanbō honbu-ron* (A treatise on an Economic Affairs General Staff Office). In 1933–4, a widely-read ten-volume collection of research papers (by authors who later became well-known, such as Arizawa Hiromi, Ryū Shintarō and Takahashi Kamekichi) on controlled economies in various countries was published by Kaizō-sha under the title *Nihon tōsei keizai zenshū* (Collection of writings on the controlled economy).

Against this background, the Japanese public came to believe that central planning and a command economy would be inevitable in wartime. In sum, Japan in the 1930s was already intellectually and spiritually prepared for the planning and socialization of its economy.

THE BEGINNING OF DIRECT WARTIME CONTROLS

The Japanese economy of the 1930s was quite dependent on foreign sources of raw materials. In March 1932 Japan set up a puppet state in Manchuria and established control over two other provinces in northern China, thereby attempting to create a yen trading bloc consisting of Japan, Korea and Manchuria. This imperial expansion sought to develop for the Japanese economy sources of key commodities unavailable at home or in the existing colonies. These commodities included cotton, wool, timber, pulp, iron ore and other metals, unrefined sugar, salt for industrial use, and crude oil and petrochemicals.

Nevertheless, securing a stable resource base did not go as smoothly as the government had expected. Japan was able to secure steady sources of certain products only, such as salt from north China and coal and soya beans from Manchuria. Most key raw materials were still sourced from the sterling and dollar blocs. These imports were financed by foreign exchange earned from exports, notably light industry products and such textiles as cotton goods.

A balance-of-payments equilibrium existed in Japan in the early 1930s. Exports were increasing at an annual rate of 18 per cent, but if imports increased faster than this, a trade deficit would be unavoidable. At the time of the Russo-Japanese War in 1904–5, the Anglo-Japanese alliance enabled Japan to depend on credits from the London money market to cover its trade deficit. However, in the 1930s, Japan had no such friendly foreign market.

With the Army's growing political influence after 1936, military expansion was promoted as national policy. The government's Six-Year Plan, the Army's 3-billion-yen Industrial Production Capacity Expansion Plan, and the Navy's 770-million-yen Third Supplement Plan (which included funds for the super-battleships Yamato and Musashi) all took effect in 1937. Moreover, the Army called for the implementation of a Five-Year Plan for Key Industries (*Jūyō sangyō gokanen keikaku yōkō*) in 1937. This aimed to sharply increase heavy industry output, including steel, automobiles, aircraft, aluminium and coal liquefaction, which would serve as a basis for the production of munitions. Large-scale plant and equipment investment in these key industries was indispensable, making import expansion inevitable (Nakamura 1994: 3–7, Nakamura 1995: 77–83). However, the arms build-up programme prevented the cost of increased imports being met by more exports. In addition, raising military expenditure and investment in plant and equipment would ignite inflation. So the government's economic policy had to achieve two incompatible goals: curbing the trade deficit and preventing inflation, while investing in large-scale plant and equipment.

Even before this period, there had been some legislation allowing government control over the economy. To take one example, in 1932 legislation was passed to prevent capital flight that weakened the yen (the Capital Evasion Prevention Law, *Shihon tōhi bōshi-hō*). Other examples were the Industry Acts for each industry introduced in 1934; these followed the lines laid down by the 1931 Major Industries Control Law (*Jūyō sangyō tōsei-hō*), the first law to impose economic controls before the War. Under the Industry

Acts, the government provided subsidies and tax relief for key military-related industries, including oil, automobiles and aircraft, and it controlled production and investment in plant and equipment. However, the 1937 Five-Year Plan for Key Industries was the government's first comprehensive set of controls over the free-market economy.

Increases in munitions production and investment in heavy industries resulted in a surge in imports, making a trade deficit inevitable. To avoid this, 'non-urgent and unnecessary' imports had to be restricted. In addition, the money supply had to be reduced drastically so that increases in government spending and investment would not cause runaway inflation. These two requirements led to the start of a planned economy. Had it not been for the widespread idealization of the Soviet-style or totalitarian planned economy, it would have been impossible for the government to initiate planning so decisively.

In September 1937, just after the outbreak of war with China, three wartime control laws were pushed through the Diet: the Law for the Application of the Armament Industry Mobilization Law (*Gunjū kōgyō dōin-hō no tekiyō ni kansuru hōritsu*) enacted a law passed in 1918; the Temporary Export and Import Commodities Measures Law (*Yūshutsu-nyū-hinra rinji sochi-hō*) imposed controls on the production, processing, trading and distribution of commodities and raw materials related to imports and exports; and the Temporary Fund Control Law (*Rinji shikin chōsei-hō*, described in the chapter by Okazaki in this volume) gave the government authority to control company establishment, capital increases, mergers, bond flotations and loans, in an effort to direct long-term funds into plant and equipment investment in key industries. The Temporary Fund Control Law thus prevented funds from flowing into industries producing 'non-urgent and unnecessary' goods. Both this and the Commodities Measures Law established only general principles, and their practical application was left to imperial and ministerial ordinances. As a result, extensive authority over economic activities was delegated to ministries, making it possible for the government to control commodities and investment funds without the Diet's approval.

At the Army's urging, the National Mobilization Law (*Kokka sōdōin-hō*) was passed in March 1938, and authority for its legislation was also delegated to ministries. It imposed broad controls in such areas as wages, employment, industrial relations, funds of financial institutions and firms' disposal of profits. Japan's wartime economic controls were formulated by detailed regulations developed under this legal framework (Maeda 1964, Nakamura 1994: 88–95).

Another legal foundation for wartime economic controls was the Materials Mobilization Plan (*Busshi dōin keikaku*), drawn up in October 1937 by the newly established Planning Board (*Kikaku-in*). The plan allocated materials (iron, steel, copper, aluminium, gasoline, kerosene, light and heavy oil, cotton and wool) to the Army and Navy and to the private sector. The plan was drawn up initially for the October–December period of 1937, and then was revised annually from 1938 to 1940 and quarterly after 1941. Additionally, mobilization plans for trade, labour, fund controls, transportation and electric power were introduced from 1939 to 1940 (Nakamura and Hara 1970). These plans were similar in structure to those initiated by the Soviet Gosplan. The Resources Agency (*Shigen kyoku*), established in 1928, had secretly made careful studies on the Soviet plans.

When war with China broke out, the authorities explained that they had no alternative but to turn to direct economic controls, as they were under increasing pressure from the military to implement economic policies. Once controls were introduced, however, they obeyed a logic all of their own, and expanded rapidly.

The transition to a controlled economy progressed rapidly and smoothly as regular government business. The basic laws and systems remained without revision. Despite such decisive changes, the government claimed that the new laws and systems were temporary and essential to meet the war emergency, and that the changes would be eliminated at the end of the war.

THE STATE OF WARTIME ECONOMIC CONTROLS

After the autumn of 1937, several regulations expanding economic controls were introduced, all based on the Temporary Export and Import Commodities Measures, the Temporary Fund Control Law and the National Mobilization Law. All key raw materials were subject to controls. Strict controls were imposed on the production and consumption of commodities dependent on imports of steel, copper, aluminium, rubber, cotton and wool. It was not long before the consumption of such commodities by the private sector was almost prohibited (Maeda 1964). Under the Materials Mobilization Plan, the military was given priority in the allocation of such materials, in turn reducing private consumption. Naturally the controls on consumption led to excess demand and market shortages. To control inflation, the government instituted an official price control system. As a result, commodities for which official prices had been set disappeared from the market, raw materials were diverted to the production of non-rationed products, and the black market grew. In order to counter the black market, an economic police force was created. At first official prices were set for only key commodities, but later the number of goods affected numbered 480,000.

In 1939–40, full-scale controls over the labour market were put into effect. Based on the National Mobilization Law, the Personal Service Drafting Act (*Kokumin chōyō-rei*) called for labour conscription. Workers in 'non-urgent and unnecessary' industries and engineers in specific areas were conscripted into service for military industries. The government assigned new graduates to jobs according to its own interests. To help control inflation, wage controls were introduced in 1940; wages were set in accordance with educational background, work experience and skills.

In April 1939, short-term funds for business transactions as well as funds for plant and equipment investment became subject to government control (Nihon Ginkō 1970). Firms' right to dispose of profits as they saw fit, which is a basis of a free-market economy, was also brought under control. At the Army's insistence, the government placed a ceiling on dividend rates. Furthermore, as the shortage of daily necessities such as rice, soya sauce, *miso* (fermented bean paste), sugar, and rice wine (*sake*) became increasingly serious in 1939, a ration coupon system (*kippu seido*) was adopted in 1941–2.

Contrary to the Army's expectations, the war with China was prolonged, with 700,000 men tied up in the occupied territory. The necessity of supplying increasing amounts of provisions resulted in the rapid expansion of economic controls. At the same time, however, both the Army and Navy allocated a considerable part of the Special Account for Temporary War Expenses, which had been intended for the war in China, to the production and storage of arms, ammunition, aircraft and warships in order to prepare for possible wars in the near future. Economic controls were introduced because an expansion in armaments was needed not only to continue to fight against China, but also to prepare for an expansion of the war (Hara 1976: 217–68, Nakamura 1976: 109–60).

THE 'NEW ECONOMIC ORDER': IDEOLOGY AND REALITY

Even before the war with China broke out, the army had urged planning for the expansion of munitions and heavy industry, to which the government acceded. The outbreak of the war saw a deterioration of Japan's international balance of payments, thus threatening inflation. In order to conduct the war and expand heavy industry while still trying to prevent inflation, Japan had no alternative but to adopt direct controls. In this sense, controls were introduced out of sheer necessity. It may be said, however, that there was also a predisposition towards a planned economy. To take one example, the National Mobilization Law, long sought by the Army, was passed without much political resistance in the wartime atmosphere. Another example was the swift passage of legislation, opposed by *zaibatsu* and major companies, which limited corporate dividends. An ongoing debate over the 'New Economic Order' (*Keizai shintaisei*) between the Army and Planning Agency and the business community exemplified the dispute over the role of planning (Nakamura and Hara 1973).

The debate over the New Economic Order started in 1939 when Ryū Shintarō, an editor for the *Asahi shinbun*, one of Japan's leading newspapers, and a member of the Shōwa Research Association (*Shōwa kenkyū-kai*), Prime Minister Konoe's think tank, published a book entitled *Nihon keizai no saihensei* (Reorganizing the Japanese economy). He argued that the Japanese economy was in the process of decline because of its poor performance in production and trade, and that it would be impossible to carry out radical reform within the capitalist framework, which was based on the pursuit of profit by individual firms. The liberal form of capitalism, he argued, had to be eliminated by controlling corporate finance and management.

Under Ryū's guidance, a 'Tentative Plan for the Reorganization of the Japanese Economy' (*Nihon keizai saihensei shian*) was drawn up by the Shōwa Research Association in 1940 (Sakai 1979: 129–34 and 356–70). This plan proposed that the owners of capital and those responsible for management should be separated in order to change corporate goals from the pursuit of profits to production maximization. Shareholders, the owners of capital, were to be given the right to receive dividends at some reasonable rate, but were to have no voice in management. Managers were to be given the status of economic bureaucrats so that they could increase production upon request of the government. This would be the beginning of a drastic transformation in corporate organizations. This transformation included the notion of nationalization or some form of governmental control of big business. Control over industry was to be exercised through cartels. Without taking corporate profits into consideration, cartels were to assign output targets to companies in consultation with the government. Cooperative marketing and purchases of raw materials were to be allowed. Moreover, companies could be merged or split whenever necessary.

With regard to the idea of direct controls, the following two facts should be noted: first, this concept denied the legitimacy of the free market and postulated a centrally controlled economy. Companies were regarded as production units to achieve targets set by the state, and this closely resembles a Soviet planned-economy model. Second, the independence of firms and the profit principle remained intact when direct controls were introduced in Japan. Basic legislation affecting companies, such as the Commercial Code, was never revised. Business society accepted controls on a tacit understanding that they were temporary wartime measures which would be removed after the war. However, Ryū Shintarō and the Shōwa Research Association completely rejected the free-enterprise principle and intended to turn corporations into an extension of the government. Ryū and Association members such as Oyama Iwao had been known as Marxian economists in the early 1930s.

In July 1940, the second Konoe Cabinet was formed. In October, under the 'Konoe new political order', Prime Minister Konoe set up the Imperial Rule Assistance Association (*Taisei yokusan-kai*), a national organization promoting the concentration of national political power and an instrument for governmental control. People from all levels of society had high hopes for the new regime. Political parties dissolved themselves in favour of the Association. On 13 September in the same year, the Planning Board drew up an Outline of the New Economic Order (*Keizai shintaisei kakuritsu yōkō*) based on the ideas of Ryū Shintarō and the Shōwa Research Association. This outline was strongly coloured with the philosophy of strict economic controls. The main goals of the group are illustrated in the following passage:

> The Commercial Code is to be amended; firms' capital function should be separated from their management function so that they may serve the public interest; those responsible for management are to assume a public character.

In a draft plan announced on 25 September (Nakamura and Hara 1973), the amendment of the Commercial Code was withdrawn, but this did not stop opposition from the business community. Seven major business organizations, including the Japan Business League, presented a joint statement of their views. They argued as follows:

> When there is a pressing need for increased production, the foundation of the economic structure must not be undermined. To do otherwise would cause decreased production. Reasonable corporate profits should be used as a stimulus for production growth, rather than being singled out for criticism. Government interference in corporate undertakings is ineffective to increase production. Since corporate ownership and management are inseparable, government interference in the appointment of company representatives is most unreasonable.

Being threatened as they were, it was natural for the business community to oppose the plan. Consequently, antagonism between the Planning Board and the business community became fierce. For example, Kobayashi Ichizō, Minister of Commerce and Industry and former president of one of the most influential firms, Tōkyō Electric Light Company (*Tōkyō Denryoku*), orchestrated the dismissal of the Administrative Undersecretary of the Ministry of Commerce and Industry, Kishi Nobusuke, a supporter of the new plans.

On 7 December 1940, the General Plan for the Establishment of the New Economic Order (*Keizai shintaisei yōkō*) was approved by the Cabinet. Since this programme had been watered down to win support from the business community, its real intention was not clearly expressed. However, the Ministry of Commerce and Industry endeavoured to achieve the plan's objectives by fleshing out the initial legislation with subsequent ministerial ordinances. In August 1941, the Principal Industry Association Act (*Jūyō sangyō dantai-rei*) was proclaimed, calling for the formation of thirteen Control Associations in key industries such as steel, coal, mining, cement, electrical machinery and automobiles, to be carried out between November 1941 and January 1942. Later, nine Control Associations were set up in the textile industry.

Control Associations (*tōsei-kai*), through which the government controlled industry, were engaged in production planning, the allocation of raw materials and cooperative marketing. In essence, they functioned as lower-echelon mechanisms of government control. But the Control Associations faced the problem of ministerial rivalry: in industries directly involved in munitions production, the Army Industrial Association and the Navy Industrial Association, both of which were similar to Control Associations, were set up under the supervision of the Department of War and the Navy Department, respectively. The ministerial factionalism that was involved in this prevented full coordination of production even in wartime.

From this brief overview, it is evident that the New Economic Order met with strong opposition from the business world and failed to achieve its original goals. In this sense, Soviet-type planning failed to be adopted. When the business world campaigned against the plan in the autumn of 1940, not only Ryū Shintarō but also those who had drawn up the Outline of the New Economic Order were attacked as 'reds' and communists. They included (Army) Colonel Akinaga Tsukizō, who was also an important official in the Planning Agency, Sakomizu Hisatsune, Mōri Hideoto (both former Ministry of Finance officials), and Minobe Yōji, a member of the Cabinet Planning Board. Afraid of being arrested in Japan, Ryū Shintarō went to Europe to work as a correspondent. In 1941, a number of officials belonging to the Planning Agency were arrested on charges of participating in the re-establishment of the Communist Party. These incidents were unfavourable to the New Economic Order movement. Nevertheless, its objectives were brought about in a different form during the Pacific War.

PLANNING DURING THE PACIFIC WAR

The Pacific War broke out in December 1941. In the preceding summer, the Ministry of Commerce and Industry had studied measures to control the economy in wartime and had secretly prepared ministerial ordinances, which were issued after the outbreak of the war. There were three important ordinances: the Business Licence Act (*Kigyō kyoka-rei*), the Business Reorganization Act (*Kigyō seibi-rei*), and the Materials Control Act (*Jūyō busshi kanri-rei*). The first created a licensing system for new businesses. It was later complemented by the Business Reorganization Act, which aimed to reorganize and consolidate medium-sized and small businesses and textile firms because of drastic shortages of goods and raw materials and the need to transfer workers to the war industries. As the war situation worsened, several business reorganizations took place, forcing most small commercial and textile firms to close and shifting their workers to war industries. This compulsion was Soviet-type policy, even though its aim was to support the war effort. The Materials Control Act was a substitute for the Temporary Export and Import Commodities Measures approved in 1937. It gave the Ministry of Commerce and Industry more authority to control the production, distribution and consumption of commodities and raw materials.

With the ever-worsening war situation, by October 1943 the government was increasingly taking the view that raising production of aircraft, steel, ships, aluminium and coal would determine the course of the war. Against this background, the concept implicit in the New Economic Order emerged again. The Munitions Companies Law (*Gunju kaisha-hō*) designated key firms as 'munitions companies' and conferred a quasi-public status on the top managers of these firms. They were required to achieve production targets in conformity with government directives. Failure brought dismissal or other punishment. All workers were regarded as having been conscripted by the National Drafting Act, and were not allowed to resign from their jobs without permission. Moreover, raw materials were allotted preferentially to munitions companies, and funding was provided through specified financial institutions. The number of firms designated as munitions companies between November 1943 and the end of the war surpassed 600.

Of course, the circumstances in 1943 were quite different from those in 1940. The New Economic Order controversy that developed in 1940 was a debate over ideology. At the time of the enactment of the Munitions Companies Law in 1943, however, there was no possibility of debating the details of the Law before it was implemented. This legislation was an extraordinary measure rammed through the legislative process by the Army, and occurred in the context of the unfavourable turn of the war. Thus, the concept of state control of the economy proposed three years earlier was finally realized. It should be noted, however, that the principle of corporate profit maximization was not eliminated. The government provided corporations with compensation for losses resulting from business activities required by the government. In other words, the position of profit-making companies was only barely preserved.

In April 1945, the Army decided to take direct control of the factories of both the Nakajima Aeroplane (*Nakajima Hikōki KK*) and the Kawanishi Aeroplane (*Kawanishi Kōkūki KK*) companies. While such munitions factories had been under the control of the Army or Navy, the companies themselves had retained managerial authority. The military now sought to take over the managerial functions, too. However, these two companies were the only ones taken over by the military. Japan was defeated before the policy could be extended to others.

EVALUATION OF WARTIME PLANNING

Economic controls were initiated to achieve urgent and complex policy objectives. Even those involved with the controls could not predict that they would be so prolonged, extensive and pervasive. Only the Materials Mobilization Plan was planned and implemented without difficulty, but this was because the Resources Agency had been working on it for nearly a decade (Bōei-chō 1967). The effects of 'planning' (the combination of regulated economic activities and the overall wartime mobilization programme) can be summarized as follows.

First, it enabled Japan, with its scarce resources, to continue the war for more than eight years. Japan had to allocate materials and funds to munitions production, reduce the production of consumer goods and commercial activities, conscript labour into the military industry, and to lower the standard of living to a subsistence level. Planning made it possible to implement these elusive policies. From 1941 to 1944, output of aircraft in Japan was around 20 per cent of that in the United States, but by June 1944 it was 35 per cent as a result of government-imposed plans.

Planning was necessitated by the outbreak of the war, but was promoted by ideology idealizing it. The New Economic Order was the most blatantly anti-capitalist idea, the official purpose of which was to increase munitions production. It criticized the capitalist system's profit motive, and advocated the intrinsic authority of management as well as restricting the owners' rights to dividends. The concept did not materialize in its original form because of opposition from the business community. However, as the war worsened, it gradually came into being. When the war ended, for example, corporate capital had increased so rapidly that individual shareholders had become unable to influence management. The separation of ownership from management was thus realized.

Planning and economic controls were not always successful. The wartime economy faced a rampant black market, confusion resulting from rationing and a shortage of daily necessities. The shortage of daily necessities became increasingly severe as the war intensified. Although the government tried to assist agriculture and fisheries and to ensure an adequately secure labour force, the effects were limited. In addition, the military mobilized engineers and workers for military industries, impeding other sectors. In order to maximize troop strength and munitions production, the military disregarded labour shortages in other industries. To make up for the lost labour, the government went to the extent of mobilizing unskilled labour, students and unmarried women. Economic planners in the government could not stop the military from taking such high-handed measures.

It is fair to assert that Soviet-style planning was pursued in the wartime Japanese economy despite numerous associated problems. In theory, the freedom of corporate management remained intact, and the profit principle was not abandoned. In reality, however, a strict separation of ownership from management was gradually realised. In wartime, even the Mitsui *zaibatsu* had difficulty raising funds. In order to secure finance, it was forced to list shares in companies it owned on the stock market and to merge the Mitsui Bank (*Mitsui Ginkō*) with First Bank (*Dai-ichi Ginkō*).

Planning pursued in this way changed when Japan was defeated. Nevertheless, the Materials Mobilization Plan and other economic controls adopted economic reconstruction goals, and continued to exist (see, for example, Arizawa and Nakamura 1990). The military was disbanded and the American occupation forces assumed authority. Since many young American bureaucrats in the Occupation were sympathetic to New Deal ideals during the Roosevelt administration, they thought that the Japanese economy could be revived through planning and control. They tried mixing price control, subsidies policies and techniques of material mobilization.

It was the American banker Joseph Dodge who shattered their ambitions. In February 1949, Dodge came to Japan on a special mission to reconstruct the Japanese economy. A Republican and out-and-out free-market economist, he abolished all planning and controls. In 1949 the Japanese economy became a free-market economy once again (Nakamura 1995).

However, it was impossible for the old system to disappear without a trace. In letter and spirit, a considerable amount of Japan's postwar government industrial policies and regulations stemmed from prewar planning. Even today, numerous government regulations remain controversial. While some of them are the remains of wartime controls, most were introduced after the war. It can be concluded that Japan's planning period ended in 1949. The economic transformation was carried out quickly and smoothly by the generation which had grown up in the prewar free-market economy.

REFERENCES

Arizawa Hiromi and Nakamura Takafusa (eds) (1990) *Shiryō: Sengo Nihon no keizai seisaku kōsō* (Documents: Conceptions of economic policies in postwar Japan), Tōkyō: Tōkyō University Press.

Bōei-chō, Bōei kenshu-sho, Senshi-shitsu (Defence Agency, Defence Research Institute, War History Department), (1967) *Rikugun gunju dōin (1) keikaku-hen* (Military mobilization (1) planning), *Senshi Sōsho* 9 (Series of war histories vol. 9), Tōkyō: Asagumo Shinbun-sha.

Hara Akira (1976) *Senji tōsei keizai no kaishi* (Commencement of the wartime economic control), *Iwanami kōza Nihon rekishi 20 (Kindai 7)* (Iwanami Lectures on Japanese History vol. 20, Modern Age 7), Tōkyō: Iwanami Shoten, pp. 217–68.

Kawai Yoshinari (1934) *Kokka kaizō no genri oyobi sono jikkō – shū toshite keizaiteki kansatsu* (Principles of national reconstruction and their implementation – mainly concerning economic observations), Tōkyō: Nihon Hyōron-sha.

Kita Ikki (1923) *Nihon kaizō hōan taikō* (An outline plan for the reorganization of Japan), Tōkyō: Kaizō-sha.

Maeda Yasuyuki (1964) *Sangyō tōsei* (Controls on industries), *Shōkō seisaku-shi* (History of policies on commerce and industry) vol. 11, Tōkyō: Tsūshō Sangyō Kenkyū-sha.

Matsui Haruo (1934) *Keizai sanbō honbu-ron* (A treatise on Economic Affairs General Staff Office), *Shin keizai zenshū 1* (Collected Works on the New Economy), vol. 1, Tōkyō: Nihon Hyōron-sha.

Nakamura Takafusa (1976) 'Sensō keizai to sono hōkai' (War economy and its collapse), *Iwanami kōza Nihon rekishi 21 (Kindai 8)* (Iwanami Lectures on Japanese History vol. 21, Modern Age 8), Tōkyō: Iwanami Shoten, pp. 109–60.

Nakamura Takafusa (1993) *Shōwa-shi I, 1926–1945* (History of the Shōwa era Vol. I, 1926–1945), Tōkyō: Tōyō Keizai Shinpō-sha.

Nakamura Takafusa (1994) *Lectures on Modern Japanese Economic History 1926–1994*, Tōkyō: LTCB International Library Foundation.

Nakamura Takafusa (1995) *The Postwar Japanese Economy* (2nd edn), Tōkyō: Tōkyō University Press.

Nakamura Takafusa and Hara Akira (eds) (1970) *Kokka sōdōin* (National mobilization), *Gendai-shi shiryō* (Documents on modern history), Vol. 43, Tōkyō: Misuzu Shobō.

Nakamura Takafusa and Hara Akira (1973) *Keizai shintaisei* (The New Economic Order), *Nenpō seijigaku 1972 'Konoe shintaisei' no kenkyū* (Annual report on Japan political science 1972 – Study on Konoe's New Economic Order), Tōkyō: Nihon Seiji Gakkai.

Nakano Seigō (1933) *Kokka kaizō keikaku kōryo* (General principles for a national reconstruction plan), Tōkyō: Chikura Shobō.

Nihon Ginkō (Bank of Japan) (1970) 'Manshū jihen igo no zaisei kinyū-shi' (History of finance and monetary policies after the Manchurian Incident), in Nihon Ginkō, Chōsa-kyoku *Shōwa kinyū-shi shiryō – Shōwa hen dai 27 kan – Senji kinyū kankei shiryō 1* (Documents on the history of monetary policies in the Shōwa period vol. 27 – Documents on wartime monetary matters 1), Tōkyō: Ōkura-shō Insatsu-kyoku, pp. 1–353.

Norman, E. Herbert (1940) *Japan's Emergence as a Modern State*, New York: Institute of Pacific Relations.

Ryō Shintarō (1939) *Nihon keizai no saihensei* (Reorganizing the Japanese economy), Tōkyō: Chūō Kōron-sha.

Sakai Saburō (1979) *Shōwa kenkyū-kai* (Shōwa Research Association), Tōkyō: TBS Britannica.

Yamada Moritarō (1934) *Nihon shihon-shugi bunseki* (An analysis of Japanese capitalism), Tōkyō: Iwanami Shoten.

2

THE IDEOLOGICAL BACKGROUND OF THE JAPANESE WAR ECONOMY

Visions of the 'reformist bureaucrats'

Ortrud Kerde

INTRODUCTION

Japanese militarism reached its zenith in the 1930s with the beginning of the Sino-Japanese War. This period is commonly referred to as the 'dark valley' of Japanese history (Fletcher 1982: 3), as a period of crises, political assassinations and rural upheavals. Militarism and ultra-nationalism both contain a strong anti-intellectual element that obstructs the free unfolding of academic creativity and usually suspiciously monitors foreign intellectual thought (cf., Morris-Suzuki 1989: 94). This attitude was reflected in the repression of socialists and communists who, from the 1920s, were persecuted and arrested. Those who upheld their views were forced to pursue their activities underground. However, according to the prominent Shōwa-period philosopher Miki Kiyoshi, this period was a time of 'anguish and crisis' (Fletcher 1982: 45) for Japanese intellectuals in general.

Anguish and crisis, however, were feelings not necessarily shared by conservative Japanese intellectuals, who often served as intellectual subcontractors to the Japanese state, and who were sometimes even called upon to mobilize public opinion in favour of expansion and military action. European political movements and ideologies such as Fascism and Nazism were brought to the attention of Japanese intellectuals in early Shōwa Japan, and they were particularly attracted to Nazi economic policies. Fletcher (1982: 160) revealed the reason for the growing fascination of prominent authors and scholars such as Rōyama Masamichi, Ryū Shintarō and Miki Kiyoshi with Fascism: they looked upon Fascism as a means of realizing the drastic reforms they deemed necessary for establishing a new social, political and economic order in Japan. The particular appeal of Fascist ideology to these writers was its emphasis on the power of the state.

As far as economic theory was concerned, many Japanese economists showed a pronounced interest in evolutionary, as opposed to analytical, theory, which is why the German 'historical school' gained popularity in the 1930s. The evolutionary character of this school's theories (unlike the static nature of the classical and neoclassical schools of the late nineteenth century) offered explanations for Japan's late economic development and helped adherents understand the country's position in the global economy.

According to the economist Taiyōji Jun'ichi (1970: 168), one problem of Japanese wartime economic policies was that the planners and ideologues neither thoroughly adopted foreign ideologies, nor did they develop original Japanese theories: 'Not only were their thoughts based on mere ideas, some practical knowledge and the superficial imitation of foreign thoughts, but they were confronted with inconsistencies due to their lack of systematic analysis and a propensity to showiness'.

But this way of dealing with foreign ideas should not be ascribed to confusion or negligence; instead, it should be seen as power-oriented pragmatism. Not feeling committed to any ideological principle, the Japanese economic strategists adopted certain policy elements, ripped them out of their socio-economic context, and combined them with other, partially incompatible, theories (Taiyōji 1970: 223) in order to bring about a blueprint for Japan's economic hegemony in East Asia.

This chapter aims to explain the Japanese understanding of these foreign ideologies and to elaborate on corresponding Japanese theories used as an ideological framework for Japanese wartime economic policies. The schools used to rationalize the economic order and justify it ideologically are examined by introducing the ideas of the Planning Board's 'reformist bureaucrats' (*kakushin kanryō*), who dominated the economy after 1937. This group based their thinking on various ingredients: traits of German universalism and the so-called 'romantic school', and the economic policies of Nazi Germany and Mussolini's Italy. These ideas were not labelled 'foreign' but were integrated into a specifically Japanese framework. With that in mind, which ideologies were used in the Japanese wartime economy, and for what purpose? Whose interest did these ideologies serve?

The first section of this chapter outlines the kind of economic thought that influenced the reformist bureaucrats. The second section introduces the reformist bureaucrats, their membership profile, and the context and environment in which they operated. The third section examines the thought of Mōri Hideoto, their chief ideologue. It illustrates the impact of foreign ideologies and economic policy on the group, and presents his conceptions of Japanese expansionism and state control as well as his critique on capitalism and communism. The fourth section illustrates how theory was translated into reality by examining the case of the Electric Power Control Law, a piece of legislation which was drafted by Okumura Kiwao, one of the leading reformist bureaucrats.

The dominant theme of the time was criticism of the capitalist order, which originated in the most diverse political camps in the 1920s. Marxist stances are exemplified by the controversy between the 'Lectures Faction' (*Kōza-ha*) and the 'Labour and Farmers Faction' (*Rōnō-ha*) over the nature of Japanese capitalism (see the chapter by Nakamura in this volume). Although Marxism was a popular ideology, especially among college graduates of Taishō and early Shōwa Japan, its influence on actual politics should not be overestimated.

Kita Ikki and Takabatake Motoyuki, both Marxists-turned-ultra-nationalists, on the other hand, exerted strong influence on the armed forces by way of their conceptions of a Japanese-style state-socialism with a strong nationalist tendency. Ryū Shintarō, journalist and member of the Shōwa Research Association, Prime Minister Konoe's think tank, displayed an anti-capitalist attitude; he argued for the control of corporate finance and management, linking the decline of the Japanese economy with the private pursuit of profits by individual companies. His ideas bear striking similarities to those of the reformist bureaucrats (cf., Fletcher 1982: 149). Economist Miyazaki Masayoshi, a favourite of the army, proposed armament and the restructuring of the Japanese economy into a 'defence economy'. Japanese wartime economic planners could thus refer to an abundance of both imported and genuinely Japanese theories to rationalize the restructuring of the economy.

FOREIGN INFLUENCES ON THE REFORMIST BUREAUCRATS

Two Austrian economists, Friedrich von Gottl-Ottilienfeld and Othmar Spann, were major sources of influence for the Japanese planners (Taiyōji 1970: 214–5, Furukawa 1992: 119–21). Translations of both authors' works were published in Japan from the early 1930s to the early 1940s. Gottl-Ottilienfeld (1932: 3–5) perceived the economy as a social construction (*Gebilde*). His ontological method as well as Spann's universalism attracted the attention of Mōri Hideoto, the chief ideologue of the reformist bureaucrats.

Their ideas were influenced by the romantic tradition and the German 'historical school' of the nineteenth century, which gave special emphasis to the description and interpretation of 'historical reality', rather than theoretical reasoning and the abstract idea of a *homo oeconomicus*. According to this school, the 'value of a people' was realized not through liberal individualism, but in the state and the nation – which, according to Spann's universalism, was an 'organic unity'. They strongly objected to the separation of the economy from the state, and they feared the social consequences of liberalism, such as pauperism and the decline of agriculture and the crafts. Pure *laissez-faire* liberalism, they claimed, would eventually destroy all human and cooperative relations, would weaken the state system (*Staatswesen*) and the sense of national identity. The historical school doubted the possibility of an automatic, smoothly operating economic process, and it opposed abstract and isolating deductive conclusions as expressions of a mechanistic understanding of economic policies (Ott and Winkel 1985: 124–5).

The historical school is generally criticized by today's economists for its lack of theory-building and the substitution of economic thinking with political considerations for the sake of the *raison d'état* (*Staatsräson*) (Winkel 1977: 120). These political considerations seem partially to explain why Spann's universalism in particular influenced the Japanese planners.

Gottl-Ottilienfeld (1932: 10–11) defines the political economy as a socio-historical discipline, closely linking the economy with social and political 'organizing tasks' (*Gestaltungsaufgaben*) (cf., Winkel 1977: 130). Likewise, Spann's universalism does not perceive society as a mere summation of individuals, but as a community of mutual responsibility (Spann 1972: 121–3). It should be noted, though, that from the early Shōwa period, Spann's 'universalism' was translated into Japanese as 'totalitarianism' (*zentai-shugi*) instead of the semantically more appropriate *fuhen-shugi* (Furukawa 1992: 119), thus giving it a somewhat stronger connotation.

The state, according to Spann, develops from individualism's mere 'necessary arrangement' (*Noteinrichtung*) to a 'moral unity', with the individual being an organ of the whole. Society takes priority over the individual, and the will of the state is not brought about 'centralistically, atomistically and mechanically' but is derived from the demands of everyday life, thus being 'superindividual' (*überindividuell*). Spann concludes that expertise and leadership are necessary in every part of life (Spann 1972: 121–3). Stressing the necessity of leadership, he sees high-ranking bureaucrats and military officials who operate relatively independently and creatively as the ideal political leaders. This is how the military and ministry officials of the reformist bureaucrats could rationalize their involvement in the planning of the wartime economy (Furukawa 1992: 120).

On a related point, economist Friedrich List, an advocate of tariff protection to stimulate national industrial development, suddenly won new popularity and was dubbed 'the grandfather of the "national" or "political" economy' (Taiyōji 1970: 216) and a precursor of the historical school in Japan. Translations of his books were published between 1940 and 1942. Gustav von Schmoller's ideas were likewise introduced to Japan at the end of the 1930s. He is considered one of the founding fathers of the historical school; his ideas of an ethical, organic political economy were of particular interest for the Japanese planners (Taiyōji 1970: 217).

Nazi doctrines (cf., Taiyōji 1970: 215) reached Japan through the translation into Japanese of three volumes on the German economy compiled by Hans-Heinrich Lammers and Hans Pfundtner. These were published in twelve volumes between 1939 and 1941. Nazi Germany's labour policies and information about the abolition and destruction of the German labour unions were introduced mainly by publications of the central bureau of the German Labour Front.

THE REFORMIST BUREAUCRATS: A MEMBERSHIP PROFILE

The reformist bureaucrats were civil servants who had graduated from Tōkyō Imperial University in the 1920s (Furukawa 1992: 18–19), and they were mainly responsible for the drafting and implementation of the state-controlled economy between 1937 and 1945. Their movement is sometimes subsumed under the broader 'reformist' (*kakushin-ha*) label, which included another reform faction within the bureaucracy, the 'new bureaucrats' (Tōkyō Imperial University graduates of the early Taishō period) and the army's 'reformists'. That these various groups called themselves reformists, however, must be taken with a grain of salt: the 'reform' label should not be allowed to obscure the reactionary character of these movements. The reformist bureaucrats are also known as 'revisionist bureaucrats' in English (a generic name proposed by Spaulding 1971: 60–1).

The central organizational unit of these reform movements was the Cabinet Investigation Bureau (*Naikaku chōsa-kyoku*) founded in 1935, and later the Planning Board (*Kikaku-in*), which was a higher-level version of the bureau reorganized in 1937. The core of the group was made up of twelve prominent bureaucrats from different ministries and army circles (Itō 1987: 129, 146; Yatsugi 1971: 127): Major-General Mutō Akira and Colonel Akinaga Gessan of the army, Iwakuro Hideo of the Military Affairs Bureau, Kishi Nobusuke, Shiina Etsusaburō and Minobe Yōji (Ministry of Commerce and Industry), Taniguchi Tsuneji, Sakomizu Hisatsune and Mōri Hideoto (Ministry of Finance), Shigemasa Seishi (Ministry of Agriculture and Forestry), Kashiwabara Hyōtarō (Ministry of Railways) and Okumura Kiwao (Ministry of Communications).

After October 1939, these individuals formed a 'Monday Group' (*getsuyō-kai*), so named because they met every Monday, before the Tuesday Cabinet conferences. Because of this, their meetings were likened to hidden Cabinet staff conferences (Itō 1987: 146). Many of the group members later joined the Planning Board and had a decisive role in the drafting of economic legislation during the New Order movement.

According to Taiyōji (1970: 223), the group's ideological foundation comprised a combination of Fascist and Marxist ideological elements as well as references to German universalism. Marxist influences should actually be considered rather indirect, however. These bureaucrats were students from after the First World War until the late 1920s, when Marxism was the ideological fashion among intellectuals, so had dealt with Marxist ideology in their university classes. After joining their ministries, however, they soon dumped Marxist and socialist concepts such as socialization.

Thus, economic planning and control according to the reformist bureaucrats should not be interpreted as a first step towards the socialization of the means of production, as in the socialist economic order. Mōri Hideoto, for instance, was rather opposed to the nationalization proposals drawn up by the Planning Board's hardliners.

MŌRI HIDEOTO: CHIEF IDEOLOGUE OF THE REFORMIST BUREAUCRATS

Mōri Hideoto was one of three key figures among the reformist bureaucrats. The other members of this triumvirate were Sakomizu Hisatsune and Minobe Yōji, with Minobe receiving most public attention. According to Sakomizu, the distribution of responsibilities among the three was such that Mōri did most of the work in the Planning Board, bringing forth ideas and plans, and was acknowledged as the group's ideologue. Sakomizu himself systematized and organized the plans, while Minobe provided for their implementation. Mōri himself never strove to be an object of public attention, publishing his ideas in influential magazines such as *Kaibō jidai* and *Chūō kōron* under the pseudonym Kamakura Ichirō (Itō 1987: 129).

After graduating from Tōkyō Imperial University's law department, Mōri joined the Ministry of Finance, and was later transferred to the Manchukuo Affairs Bureau (*Manshū-koku kokumu-in sōmu-chō*). He joined the China Expeditionary Army Headquarters (*Shina haken-gun shirei-bu*) in 1937 and after working briefly at the Ministry of Finance, he moved on to the Asian Development Agency in 1938. There he developed connections with prominent military representatives, who came to have a strong influence on his economic thinking and later made him the intermediary between the Planning Board and the military. In 1941 he joined the Planning Board, where he remained until its merger with the Ministry of Munitions in 1943. He worked in various ministries until September 1945 (Itō 1987: 129–30).

Recognizing that the world order had undergone severe changes, Mōri argued that Japan, while choosing a path to secure its political and economic independence, had to make plans to stimulate rapid economic growth without becoming entangled in economic theory. He proposed the formation of a system of economic blocs, each consisting of the countries of a different region of the world; he supported the transformation of the political system into a totalitarian regime; and he advocated the introduction of a planned economy.

In 1939, Mōri criticized the planned economy of Japan as lacking an ideological foundation, arguing that it had descended into mere claptrap from which no progress was possible. He further argued that the introduction of a capitalist order to the occupied territory in China would end up with exactly the kind of exploitation typical of the world powers (by which he meant both the United States and the Soviet Union), and added that 'the masses' were longing for 'reform' (*kakushin*) (Furukawa 1992: 118).

Needless to say, he considered reform a task for the bureaucracy. But to his mind, the bureaucracy itself needed reform, too. Mōri sought a redefinition of the tasks and functions of high-ranking bureaucrats, demanding that they change from 'legislative' (*hōsei-teki*) to 'creative' (*sōzō-teki*) bureaucrats, since their tasks would shift from 'inspection' to 'management' (Furukawa 1992: 117).

Economic expansionism and state control

The influence of the military's ideology on Mōri's thought is mirrored in his vision of a new world order, which he anticipated would result from a victory for Nazi Germany in the Second World War. According to Mōri, the economy would undergo a global restructuring resulting in the formation of four economic blocs: an East Asian bloc (under Japanese leadership), a European bloc (controlled by Germany) plus a Soviet and an American bloc, obviously borrowing from Nazi visions of a *Großraumwirtschaft* (unified economic region, *kōiki kokumin keizai*) (Itō 1987: 142, 145).

Mōri distinguished between a 'defence economy' and a war economy. He defined the former as a means of securing the 'peace economy' which the defence economy would eventually result in. The most crucial burden a nation has to struggle with, Mōri claimed, was the acknowledgement of its inability to defend itself, as a people's main concern was its 'everlasting existence'. He concluded that Japan's stability and security were dependent on her 'defence economy' (Kamakura 1939b: 31), a popular euphemism at the time for wartime economy.

In his writings, Japanese expansion comes across as a natural right. In an article published in 1940, Mōri explains the Meiji Restoration using a geopolitical approach (Kamakura 1940). He draws on the German political geographer Karl Haushofer, a leading proponent of geopolitics, who had claimed that Japan was a 'people without *Lebensraum*' ('living space', *seikatsu kūkan*) and consequently had to seek 'self-expansion'. (The *Lebensraum* idea was also part of Nazi ideology.) Mōri pointed out that after the Meiji Restoration, Japan perceived the Pacific region as an area offering the 'self-liberation' and room for expansion needed to gain complete political autonomy and self-sufficiency. By being subsumed into the capitalist world, he argued, Japan had transformed itself into a capitalist state and as such would have to expand.

Due to the changes in the world economy and the economic crises after the First World War, Japanese economic thought regarding the 'East Asian–Pacific hemisphere' began to undergo some changes. Japan, according to Mōri, developed a new consciousness for *Lebensraum* and self-sufficiency which was directly expressed in the 'emergence of Manchukuo' (Itō 1987: 134), by which he meant the Japanese occupation of Manchuria by the Kwantung Army in 1931. For the first time, he claims, Japan had left its old path of a free-market maritime economy and had instead embarked on a new policy of a self-sufficient continental economic sphere in East Asia. Mōri ascribes this to Japan's dual political nature; based upon a maritime, free-market economy, it was at the same time developing a new, continental character, which demanded the establishment of a planned economy (Itō 1987: 134). Mōri euphemistically referred to Japan's expansion in East Asia as a 'new continental order', claiming that this would 'liberate' both the Manchurian and the Chinese economy (Kamakura 1939b: 32).

Although he emphasized that trade was not solely for the pursuit of profits and material acquisition, he also cited high economic growth as a main objective of his envisioned new economic order in East Asia. The pillars of this were supposed to be the key manufacturing, machine tool and precision machinery industries (Kamakura 1939c: 88). He considered technological innovation one of the keys to economic growth, referring to himself as an 'economic engineer' (*keizai gijutsu-sha*) in his pursuit of achieving that aim (Itō 1987: 140–1).

Mōri regarded the 'Chinese Incident' (the Marco Polo Bridge Incident in 1937 that led directly to the Sino–Japanese War) as an East Asian revolution against 'international capitalism and communism', as an action that would eventually lead to the unification of the Asian people. He argued that the incident had made Japan the manager of her own economy for the first time in history (Itō 1987: 134–5, Kamakura 1939b: 26). Further spreading nationalist propaganda, he saw Japan, China and Manchuria as a single political power in which productivity would rapidly increase if a 'totalitarian planned economy' (*zentai-shugi-teki na keikaku keizai*) could be established. This abandonment of the liberal order in favour of a totalitarian state is epitomized by one of his key political slogans, 'One ruler, all the people' (*ikkun-banmin*) (Kamakura 1939a: 24, Itō 1987: 136).

Free-market benefits vs. visions of a planned economy

Mōri considered political power the key factor for the establishment of his envisioned totalitarian planned economy. His conviction can be summed up as 'not control of politics by the economy, but control of the economy through politics' (Itō 1987: 136–7, Kamakura 1939b: 26).

Nevertheless, like many planners of his time, he did not pursue the idea of a controlled economy in a very resolute and consistent way; rather, he indicated that state control does not have to amount to a complete transformation of the existing private enterprise system. Although he was convinced that an economy striving to provide for the well-being of all strata of society best be kept under state control, he did not at all imply that all free-market elements had to be abandoned. He thought it possible and even necessary for elements of both a controlled and a private economy to exist simultaneously, and expressed contempt for both economic orders in their pure forms (Kamakura 1939b: 28–9). He considered a state-controlled economy that provides no room for independence or individual initiatives as much a menace to the people's livelihood as a private economy that shuts out the state completely. This toned-down version of a planned economy was obviously aimed at pacifying big business, which right from the start fought the Planning Board's ideas as unacceptable attempts at forcing a socialist economic order upon Japan (Taiyōji 1970: 222–3), thus equating planning with socialism.

The 'socialist' label, however, did not fit Japan, since the socialist economic order aims at the socialization of the means of production and the complete bureaucratic levelling out of all former independent economic entities, not accepting any form of individual economic autonomy. In contrast, in Japan there was still room for private influence on the economy at least until 1941 (Taiyōji 1970: 222–3), when the escalation of the Pacific War resulted in stricter state control. By examining who held equity in the National Policy Companies (*Kokusaku-gaisha*) and the membership profile of the forced cartels known as control associations (*tōsei-kai*) in each branch of the economy, one sees that *zaibatsu* representatives held considerable sway (cf., Otto's contribution in this volume).

Given the blunt anti-communism and anti-socialism that was prevalent in wartime Japan, the often-invoked argument of the 'socialist' character of the Japanese wartime economy loses much of its validity. Socialist and communist thinkers were purged, and big business pressured the government to have hardliners who favoured a planned economy removed from the Planning Board and ultimately arrested (in the Cabinet Planning Board Incident, see Fletcher 1982: 153).

Ryū Shintarō, one of the most ardent and prominent supporters of state control, whose work was a favourite of these planners, was labelled an 'unpatriotic communist' and felt forced to set off for Germany, where he worked as a foreign correspondent on the daily newspaper *Asahi shinbun*. Pro-planners were accused by the business world of attempting to introduce a socialist economic order to Japan under the cloak of supporting the defence economy. The consequences of this showed that capital was still a very powerful force (Fletcher 1982: 129, 152–3). In particular, the powerful *zaibatsu* lobby still had enough sway to prevent any more radical attempt at restructuring the economy against its interests.

It should be noted, though, that increased government control of the economy was part of a global wartime trend and was frequently referred to as such by Japanese officials and intellectuals who supported it. This trend was demonstrated in 1941, for instance, by emerging American ideas of a 'managerial revolution' that 'would sweep away the old bourgeois ruling classes and place control over the means of production in the hands of a managerial elite' (Duus 1984: 822).

The combination of state planning with the maintenance of certain private economic elements was also demonstrated in Nazi Germany's economic policy. Leading reformist bureaucrats like Mōri and Okumura did not deny this source of influence (Furukawa 1992: 56–7, 119). Blunt anti-Marxism was demonstrated in Nazi Germany in order to win over the economic establishment. At the same time, certain anti-capitalist expressions aimed to appeal to social strata (such as small and medium-sized craft workshops and blue- and white-collar workers) who felt they could not compete against big capital (cf., Kühnl 1971: 90–2).

However, centralized state control or a bureaucrat-led levelling of all former independent economic entities had not been completely realized in Nazi Germany. While labour and trade unions had been broken up and abolished, the big industrial groups and banks maintained considerable independence and power. Restrictions were imposed on individual entrepreneurs' freedom to secure the economic interests of business as a whole (Schweitzer 1964: 529, Kühnl 1979: 125).

In Japan, this dichotomy between monopoly capital and small capital was manifest in the conflict between the dominant *zaibatsu* and small businesses. The Planning Board as well as Ryū Shintarō actually sought the dissolution of small businesses and their reorganization into large-scale enterprises (Fletcher 1982: 122). Mōri, though, tried to evade any explicit statement that could antagonize any of the opposing groups, which led to the rather vague content of his economic policy.

The combination of state planning (as exemplified by the Four-Year Plan of 1936) and free enterprise was not considered contradictory in Germany. An ideologue of the time held that:

> Political control of the economy by the state culminates in the state economy. State control of the economy does not mean general, direct state economy, however. It does not mean that the state itself runs the economy in all cases by its own instruments. Rather, it [. . .] allows economic activity by private entrepreneurs and non-governmental associations.
>
> (Huber 1936: 28)

The same point of view is presented in an article published in the economic journal *Der Deutsche Volkswirt* (The German Economist) in 1941, maintaining that the state only wanted to guide the economy, leaving the actual implementation of economic policy and management to the initiative of private industrialists, and maintaining competition and private property (Neumann 1981: 217).

In Germany, individual state interventions in the economy were treated as exceptions to the rule. An example is state control of the power supply industry, which was considered particularly important for the economy and the 'livelihood of the people' (Huber 1936: 28–9). At least on a theoretical level, therefore, the influence of German wartime economic thought on Japanese planners like Mōri should not be neglected.

Relationships between the state and the individual

Mōri expected the new economic order to serve his vision of an East Asian community under Japanese rule, in which all aspects of life – culture, literature, law and the economy – were to be regulated (Kamakura 1939b: 25–6). He agreed with Friedrich List, who held that a nation's wealth is represented not by stocks of commodities but by the abilities and skills of its people. Unlike the classical economists, List also considered education, legislation and science to be historically important productive forces.

Mōri pinpointed the Marco Polo Bridge Incident as the beginning of the controlled economy (*tōsei keizai*), which he asserted had transformed the Japanese people from economic objects into economic subjects (Kamakura 1939b: 25–6, Itō 1987: 137, 140). Man was no longer the abstract, universal human being as depicted in (neo-)classical economic theory, but rather became an active participant in the economy, influencing market processes as he deemed himself a part of the economy. In this way, Mōri bade farewell to the classical *homo oeconomicus*, and farewell to the concept of individuals being objects capable of unlimited rationality. Instead, he promoted an economy bare of abstractions, one that was an 'integral part of the people's life', as he put it.

Under the new economic order, the 'industrialist' (*kigyō-sha*) was not defined as a capitalist, but rather as an 'enterprise engineer' (*kigyō-gijutsu-sha*) who as such was eligible for state protection (Kamakura 1939c: 88, Itō 1987: 140). Mōri envisioned cooperation between the state, acting as a superordinate monitoring body, and managers, working as administrators of capital and putting their technical know-how at the state's disposal. His new economic order was to ensure that employees and 'enterprise engineers' would no longer compete against each other as opponents, no longer be controlled by the desire for higher income, because they would be protected by the state. Both workers and 'enterprise engineers' would act for the benefit of the company, whose main objective was supposedly the pursuit of public well-being.

The dominance and superiority of the 'human factor' in this new economy would 'liberate' labour, technology and the companies themselves from the restrictions of 'capital'. The state would set certain economic objectives. The economic order would be supported and maintained through the regulation of production, profits, and competition (Kamakura 1939a: 26, Itō 1987: 140).

Mōri's vision of the relationship between workers and the state remained opaque, just like that of the German universalists and romanticists he was obviously influenced by. As to how that consciousness to act according to the principles of the state could be brought about in workers or how it would be expressed, he proposed the mobilization and organization of all strata of society. As neither 'one-man leadership' nor a majority party would be appropriate for Japan, he advocated the establishment of a united political organ, acting as an 'advisory body of all the people' (Itō 1987: 138–9).

Mōri aimed at ideologically legitimizing the economic order, i.e., the controlled economy, rather than hammering out a profound economic theory. He directed his economic considerations to meeting the demands of a Japanese state that was aiming at expansionism, and thereby became a tool of national power politics. By spreading nationalistic propaganda, he tried to rationalize Japanese expansionism and dominance in East Asia. In the following section, a closer look will be taken at how this ideology translated into reality.

VISIONS INTO PRACTICE: STATE CONTROL OF THE POWER SUPPLY

The ideas of the reformist bureaucrats were realized in 1937 through the Electric Power Control Law (*Denryoku kokka kanri-hō*). This law was an unprecedented example of Japanese wartime economic control, since it provided the government with considerable sway over the national power supply. In order to justify this *modus operandi* the Planning Board referred to the priority of public over private interest and profit maximization (Ikeo 1938: 2, Taiyōji 1970: 222), claiming that the distribution of electricity was of ultimate concern for the functioning of the Japanese industry and defence (Fletcher 1982: 74, Furukawa 1992: 57), since electricity could only be produced centrally and then distributed nationwide.

The reformist bureaucrats were among those who demanded that the 'anarchy of [capitalist] production' (*seisan no museifu*) (Fletcher 1982: 74) be brought to an end. The private enterprise system, according to their assessment, had led to regional bottlenecks and sometimes power surpluses, creating severe domestic differences in prices which could only be corrected through state control (Matsuzawa 1941: 37). The law was thus tantamount to a revolution against the then-dominant management by private enterprise. It produced protests from business leaders who felt deprived of their autonomy and profit opportunities (Ikeo 1938: 25, Fletcher 1982: 74).

A supplement to the law, the Japan Electric Power Company Act, passed on 6 April 1938 and scheduled to be implemented on 1 April of the following year, provided the legal framework for the establishment of the Japan Electric Power Generation and Transmission Company (*Nippon Hassōden KK*). The priority of public over private interest is demonstrated by the company's classification as a 'special-purpose company' (*tokushu-gaisha*), alluding to its semi-governmental character. The government planned to implement state control of the national power supply through the *Nippon Hassōden* (Art. 2 of the Electric Power Control Law), aiming at lowering electricity prices and maintaining and increasing the electricity supply. Article 1 of the law put the *Nippon Hassōden* in charge of power generation and supply (Matsuzawa 1941: 37).

Regarding the state's capital share of the *Nippon Hassōden*, however, the worries of the former shareholders and entrepreneurs appear to have been premature. Although Art. 8 of the law provided for state shares in the equity capital of the company, there were no such shares as late as September 1939. But already after the first fiscal year, the government had to subsidize the legally guaranteed payment of dividends and had to provide compensation for losses (Matsuzawa 1941: 68, Obama 1940: 70).

All important decisions, ranging from power distribution and setting of the electricity price, to logistics and the establishment of new plants, were to be made by the government and implemented by the *Nippon Hassōden*, which acted as a manager (Ikeo 1938: 2–3). Thus, despite the continuing principle of private ownership, the government got its stake in what used to be monopoly capital.

That the law clearly reflects the conceptions of the reformist bureaucrats should not be surprising, since it was conceived of primarily by Okumura Kiwao, the Shōwa group's secondary ideologue. Okumura had gained experience relevant to state control during his deployment in Manchuria, where he was occupied with the establishment of the Manchurian Telegraph and Telephone Corporation (*Manshū Denshin Denwa KK*), a semi-governmental joint venture that started operating in 1933. After visiting both Europe and the United States in 1937, he became particularly interested in German and Italian totalitarianism and Fascism. His sources of influence were finally revealed in a book published in 1938, which demonstrated a heavy reliance on German social science and economics (particularly that of Werner Sombart) as well as on Nazi economic doctrines (Furukawa 1992: 56–7).

It therefore does not come as a surprise that the drafting of the bill was mainly influenced (and welcomed) by the armed forces (Fletcher 1982: 74, 148). The reorganization of the power supply sector was consequently categorized under the generic term 'reform policy' (*kakushin seisaku*), thus demonstrating its proximity to its intellectual originators, the reformist bureaucrats.

CONCLUSIONS

Japanese wartime economic planners drew on a variety of ideological sources, many of them foreign, in order to rationalize an economic order which would assist a state aiming for expansion. The main problem confronting the planners was how to introduce these foreign ideas to a Japanese audience and integrate them into a specifically Japanese context. This task was made easier by a considerable amount of preliminary work which had been undertaken in the 1920s by Japanese ideologues such as Kita Ikki and Takabatake Motoyuki, who had devoted themselves to the conception of ultra-nationalist, etatist state systems fashioned according to the Japanese political and historical context.

The intellectuals who offered their services to the Japanese empire were very rarely economists; rather, they were mostly foreign policy propagandists who sought broad acceptance for Japanese expansion on the Asian continent. Along the way, they spread slogans on the necessity of a national defence economy. For that purpose, they had to unite a diverse assortment of groups, which ultimately led to a watering down of their economic concepts. The economic order eventually brought about was thus neither that of a pure (Soviet-style) planned economy nor strictly oriented towards free enterprise.

Goals set by hardliners within the Planning Board such as the strict economic planning by the state through a central planning agency, the state control of profits, and the separation of capital ownership and management, had to be set aside for a long time, because the big business lobby, represented by the *zaibatsu*, was too powerful. This lobby devoted all its energy to maintaining its influence. Five-Year Plans and shows of anti-capitalism aside, the Japanese controlled economy fell far short of a socialist economic order. Key elements of socialist economies such as the socialization of the means of production and the abandonment of the profit principle were not put fully into practice in Japan. Like Nazi Germany's planners, the Japanese counterparts could not, and did not want to, do without the support of big capital. Big business, on the other hand, derived benefits from expansionism, resulting in the opening up of new markets and the tapping of resources.

The intellectuals most willing to serve those wartime demands were the reformist bureaucrats, whose plans for a new economic order were not all that new, since they mainly combined fragments of already well-known economic thought. The result was an ideology that was both anti-communist and anti-capitalist, and that stressed the indispensability of a powerful state. These intellectuals rationalized the establishment of an East Asian Co-Prosperity Sphere under Japanese dominance, the goal of which being Japanese self-sufficiency, by emphasizing the 'economic struggle for existence' of all nations.

The economic order that was devised by the reformist bureaucrats combined the centralistic principle of state planning with the maintenance of key elements of free enterprise. Japanese wartime planners did not establish a new economic system; they simply imposed greater state control on an economy that still rested upon private ownership and private profit. This remained so until the escalation of the Pacific War resulted in a gradual decrease of the freedom of corporate management. However, big business often benefitted quite directly from the policies of the bureaucrats.

ACKNOWLEDGEMENTS

The author is indebted to Gerd Hardach, Erich Pauer, Jason Truesdell and three anonymous readers for helpful comments and criticisms on earlier versions of this manuscript.

REFERENCES

Duus, Peter (1984) 'The reaction of Japanese big business to a state-controlled economy in the 1930s', *Rivista Internazionale di Scienze Economiche e Commerciali* 9: 819–32.

Fletcher, William Miles (1982) *The Search for a New Order*, Chapel Hill: University of North Carolina Press.

Furukawa Takahisa (1992) *Shōwa senchū-ki no sōgo kokusaku kikan* (National policy instruments of the Shōwa wartime period), Tōkyō: Furukawa Kōbunkan.

Gottl-Ottilienfeld, Friedrich von (1932) *Der Mythus der Planwirtschaft: Vom Wahn im Wirtschaftsleben* (The myth of the planned economy: illusion in economic life), Jena: Gustav Fischer.

Huber, Ernst-Rudolf (1936) 'Staat und Wirtschaft' (State and economy), in Hans-Heinrich Lammers and Hans Pfundtner (eds) *Die weltanschaulichen, politischen und staatsrechtlichen Grundlagen des nationalsozialistischen Staates* (The ideological, political and constitutional foundations of the National Socialist state), Vol. 1, Art. 19, Berlin: Industrieverlag Spaeth & Linde.

Ikeo Yoshizō (1938) *Denryoku kokka kanri-an ni tsuite* (On the Electric Power Control Bill), Tōkyō: Tōkyō Shōkō Kaigisho.

Itō Takashi (1987) 'Mōri Hideoto ron oboegaki' (In commemoration of the views of Mōri Hideoto), in Kindai Nihon kenkyū-kai, *Senji keizai* (The wartime economy), *Nenpō kindai Nihon kenkyū* (Annals of modern Japanese studies), 9: 129–50, Tōkyō: Yamakawa Shuppankai.

Kamakura Ichirō (1939a) 'Kokumin soshiki to Tō-A kyōdōtai no fukabunsei' (The indivisibility of the national structure and the East Asian community), *Kaibō jidai* 1: 22–8.

—— (1939b) 'Nihon kokumin keizai no keisei to seiji – hōtoshite no "Tō-A no shin-chitsujo"' (Formation and politics of the Japanese national economy – 'The new East Asian order as a rule'), *Kaibō jidai* 4: 25–32.

—— (1939c) 'Kokumin keizai to shieki' (The national economy and private profit), *Kaibō jidai* 5: 83–9.

—— (1940) 'Taiheiyō kūkan no seikaku kakumei – sekai seiji to Tō-A kyōei-ken no hensei' (The revolution of the Pacific region's character: world politics and the formation of an East Asian co-prosperity sphere), *Chūō kōron* 55, 11: 34–42.

Kühnl, Reinhard (1971) *Formen bürgerlicher Herrschaft: Liberalismus–Faschismus* (Forms of civic governance: liberalism–fascism), Reinbek bei Hamburg: Rowohlt.

—— (1979) *Faschismustheorien: Texte zur Faschismusdiskussion 2 – Ein Leitfaden* (Theories on Fascism: Texts on the discussion of Fascism 2 – An introduction), Reinbek bei Hamburg: Rowohlt.

Matsuzawa Isao (1941) *Kokusaku-gaisha ron* (On National Policy Companies), Tōkyō: Daiyamondo-sha.

Morris-Suzuki, Tessa (1989) *A History of Japanese Economic Thought*, London: Routledge.

Neumann, Franz L. (1981) 'Die Wirtschaftsstruktur des Nationalsozialismus', in Helmut Dubiel and Alfons Söllner (eds), *Horkheimer, Pollock, Neumann, Kirchheimer, Gurland, Marcuse: Wirtschaft, Recht und Staat im Nationalsozialismus: Analysen des Instituts für Sozialforschung 1939–1942* (Horkheimer, Pollock, Neumann, Kirchheimer, Gurland, Marcuse: Economy, law and the state under National Socialism: analyses by the Institute for Social Research 1939–1942), Frankfurt: Europäische Verlagsanstalt, pp. 129–233.

Obama Toshie (1940) 'Kokusaku-gaisha to kanryō' (National Policy Companies and the bureaucracy), *Bungei shunjū* 18, 9: 66–72.

Ott, Alfred E. and Winkel, Harald (1985) *Geschichte der theoretischen Volkswirtschaftslehre* (History of theoretical political economy), Göttingen: Vandenhoeck & Ruprecht.

Schweitzer, Arthur (1964) *Big Business in the Third Reich*, Bloomington: Indiana University Press.

Spann, Othmar (1972) *Der wahre Staat* (The true state) (Gesamtausgabe vol. 5), Graz: Akademische Druck- und Verlagsanstalt (first published 1938).

Spaulding, Robert M. Jr. (1971) 'The bureaucracy as a political force, 1920–45', in James William Morley (ed.) *Dilemmas of Growth in Prewar Japan*, Princeton, New Jersey: Princeton University Press, pp. 33–80.

Taiyōji Jun'ichi (1970) 'Die geistigen Grundlagen der industriellen Entwicklung in Japan' (The intellectual bases of industrial development in Japan), in Ikeda Kōtarō, Katō Yoshitarō, Taiyōji Jun'ichi, *Die industrielle Entwicklung in Japan unter besonderer Berücksichtigung seiner Wirtschafts- und Finanzpolitik* (Industrial development in Japan with special consideration of its economic and financial policies), (*Schriftenreihe zur Industrie- und Entwicklungspolitik*, vol. 1), Berlin: Duncker und Humblot, pp. 167–84.

Takada Yasuma (1944) *Tōsei keizai ron* (On the controlled economy), Tōkyō: Nihon Hyōron-sha.

Winkel, Harald (1977) *Die deutsche Nationalökonomie im 19. Jahrhundert* (The German political economy in the 19th century), Darmstadt: Wissenschaftliche Buchgesellschaft.

Yatsugi Kazuo (1971) *Shōwa dōran shishi (chū)* (A private history of Shōwa agitation, vol. 2), Tōkyō: Keizai Ōrai-sha.

3

JAPAN'S TECHNICAL MOBILIZATION IN THE SECOND WORLD WAR

Erich Pauer

INTRODUCTION

After its 'industrial apprenticeship' from 1850 to 1870, when Japan imported, copied and used Western equipment, Japan's industrial development made remarkable progress until the 1930s. The First World War provided further economic stimulus, and by 1920, Japan can be regarded as an industrialized nation. Although writers in the Meiji, Taishō and even the Shōwa periods often disregarded Japan's own creativity and denigrated the Japanese as 'copycats', studies show that Japan's technological development was by no means slower than in the West. Observers forget that only a few decades before, copying was as common in the West as in Japan. Japanese scientists actually displayed creativity, but the world took little notice of their innovations before the Second World War.

An improved educational system, new university faculties of science and technology, the establishment of private and national research laboratories, and better industrial vocational training after the First World War all meant that in the 1930s Japan rapidly closed the technological gap between itself and other industrial nations. Earlier generations of Japanese engineers and natural scientists went overseas to study, but by the 1930s education in most fields in Japan was highly rated, and Japanese scientists received most of their academic training at Japanese universities. Visits to industrialized countries were no longer exclusively for study or research; instead, scientists went mainly to collect information on technical developments useful to industry at home. Successful marketing of their products in the USA and Europe boosted Japanese engineers' confidence, and they gained respect in society and industry. In Manchuria, electricity and communication networks were quickly built, and industry was developed rapidly. These successes stimulated a 'technocratic consciousness' among engineers and technicians. In 1934, some engineers in the Communications Ministry began to move beyond their small technical arena: they railed against the 'omnipotence of the law' (*hōritsu bannō-shugi*, as they called it), challenging the powerful bureaucracy that made decisions without sufficient technical expertise. Similar complaints had been heard in western countries, especially Germany, where protests against the 'Juristenmonopol' shortly after the First World War (Willeke 1995a: 149, Willeke 1995b: 223) presaged a technocratic movement that would last two decades. The Japanese moves in the 1930s resulted from a movement within the engineering world that began in the 1920s, and which shows similarities to the technocratic movement in the United States and Germany.

THE TECHNOCRATIC MOVEMENT IN JAPAN

In 1918, leading figures of fourteen Japanese engineering associations established a forum called *Kōsei-kai* (Ōyodo 1989: 100). This forum was to represent the engineering world in countering civil servants, who were seen as lacking engineering or scientific understanding. Students at the engineering faculties of three universities in Tōkyō also established a *Kōgyō rikkoku dōshi-kai* (Association of persons of the same mind for establishing an industry-oriented state) (Ōyodo 1989: 104).

In 1920, Miyamoto Takenosuke (1892–1941) (later a leading technocratic public engineer) and nine colleagues proposed a 'Soviet of Technicians' (*gijutsu-sha no sobietto*) (Ōyodo 1989: 110). This phrase came from a chapter title in a book by Thorstein Veblen, the intellectual godfather of the technocratic movement in the United States (Veblen 1994: 138). Shortly afterwards, Miyamoto and his colleagues (all graduates from the Civil Engineering Department of Tōkyō University) founded the *Nihon kōjin kurabu* (Japan workmen club), which later became an important driving force within the technocratic movement. The name of this club shows Miyamoto's deep interest in social matters. Between 1923 and 1925 he travelled to Europe and the United States, where he collected information on his scientific interests (torsion of ferro-concrete) at various universities. While abroad he also showed interest in social movements of engineers, and collected ideas on the European and American technocratic movement (for details of his trip, see Ōyodo 1989: 88–91).

Veblen's multifaceted ideas may have had more influence on Japan's technocratic movement than assumed hitherto. Other writings of the American technocratic movement also became known in Japan during the 1920s. The ideas of the chequered figurehead of the American technocratic movement, Howard Scott, which are heavily based on Veblen, became known in Japan in the early 1930s. In 1933 a public discussion on technocracy (*Tekunokurashii zadan-kai*) resulted in the establishment of an 'Association for Technology and Economy' (*Gijutsu keizai kyōkai*), which aimed 'to take a new look at society from the standpoint of technology' and to create a new society based on this. Miyamoto Takenosuke was a member of this association; in his diary he refers to the need for scientific, technological and statistical studies to formulate plans for such a new society (see Ōyodo 1989: 207–8).

Frederick W. Taylor's writings on Scientific Management created a new way of thinking among engineers, and the widespread use of his approaches broadened the basis for technocracy in Japan. Taylor's ideas of efficiency, based on the engineering concepts of measurability and precision, also enlarged engineers' egos. The organization of scientific production required 'experts' or 'specialists' (terms often used by technocrats).

American ideas were not the only influence on Japan's technocracy. Friedrich von Gottl-Ottilienfeld's *Wirtschaft und Technik*, published in German in 1914, and in Japanese in 1931, pointed at a 'rational technology'; it was read by engineers and technicians who later became leading figures in Japan's technocratic movement (see Ōyodo 1989: 216 and 229, footnote 54). Other German influences included Sombart, Eugen Diesel, Friedrich Dessauer and Eberhard Zschimmer: their views of technology's relationships with mankind and economics, and their critiques of capitalist economics, promoted state influence and control (see Iwasaki 1995: 192). These ideas fell on fertile soil in Japan because of similar criticisms of the capitalist economy in Japan itself.

Despite fundamental differences in the technocratic movements in the USA, Germany and Japan, a basic feature of their success can be seen. In Japan, Europe and the United States, there was a widespread feeling that politicians and economists had failed to deal with the political and economic crises of the 1920s and 1930s. It was not a forced influx of ideas from Germany and the USA which lead to the growing technocratic consciousness in Japan; rather, Japanese technocrats took up outside ideas because they already held similar views on economy and society.

Veblen frequently used the term 'science and technology', denoting standardization and systematization in industry. The Japanese equivalent, *kagaku gijutsu* (science [and] technology), grew in popularity (for this see also Yamazaki 1995: 180, footnote 11). Another of Veblen's terms common among Japanese technocrats and military leaders was *gijutsu sanbō honbu* (technical general staff) (see Matsumae 1941: 148–76, Ōyodo 1989: 327–8), derived from the 'General Staff of the industrial system' (for example Veblen 1994: 71).[1] The idea of an 'alliance between engineers and workers' was reflected in the weekly mouthpiece of 'national policy', the *Kokusaku kenkyū-kai Shūhō*, which criticized technical professors and demanded an alliance with industrial workers to strengthen Japan's military potential (Kokusaku kenkyū-kai 1944: 6: 41: 2 (388)).

Examples of the affinity between Japanese and German ideas of representatives of the technocratic ideology are also legendary. Sombart's ideas of a *Bedarfsdeckungswirtschaft* (an economy for the satisfaction of needs) with a more totalitarian touch found no objection in Japan. The anti-Americanism and anti-capitalism of Zschimmer and Eugen Diesel had their counterparts in Japan (for example Ōkōchi 1938; see also Iwasaki 1995: 193). Diesel's demands for engineers to extend their power beyond formulas and machines to the whole of society (Willeke 1995a: 172–3, 277) was expressed in a similar way by many Japanese technocrats. Dessauer saw the possibility to transfer *Plantechnik* (a planning technique developed around 1920; see Willeke 1995a: 137) from natural sciences to economics, thereby creating a 'planned economy' in the form of a *Gemeinwirtschaft* (social economy). This bore a strong affinity to the Japanese idea of *kyōdōtai* (*Gemeinschaft*, 'community'), which was seen as the future basis of society. Germany and Japan also shared the idea of a *Gemeinwohl* (commonweal), to which engineers should contribute (Willeke 1995a: 141) and in which they should take a leading role because of their technical competence.

These discussions on technocracy reached a peak in the first half of the 1930s. They had an enormous influence on broader views of science and technology. More than two dozen books by Japanese authors on technology and its philosophy and relationship with society were published in just three years between 1937 and 1940 (for a list, see Iwasaki 1995: 190–1). Books focusing on the relationship between technology and civil administration indicate the main aim of the technocrats: rule by technologically competent people, i.e., engineers and natural scientists.

Both Japanese and German technocrats followed a system of *Technik-Kultur-Synthese* (synthesis of technology and culture), in which technology was seen as a material precondition, integral part or stabilizing superstructure, of a culture or nation (Willeke 1995a: 120). The Association of Japanese Engineers (*Nihon gijutsu kyōkai*) stated in a 1937 prospectus that Japanese culture was in many ways based on technology (Ōyodo 1989: 214). Therefore, all Japanese engineers and technicians should support technology and use it to serve their country. Compared with earlier demands, this prospectus is not so open in its advocacy of technocratic ideas, but its targets are still identifiable as technocratic in nature. After 1936 the technocratic movement continued to follow its previous course, but the term 'technocracy' was used less frequently. This may be because of attempts (begun in 1935) to unite engineers in a single association, thereby including factions less strongly associated with technocratic ideas. These ideas were promoted strongly nevertheless, as is shown in the programme of a Conference of Engineers of Six Ministries (*Rokusho gijutsu-sha kyōgikai*) in the mid-1930s, which stated that 'an indispensable precondition for the development of the national power, is a new movement which makes concrete the request for respect for technology and the respect for the experts' (Ōyodo 1989: 216).

Whereas the technocratic movement in the United States was anti-democratic and lacked technological or economic ideas for national renewal, the German technocrats aimed to prepare a technological state based on techno-scientific planning, jurisdiction and expertise. The German technocrats wanted to establish a competent planning body to use science and technology for the welfare of the whole people (Willeke 1995a: 100). The infusion of scientific intelligence into the political infrastructure, making use of technical and scientific instruments as authoritative guides to decisions, would lead to rule by engineers and technicians. In Japan, by contrast, the technocrats did not need to move into government: they already sat there. Most of the leading technocrats were civil engineers in government ministries, with the Communications Ministry having the most influential and imaginative men. These civil servants became the leaders of a 'technocratic movement' in the late 1930s, though they no longer used the term 'technocracy'.

THE 'TECHNOCRATS' IN ACTION

Shortly before hostilities with China began in mid-1937, a small group of Communications Ministry engineers began networking with engineers of other ministries and government institutions. The resulting partnership sought to promote the social and economic importance of technology to the broader public. Without using the term 'technocracy', it demanded more respect for the expertise of engineers and technicians (clearly a technocratic demand). Within a year, this movement had gained much support from engineers in other ministries and institutions.

At a 'Meeting of Engineers for a Technology-Oriented State' (*Gijutsu rikkoku gijutsu-sha taikai*) at the end of 1937, 1,600 technicians passed a resolution asserting the importance of mobilizing engineers and technicians to establish a technology-oriented state (*gijutsu rikkoku*). The resolution argued for laying the foundations for such a state through:

- the scientific development and exploration of raw materials,
- making Japanese technology independent from foreign countries, and so able to manufacture important goods in Japan,
- controlling the export of Japanese technical knowledge, and
- improving technical training and expanding technical research institutions.

Japanese power was to be based on the Japanese way of thinking, coupled with Japanese technology. Since industrial development results from the development and the utilization of technology, the engineers argued, the government should employ far more engineers, particularly in positions where technical decisions were concerned (Ōyodo 1989: 219–21).

This resolution was clearly aimed at technological revolution. Because the state and its technology policy were also involved, one could say that the engineers aimed towards a Japanese kind of technocracy, where social and political decisions would be made according to the needs of technical methods and systems. Shortly afterwards, concrete demands were made for technicians to participate in the civil administration, for them to take up leading government posts, and for laws to enforce these demands (Ōyodo 1989: 231).

How did the group of engineers proceed with their demands to establish a more technology-oriented state? How much support did such technocratic ideas have to offer wartime mobilization? What results stemmed from the technocrats' efforts? Did the technical mobilization they planned support the Japanese armament industry? And on what level did technical mobilization proceed?

To answer these questions, this chapter first examines the development of several mobilization plans, and considers who helped to draw them up. It then addresses the issue of re-educating the work force, which was one purpose of mobilization. The closing section deals with the problems resulting from a lack of systematic thought during the product-design process, which was the main reason for difficulties in introducing mass production into Japanese companies.

MOBILIZATION AND TECHNOCRATIC IDEAS

After the outbreak of the Sino-Japanese War, bureaucratic engineers such as Miyamoto Takenosuke and Matsumae Shigeyoshi gained influence in the government, especially within the Konoe Cabinets between 1937 and 1941. They successfully networked the various engineers' associations, thereby gaining influence over both the Cabinet and public opinion. But not only did they aim for a future Japanese technocracy; they also turned their attention to the war on the continent. A meeting of leading technocrats in 1938 discussed both what engineers could do to promote the development of Japan, as well as Manchuria and China, then occupied by Japanese forces. The meeting emphasized the exploitation of raw materials for the future industrial prosperity of Japan – but this exploitation also meant the economic development of Manchuria.

The engineers formed an Association for the Technical Development of China, which demanded the creation of an office to work with the Konoe Cabinet, charged with developing the technology policy for the continent and supporting its realization (Ōyodo 1989: 239). Within this office, a special department was to be set up to deal with general technical development (*Gijutsu no sōgōteki shidō-bu*).

The various engineers' associations and study groups were all privately organized, but the leading figures were government bureaucrats. This meant that a strong connection between the group's aims and government policy could be established. The engineers saw their role as technical bureaucrats. They aggressively sought to influence decisions involving technological matters. For them, technology could, and should, be used as an instrument for Japanese development; technology was regarded as 'raw material'. In their minds, technology was the way, the primary means to development; politicians, entrepreneurs, and indeed the entire population should be trained as 'scientific technicians' (*kagakuteki gijutsu-sha*). Technology was practical science, science with function (Ōyodo 1989: 251–2).

This technocratic ideology also influenced economists such as Mōri Hideoto, one of the leading ideologists of the time, who identified himself as a 'technical economist' (*keizai gijutsu-sha*). He regarded new technology and a new technological orientation as the driving force for economic development not only in Japan but in the whole yen-bloc: Japan, Manchuria and China. For him, technology was an unlimited source of power (Itō 1987: 140).

Beginning in 1938, these technocrats expanded the scope of their plans. No longer limiting themselves to Japan, they now focused on the entire Asian continent, particularly on China. The primacy of politics and economics in 'pan-Asianism' were now accompanied by a 'technological Asianism'. The advance of Japanese technology would be the core for the development of Asian technology. In addition to this primary element, other political elements would be introduced: slogans such as 'coexistence and mutual prosperity' (*kyōson kyōei*) and a 'new community' (*shin kyōdotai*) were similar to those used in Konoe's 1938 speech, 'New Order in East Asia'. The technocrats believed the new community should be founded not only on political and economic devices, but also on technology, as technology was regarded as an important pillar for the new Asia.

For the plan to succeed, technicians would have to be mobilized. The basic ideas promoted were:

- to establish an independent technology, i.e., to become independent from foreign (technological) ideas, patents, licenses and so on; and
- to control technology and broaden engineers' minds to make them aware of economics, politics and culture. Such awareness would lead to a much broader development of technology. This could be achieved via technical education.

The technocrats planned to combine the raw materials of China with Japanese technology to establish a 'Greater East Asian Co-Prosperity Sphere', as it soon came to be called (Ōyodo 1989: 273).

In 1938 the 'Asian Development Board' (*Kō-A-in*) was established, chaired by the Prime Minister himself, and four of its five departments (general affairs, politics, economics, culture and technology) were headed by bureaucratic engineers from different ministries. All of them can be characterized as technocrats (for details, see Ōyodo 1989: 258–61). Another technical advisory body (*Kō-A gijutsu iinkai*, Asian Development Technology Committee) was established at the Prime Minister's office, and was staffed with 44 engineers from various ministries. This committee, too, emphasized the development of China, although they were actually more interested in the exploitation of China's raw materials to supply Japanese industry. Japan was to strengthen its (industrial) power by using China's raw materials. Japan was to gain self-sufficiency by developing its defence capabilities and by controlling raw materials (Ōyodo 1989: 264).

This ideology was based on a conception of the state and economy critical of free-market economics. In a 'defence-oriented state' (*kokubō kokka*), which was then the most widely accepted conception of the state in Japan, technology was considered to be one of the most important tools: only technology made the exploitation of raw materials possible. In a free economy, exploitation of raw materials is entrusted to private entrepreneurs. But, in modern times, it was argued, technology and the raw materials won by it must be used for the prosperity of the whole country. State control over technology and raw materials was therefore considered necessary (Ōyodo 1989: 420). These concepts of state control (by bureaucratic engineers) over technological development clearly reveal the lasting strength of technocratic ideas among the public. Such an idea of 'rational technology' (strongly connected with technocratic ideas of the German writers described above) gained further support in 1939 after the surprising success of the German Wehrmacht in the war against Poland. Japanese economists explained Germany's military success as resulting from its scientific and technological power. The technocrats introduced their ideas to the Cabinet, and in 1940 they published various drafts of them on behalf of the second Konoe Cabinet.

This clearly shows the level at which technological mobilization was planned. It was not the military and its engineers, but government technocrats who were responsible for planning the mobilization. Their plans were influenced not so much by military targets, but by the goal of the 'defence-oriented state', for which technology was regarded as an important pillar. 'Technical mobilization' was not so much a mobilization for war, but a move towards a kind of a technocratic state – Japan – that would lead the entire continent of Asia.

MOBILIZATION OF THE SCIENTIFIC COMMUNITY

The first step towards mobilizing scientists was undertaken by the government itself. Article 25 of the National Mobilization Law (*Kokka sōdōin-hō*), enacted in 1938, permitted mobilization measures in emergencies. An ordinance (*Sōdōin shiken kenkyū-rei*) of 30 August 1939, which was based on this law made it possible for the government to require research laboratories to carry out certain research and tests (*shiken kenkyū*). A 'Committee for Mobilization of the Scientific Community' (*Kagaku dōin iinkai*) was designated to draw up a plan for the mobilization of the scientific community. This committee consisted of 39 engineers and technicians from various government offices (for a list see Ōyodo 1989: 316–18), supported by 45 persons recruited from several ministries. It was headed by the Vice-Chairman of the Planning Board (*Kikaku-in*).

The committee completed its Sciences Mobilization Plan (*Kagaku dōin keikaku*) in May 1940. This aimed to facilitate stronger coordination between science and industry, since current levels of scientific guidance were regarded as inadequate for the continuous improvement (*kaizen*) of industry and for converting scientific results into industrial goods. The Plan's goals were:

- the scientific exploitation, development and use of raw materials in Japan, China and Manchuria to promote the self-sufficiency of Japan
- the support and control of scientific research and the scientific development of industry

According to the guidelines in this Plan, each ministry was to establish its own mobilization plan and submit it to the Planning Board for approval. The Planning Board was to keep in close contact with other agencies regarding the training of researchers and the allocation of funds. The purpose of the research being conducted was also evaluated, and studies which could help Japan reach self-sufficiency in various areas were classified as 'essential' (i.e., military related). This particularly concerned research on metals, chemicals, fuels, mining, food, replacement parts, precision engineering, chemical equipment, electronic equipment, transportation technology (aircraft, automobiles, trains and ships), electronic communication and weapons (Ōyodo 1989: 319–20). More than 500 research projects were initiated by the Planning Board in the following three years (Morris-Suzuki 1994: 147).

The Mobilization Plan actually encompassed nothing surprising. Its contents had been discussed previously at both formal and informal levels, in government as well as private associations, and in various clubs and committees. The Plan was nothing more than a repetition of the technocrats' ideas. The close connection between the government technocrats and Cabinet members made a Plan based on these ideas possible.

The Plan also included provisions for supervising scientific research. Every government agency was to encourage 'essential research' within its affiliated research bodies, and research topics and funds were to be reported to the Planning Board. Grants were also expected to be reported. When researchers needed to requisition materials for projects, they were to report their needs to the Planning Board, which would then distribute the materials requested. By developing this system, the Planning Board intended to establish a general communication network to support research (Ōyodo 1989: 321–2).

According to the Plan, a general scientific body (*Chūō tōkatsu kikan*) was to be established in 1940 to coordinate the visits of researchers to various countries to inquire into technical matters. This body was also to be responsible for the so-called 'pooling' of patents, for establishing a technical advisory group, for coordinating basic and applied research, and for drawing up plans for joint research projects involving private and government research laboratories. The intention was to establish tight government control over technological research and development (Ōyodo 1989: 325–6).

The participation of technicians in political administration, a demand by the bureaucratic engineers already mentioned, was strengthened in 1940 when Konoe put into practice his 'New Order' (*Shintaisei*). In the same year, the various ideas concerning the mobilization of technology and the sciences culminated.

A leading body was the Technical Committee for the Defence State (*Kokubō gijutsu iinkai*), initiated by Matsumae Shigeyoshi. This was formed within the Association of Japanese Engineers (*Nihon gijutsu kyōkai*) by a group of about 150 military engineers interested in planning the defence state. These engineers came mostly from the middle bureaucratic level (*kachō*, head of section) of various ministries. The committee was subdivided into ten smaller sub-committees; Miyamoto Takenosuke headed the most important one on technology policy. The targets set by the committee did not differ dramatically from those identified in the mobilization plan, but they were discussed in more detail in the committee's meetings (Ōyodo 1989: 335). The main points of discussion were:

- (At the committee's first meeting): State control of technology research and development;
- (Second meeting): Technical education, starting from elementary school for both boys and girls; education for apprentices and adults (ideas similar to those of the *Shōwa kenkyū-kai* [Shōwa Research Association], a brains trust for Prime Minister Konoe).
- (Third meeting): Administration of technology (*gijutsu gyōsei*) aiming to raise the technological level, the distribution of technical experts, registration and categorization of technicians according their abilities, controls on technology imports, establishment of 'patent-pools', dispatching of 'technology attachés' in foreign countries, etc.

The essential goal was the technological independence of Japan (for details see Ōyodo 1989: 342–74). Especially in this case, the reciprocity and tight connections between government officials and private organizations can be observed clearly. Because they were engineers as well as bureaucrats, the technocrats from the engineers' association were able to influence laws and ordinances in the interests of technocracy. In this way, the technocratic movement gathered momentum and influence before 1940.

Not surprisingly, therefore, technology was a major portion of the 'Ten-Year Plan for a National Policy' (*Sōgō kokusaku jū-nen keikaku*). A major section of this plan was dedicated to 'Technology Policy', and it covered the following points:

- the promotion and encouragement of technical education;
- the encouragement and control of scientific research (including private research);
- the guidance of scientists to fit their role as inventors and innovators for their country; and
- the tightening of controls on technicians and technology (Ōyodo 1989: 338).

This plan, drafted under the guidance of the Yonai Cabinet in the first half of 1940, was re-introduced by the following Konoe Cabinet with only slight modifications. Although drafted by a different body, the plan was quite similar to what the *Shōwa Kenkyū-kai* had advanced some years before (Ōyodo 1989: 339).

The technocratic ideology viewed political parties as superfluous. Efforts to network engineers and technicians were realized in August 1940 with the founding of the All-Japan Board of Associations of Scientists and Engineers (*Zen Nihon kagaku gijutsu dantai rengō-kai*; abbr. *Zen-ka-gi-ren*). This aimed to reach every scientist, engineer and their associations, and to bind them to national policy goals. The leading technocrats regarded scientists and engineers as important people at the forefront of political and economic leadership.

With their close connections to political and economic power in government, the technocrats then began putting their goals into practice. With respect to the Greater East Asian Co-Prosperity Sphere, the technocrats moved towards establishing Japan's leading technological role in Asia, funding research to match Japan's technical capabilities with those of the US and Europe. Their technology policy aimed to support both the 'defence state' and Japanese self-sufficiency, and sought to establish a 'New Order for Science and Technology'. Various new committees, councils, bodies and institutions were founded, the most important being the 'Technology Deliberation Council' (*Gijutsu shingi-kai*) and the 'Technology Board' (*Gijutsu-in*). The latter was the leading body for technical mobilization (Ōyodo 1989: 389, 391); it brought under its roof the diverse technology policies of various government organizations. It also controlled the funding of all government and private research institutions (Morris-Suzuki 1994: 148). Several people in the various committees and bodies were engaged in drafting new political platforms, plans, outlines and bills, which were then intensively discussed, rewritten and re-discussed. Though their words differed from earlier plans, these documents had the same aims and made the same proposals (for various plans, drafts and outlines see Ōyodo 1989: 392–412). Reconciling the different documents took time; but the 'General Plan for the Establishment of a New Science and Technology System' (*Kagaku gijutsu shintaisei kakuritsu yōkō*) (for the text see Ōyodo 1989: 426–30), was adopted by the Cabinet in May 1941 and published in *Shūhō* (Weekly Report) in early June. This was the first policy on science and technology in Japan.

The General Plan intended nothing less than a revolutionary promotion of science, dramatic technological development, and the cultivation of a science-oriented society (Commission 1991: 44). It was designated as the main pillar of the new system, aiming for the 'completion of the Japanese character of science and technology based upon resources in the Greater East Asian Co-Prosperity Sphere' (Yamazaki 1995: 168, Morris–Suzuki 1994: 148). It was several months before the basic draft for the establishment of the Technology Board could be enacted as an imperial decree (*chokurei*) at the end of January 1942.

In the meantime, however, strong opposition from the Ministry of Education and the Ministry of Commerce and Industry (both of which had their own plans) had reduced the push for a new technology policy (Yamazaki 1995: 169). Momentum was probably also lost because of the political and military developments in the previous months. Another blow was the death in late 1941 of Miyamoto Takenosuke, one of the most important promoters of technical mobilization. Not surprisingly, therefore, the organizational level and power of the Technology Board was much smaller than the technocrats had hoped. The Board was neither strong enough to advance technocratic ideas, nor did it have the authority to coordinate the work of government bodies and institutions.

The process of organizing the Board started when Japan was already at war with the US, and this situation hampered work. The Board prepared reports on the most sophisticated fields of science and technology where research should be promoted. Programmes of a more general character as well as definite ones – e.g., a 'Five-Year Plan for an Aeroplane Research System' – were included. The target was to create a coordinated group of research institutions dealing with basic and applied research, pilot production and production. For this, no new research institutions had to be established. Instead, the Board was to connect and control existing institutions – public, university, and commercial (for details see Yamazaki 1995: 170–1). This fulfilled one long-standing aim of ensuring the cooperation of research institutions.

Along with the establishment of the Technology Board, a Science and Technology Deliberation Council (*Kagaku gijutsu shingi-kai*), was to replace the existing Science Deliberation Council (*Kagaku shingi-kai*). Formed only in December 1942, this Council included nearly 200 people from various ministries, agencies and other public organizations as well as experienced scholars. It was headed by the Prime Minister, and the President of the Technology Board as his deputy (see Ōyodo 1989: 449–50). The Council held its first meeting in January 1943; it immediately began passing resolutions for mobilization, but it was much too late to have a concrete influence on wartime technology policy. The centralization of scientific and technical research continued to be discussed as late as mid-1944. The need for control, mobilization of research, the 'pooling' of scientists, and other issues were then still under discussion, still not put into practice. New plans were drawn up for this centralization and for using political power to achieve it. Despite the Technology Board's many attempts to systematize research institutions and foster cooperation among them, complaints about the gap between research and manufacturers continued (Kokusaku kenkyū-kai shūhō 1944: 6: 41: 2–8 (388–91)). The fact that the same issues still came up shows that almost none of the plans had materialized.

A further step towards the scientific mobilization of human resources was the establishment of the Research Mobilization Committee (*Kenkyū dōin kaigi*), which was based on a bill for Total Measures for Science and Technology Mobilization (*Kagaku gijutsu dōin sōgō hōsaku kakuritsu ni kansuru ken*), passed by the Cabinet in October 1943 (Kagaku gijutsu seisaku-shi kenkyū-kai 1990: 40). This Committee consisted of senior politicians, representatives of the Army and Navy, and outstanding scientists such as Ōkōchi Masatoshi (president of the Institute of Physical and Chemical Research [*Rikagaku kenkyū-sho*, abbr. *Riken*]), and Yagi Hidetsugu (President of the Tōkyō Institute of Technology *(Tōkyō kōgyō daigaku*]). But despite its prestigious membership, the Committee was destined to fail, too. It discussed plans and produced various documents, drafts and plans for mobilization. But even such priorities as improving the manufacture of vacuum tubes (necessary for radar) or reorganizing aeroplane science and technology were not put into effect. One reason was the strong opposition from the Army and Navy, which argued that the Technology Board should handle only scientific and technical problems, and not interfere in manufacturing. The Ministry of Education also opposed any plans that might diminish its leadership in science and technology. This ministry's idea was to cut the Technology Board down to a small body that would not be involved in research (for details see Yamazaki 1995: 173–8).

Despite all the false starts, planning for mobilization continued on various levels. At the end of 1944, propaganda supporting mobilization did not differ much from that in previous years (for examples, see Inamura 1944). In early 1945, a list prepared by the Information Bureau of the Imperial

Rule Assistance Association (*Taisei yokusan-kai*) describes the Technology Board as responsible for an overall year-long Campaign for the Diffusion of Science and Technology (*Kagaku gijutsu no fukyō undō*) (Akazawa *et al.*, 1984: 12: 349–356). This seems to have been a last attempt to popularize its goals and gain support from the masses.

The Technology Board had clearly failed to unite Japan's 250,000 engineers and technicians to support the wartime mobilization of science and technology. The only results of all the planning were piles of paper. The blame for this failure lies squarely on the technocrats, who were less concerned with practical issues than with science.

Despite all the failures, earlier measures based on the National Mobilization Law of 1938 and later the Sciences Mobilization Plan of 1940 led to a sudden increase in the number of research laboratories, researchers and projects from the late 1930s to 1942. At the end of this period, about 1,150 public and private laboratories existed (doubled in number in 1935), employing 50,000 researchers. More than 10,000 non-military research projects were counted in the same year (Morris-Suzuki 1994: 150, 148). As the technocrats clearly saw, these laboratories were independent from one another, and liaison among them was weak; they strove to improve the exchange of research findings to support the war effort, and for Japan's overall development. These ideas were clearly those of non-business people, and they neglected some basic rules. Entrepreneurs do not run their businesses in support of the country's far-reaching goals and future prosperity, but for their own (or their shareholders') profit. Accordingly, the big *zaibatsu* companies either sought, and usually found, ways to escape the strong state controls based on the new special economic laws (*Keizai-hō*), or they simply rejected unwelcome regulations. Laboratories and research institutions worked autonomously on projects important to their parent companies. Even during the war, Japanese companies emphasized long-term, basic research, though this was often blocked by short-term demands from the Army or Navy (Morris-Suzuki 1994: 151). As it was widely accepted that technological interchange was indispensable for the development of mass production, companies were sometimes forced to reveal certain technological developments (Yoshida 1990: 115–16, 120, cites examples of this), but even then the companies delayed transferring documents. This can hardly be called technological cooperation. In 1944, Ōkōchi Masatoshi noticed the failure of technological diffusion within industry, but was unable to understand its actual reasons. He thought that companies lacked only (public) acknowledgement of their services; but the companies themselves looked rather for financial compensation, not for awards (Yoshida 1990: 120).

The plans to centralize, systematize and control research in science and technology for the war effort also failed because of bureaucratic rivalries. Whereas on the one side, the technocrats struggled for power, on the other side, private-sector engineers and scientists made remarkable progress in their research, but sometimes had lacked the experience to put their findings into practice.

The ideas of a technocracy still bubbled in the heads of the elite bureaucratic engineers, but they never managed to establish a technology-oriented state as they had announced in the mid-1930s.

EDUCATING THE LABOUR FORCE AND INTRODUCING A NEW PRODUCTION SYSTEM

One reason for the failure of technological mobilization was the war situation. Another was the indifference of military and political leaders: they were accustomed to a system of giving and taking orders, not to one where those with the best technical ability made the decisions. But the third, and most important, reason lay in quite a different arena.

Mobilization was planned by the technocrats, most of whom were highly educated. In the planning period before 1940 most ignored the difference between theory and practice because their sights were on the higher goal of a technocracy. But when the time came to put the plans into action, theory and practice diverged, and a gap between practically oriented engineers and the bureaucratic engineers became apparent. The bureaucrats tried to act as administrative engineers, changing policy according to their latest ideas. This widened the gap and led to contradictions.

In addition to terms such as 'exploitation', 'control', 'coordination', 'pooling' and so on, two more terms are key to the discussion on technological mobilization in the late 1930s: 'education' (especially technical education), and 'production' or 'production engineering'.

In 1938 the chairman of the Riken concern and President of the Institute of Physical and Chemical Research, Ōkōchi Masatoshi, clearly pointed to a crucial issue: mass production. He said that Japan was able to manufacture two or three cars for a huge amount of money, but nobody knew how to make 10,000 cars a year. Nobody knew what equipment was necessary to mass-produce cars or other goods. He clearly saw that this problem could not be solved simply by multiplying existing tools by the hundredfold, but that a new manufacturing system based on a new way of thinking was necessary. A central problem for such mass-production engineering was the workforce, which would have to be educated in a new, and different, way. Technical mobilization thus depended upon education, and would have to start in elementary schools and continue all the way through to universities. But, as Ōkōchi saw it, education in technical fields could not remain merely theoretical in approach. As there were many innovations being made in Japan, but little in the way of means for converting the ideas into commercial goods, it would be necessary to change the teaching focus from production technology (*seisan gijutsu*) to production engineering (*seisan kōgaku*) (Kyōchōkai 1938: 5–7).

The technocrats were not opposed to such ideas. For them, too, increasing the number of technical schools and universities with departments of scientific and technical fields was the only way to solve the shortage of technically trained workers. The demand for university graduates in science and technology was three times greater than the supply; in 1940, the demand for graduates from technical schools was five times the supply (Miyamoto 1941: 201). The technocrats agreed that engineering education should be improved, seeing it as a basic requirement for satisfying the needs of mass production. Only by teaching technology from the very earliest levels of education would a technologically oriented people with the necessary understanding of technical methods develop (Miyamoto 1941: 203).

Shortly after the outbreak of the Sino–Japanese War, the lack of adequately trained technical workers led to laws controlling the employment of technical-school graduates. These laws were enacted in June and August 1938 (for details on these and other ordinances see Kōseishō 1988: 355, 357, and Ōyodo 1989: 274–5). A study of the distribution of technicians was to be done, and efforts were to be made to employ graduates more in concert with war needs (Cohen 1949: 309). The new laws also emphasized the training of technicians. The Ministry of Health and Welfare issued a Relative Ordinance (No. 55, April 1939) based on an October 1938 'Summary Draft of an Imperial Ordinance Concerning the Training of Technicians at Factories and Other Industrial Institutions', which required factories with more than 200 employees to implement compulsory training programmes for their technicians:

> The technicians are to be trained to qualify as 'soldiers of industry' and to qualify intellectually and technically as technicians of more than medium standing, with technical knowledge enabling them to pass extensive technical judgements on productive activities and carry on operations even when left to their own direction.
>
> (Department of Welfare 1939: 23; see also Sumiya 1977: 2: 292–307)

These ideas concerning the advancement of technical ability and the broadening of the qualifications of technicians within the labour force were seen as very important within the whole movement for technological mobilization, but success was limited to a small part of the industry. Only larger companies could afford such training programmes. A number indeed established training departments and developed curricula; aviation, shipyards, and iron and steel industries took the lead. By 1942, more than 1,500 training facilities were established, but the number of technicians produced was only 30,000 in 1941 and about 40,000 in 1942 (Sumiya 1977:

vol. 2, 299–302). The Ministry of Health and Welfare ordinance proposed training technicians only in larger firms, and as a result, a gap arose between the technical abilities of workers in larger firms and those of their subcontractors, where most of the parts necessary for the assembly lines were made.

News of the lack of trained workers must have reached the ears of the Industrial Patriotic Association (*Sangyō hōkoku-kai*), the organization established to control labour after the dissolution of labour unions in 1941. This association also included engineers employed by companies. With their practical experience and involvement in production, they had very different attitudes from their bureaucratic colleagues in the ministries. Whereas the government found it expedient to stimulate workers' spirits to make greater efforts, and the technocrats searched eagerly for new instruments to gain power, the practical engineers had to deal with real problems on the shop-floor. Meetings of engineers in the Industrial Patriotic Association (in late 1941 and late 1942) put practical matters in the forefront. Both meetings (for the texts see Kanda 1981: 288–90 and 371–6) made demands that corresponded exactly to demands made by the technocrats, but focusing only on the manufacturing process. They include demands for measures to increase efficiency, train technicians, educate shop-floor workers, establish study groups to improve workplaces, open technological knowledge to the public, manage labour. Besides references to the importance of technology for the country and that technology is a 'raw material', the lack of a spiritual tone is apparent – indicating a widening gap between the government technocrats and practical engineers. Making resolutions is one thing; putting them into practice is another.

The problems were to grow. The poor quality of goods made by the huge number of small subcontractors hampered production throughout the war. The shortcomings of the technical bureaucrats are again apparent: they were unaware of the practical concerns of mass production, subcontracting and such details. They also failed to see that improvements in elementary school education would have no immediate effect on the manufacturing work force. In 1942 in the airframe and engine industries, concern over 'a shortage of specialists and foremen' was voiced. Efforts to train workers were already underway: 'almost all of the larger factories have their own workshops to train workers and have provided for extended training of apprentices' (Information 108). But especially in the aircraft industry, the situation clearly changed for the worse in the following years:

> The systematic training of apprentices for several years can relieve the lack of specialists only slightly. The majority of workers [who are either] unfamiliar with the work or [come] from other factories[,] are schooled or instructed only briefly. The situation of technical personnel, however, is especially critical. The management

> of several plants which expanded rapidly in recent year (sic), is not competent to handle such expansion. Thus personnel often fail to distinguish clearly between commercial and technical problems. The number of experienced assistant managers is especially small. Builders are not yet sufficiently adjusted to economize in work and material.
>
> (Information 146)

The problem was seen to result from workers' inability to act for themselves and their lack of initiative. 'The latter causes serious production losses where factory organization is lacking'. But what in fact was lacking was an understanding of mass-production engineering, even though Ōkōchi Masatoshi had advocated this back in 1938. Education could overcome this problem, as Ōkōchi, Miyamoto and others had argued, but changing curricula and teaching students in a new and different way takes time. Graduates cannot be mass-produced.

The lack of specialists and technical personnel continued to be a problem. In late 1943 and early 1944, the government began converting commercial schools to technical schools (Cohen 1949: 274), but these measures came too late to help industry.

IN SEARCH OF MASS PRODUCTION

Several other obstacles hampered the introduction of mass production. In the late 1930s, the technocrats addressed the inadequacy of interaction between research and manufacturing. Ōkōchi's demands for improved technical education were based not only in theory but also in practice: on his work with the Institute of Physical and Chemical Research. Here, he had demanded that the Institute not only present its research findings to the public, but also try to convert them into commercial goods. He promoted tying research in with manufacturing, and most of his technocratic colleagues agreed. As a result, demands for a connection between research and manufacturing appear in nearly all plans and drafts made in the late 1930s.

The beginning of the Sino-Japanese War quickly increased the demand for military goods, but this required a complete transformation from exclusively manual labour to machine-based manufacturing (Information 109). The lack of appropriately trained personnel made such a change impossible.

Shortly before the beginning of the Pacific War, two different types of technocrats had emerged. Some stuck to their plans to introduce engineers into the political administration, and produced mountains of paper but little else. Another, more realistic, group dissociated themselves from these ambitious plans, and tried to make immediate changes. The latter group tried to overcome what they called 'sectionalism' (this term referring to the lack of contact among research institutions, and between researchers and industry). Each research institute, university, and indeed individual researcher, worked alone and did not try to communicate with others (see Matsumae 1944: 18–19). One reason for this lay in inadequate university education, where science and technology were not taught in a coherent and comprehensive way. The university graduates lacked the ability to systematize what they had studied and to set up mental maps connecting various theoretical or practical fields.

Most of the leading technocrats failed to understand the issues concerning assembly-line manufacturing. They regarded themselves as scientists, and they saw it as self-contradictory for scientists to deal with mundane assembly-line problems. Engineers were regarded as leaders; to cope with actual manufacturing problems was beyond their scope, even though the term 'production-engineering' was used quite often. Because of this, plans for the transformation of manufacturing techniques were not introduced by the technocrats, but by individuals more directly involved with manufacturing realities.

The aviation industry serves as a good illustration of the lack of a production-engineering orientation. Japanese aircraft production had grown in the 1920s and 1930s, with manufacturers achieving some independence from their foreign counterparts. Education in the fields of aerodynamics and aircraft mechanics had reached an advanced level, but nearly all of the young designers sought to apply their theoretical knowledge to developing an ideal aeroplane, not to actual production needs (Maema 1993: 137). For example, engine designers gave little consideration to the availability of machine tools necessary to build the engines they designed, and often approached design without due regard for production (BIOS/JAP/PR 1296: 15). They lacked interest in such practical issues as the equipment needed to make planes, the experience of pilots, and the need for additional testing. They therefore left the design and manufacture of equipment other than the airframe to second- or third-class manufacturers (Okamura 1953: 384–91, Katō 1993: 158).

The military itself actually supported such attitudes. They did not push designers to put as much emphasis on the design of the airframes as on the equipment; instead, they generally took frame designs from commercial industry, and then combined them with the most powerful engines and most efficient equipment available. They believed that this would result in the most efficient plane (Maema 1993: 155). Efficiency was the basic concern – and it did indeed sometimes result in powerful aircraft. But the manufacturers and the machinery industry lacked the ability to mass-produce such designs (Maema 1993: 144). As late as 1944, analysts commented that 'the design of Japanese flight instruments was not sufficiently suited to the demands of mass production until now'

(Information 141). Insufficient standardization and incomplete worker training – especially in smaller companies – for proper manufacturing were the main obstacles.

Although limited human resources, poorly educated workforce, inadequate equipment, and the lack of high-quality raw materials were all serious problems, the biggest obstacle was the lack of systematic thought in development. For example, in designing an airframe, designers neglected to consider the impact of the equipment on their design needs. And to design for mass production, the designer needed to consider available production methods. Consequently, the imbalance between the high-quality aeroplane designs and the limitations in production engineering (which was still mainly manual work) led to faults and even fatal accidents (see examples in Maema 1993: 137). Another example illustrates this: because the basic purpose of fighter planes was to attack, designers did not even begin to address defensive measures and bullet-proofing of fuel tanks before 1942 or 1943. In addition, designers lacked an understanding of the practical problems of combat. It was not the engineers' technical inability, but rather their laziness, that prevented an earlier start to research in such fields (Katō 1993: 159).

Such examples led some technocrats to demand the introduction of production engineering into technical education so that designers would consider the needs of assembly-line mass production. For Ōkōchi, a 'new type of engineer' seemed necessary – one who would major in production engineering (*seisan kōgaku*). But technocrats like Miyamoto Takenosuke favoured 'comprehensive engineering' (*sōgō kōgaku*). On this point the opinion of technocrats and production-oriented engineers differed significantly. Later discussion focused on whether the science-oriented engineers (*kōgaku-sha*) and designers (*sekkei-sha*), or the production-oriented engineers (*seisan gijutsu-sha*), would receive this new education. At the same time educational institutions had to decide whether to provide more scientific-oriented technical education (*kōgaku kyōiku*) or a more application-oriented one (*kōgyō kōgaku*) (details of this discussion in Ōyodo 1989: 278–9).

There were some exceptional cases in the aircraft-engine manufacturing industry (for an overview of the Japanese aircraft industry in prewar and wartime period see Samuels 1994: 114–29). Under the guidance of an American engineer, Nakajima Aircraft (*Nakajima Hikōki*) had modernized its engine production before the war and became one of the best-known aircraft makers during the war. Noted for having the most reliable engines, Nakajima employed well-educated production engineers who advised the designers on production feasibility. They focused on the engine as a system and advised designers that by changing one part of the engine, consideration of the 'neighbouring' parts was important (Maema 1993: 147). But Nakajima, with its modern assembly lines, must be seen as an exception. Although a German engineer reported in 1944 that 'the assembly lines make a favourable impression' (Information 25; for another description of the manufacture of aircraft engines at Nakajima see Takahashi 1988: 232–48), most of the other companies did not make much use of modern manufacturing methods.

The reason for this may be political. Although the Konoe Cabinet pushed for scientific and technical mobilization within its 'New Order', the successive military Cabinets under Tōjō Hideki failed to improve manufacturing conditions. Military propaganda hailed the inevitability of victory, saying that the Japanese fighting spirit would result in a very short war. If that was true, then new production methods seemed unnecessary, so change was always hesitant. All of the previous plans for increasing technical capabilities seem not to have advanced. Matsumae Shigeyoshi himself 'realized [in early 1942] that [in the Kawanishi Aircraft Factory], there was no attempt at continuous production and no thought of introducing mechanization; there were simply crowds of people working in primitive conditions' (Matsumae 1981: 18). All efforts obviously aimed towards increasing the output of manual work rather than towards improving production-engineering methods and thereby product quality. The military Cabinet also retreated from the idea of a revolutionary transformation into a technocratic state; it gave priority instead to a steady reorganization of industry (Ōyodo 1989: 419).

Nevertheless, the government had to respond to the increasing demand for weapons from the Army and Navy. Since the science-oriented engineers obviously failed to design goods suitable for mass production, production-oriented engineers and technicians were to encourage and promote research. This change in technology policy in 1942 may also be seen as a result of an Army delegation's visit to German armament factories in 1941 (Nihon kōkū gakujutsu 1990: 214). In the same year, two new associations were formed, the Japan Productivity Association (*Nihon nōritsu kyōkai*, founded in March 1942) and the Great Japan Aero-Technology Association (*Dai–Nihon kōkū gakujutsu kyōkai*, founded in May 1942). Members of these associations, who were usually production-engineering oriented, investigated the production system of various factories, then advised changes resulting from each 'factory diagnosis' (*kōjō shindan*). But even then, production engineering progressed only slowly.

The German aircraft industry sent specialists to Japan in submarines to offer technical assistance to their Japanese counterparts. In 1944, most were employed to equip new aircraft plants for modern mass production, convert plane designs for mass production, and to assist in the construction of mass-production facilities (Information 144). A German engineer working at the aircraft manufacturing company Aichi Kōkū reported in 1944, 'Redesigned wing is now on the assembly line. This line is the first one correctly employed by the Japanese. Time saving[s]: 60%. I acted as technical adviser for all assemblies' (Information 19).

But most of the Germans did not end up doing what they were sent to do. Their reports describe conditions in plants beyond their comprehension. 'Everyone wants to give orders, no one will assume responsibility' the reporting engineer stated, and 'suggestions for improvements to save time are accepted with extreme hesitation, even when the necessity of such measures is realized by the plant management' (Information 14–14a).

In November 1944, the general German consensus was that:

> despite intensive study of recent foreign production methods, their use in Japan has not been carried out with sufficient understanding. It appears that Japanese engineers do not understand modern production properly. In addition, the Japanese mind is opposed to a workers card [*sic*] system, before and after calculation, piecework system, assembly lines and belt production. Wherever they have been set up, the impression is that often they are not fully utilized.
>
> (Information 141)

That a considerable number of Japanese engineers were unfamiliar with mass production engineering as late as 1945 was described in another report from a German engineer, who wrote: 'Basic construction was made according to my recommendations. Organization details not included in the Heinkel data were completed according to Japanese concepts and are not suited for expedient mass production' (Information 31).

Knowing that the aircraft industry was one of the best-developed branches of industry during the war, one can imagine the state of mass-production engineering in minor industrial branches.

CONCLUSION

The technocrats started in the 1930s with demands for a better use of their abilities and competence within the government to lead the country to prosperity. Their unrealistic targets, imperfect understanding of reality, and unfamiliarity with manufacturing failed to lead to their hoped-for results. Technocracy had failed.

During the war, increasing production was a primary goal. Government and military leaders often relied on stimulating the Japanese spirit to spur efforts for mobilization. The technocrats searched for a new technologically based system, had laws enacted, wrote plans and started campaigns – but also failed. To accomplish their goals better quality equipment, a technically trained workforce and modern production-engineering would have been necessary. But industry could not fulfil any of these three needs. Production increased mainly by increasing manual work, as an Armament

Ministry official publicly admitted in May 1944 (Kokusaku kenkyū-kai shūhō 1944: 6: 19: 12 ([216]).

One could therefore conclude that all the efforts towards a scientific and technical mobilization had failed. But that conclusion would be both too general and too hasty. Although technical mobilization was not so much dominated by the military as it was by technocrats, even as civilians the technocrats could not escape the pervasive (including psychological) militarization. They saw their chance to play a role in political administration, and they thereby supported the government's expansionist plans. Their broad plans for a scientific and technological mobilization sought to promote Japan's technology so Japan would become the leading country of Asia. They fostered a climate in which important armament industries quickly enlarged their research facilities. The Army and Navy also hired more researchers. This was one clear – but unintentional – success.

The technocrats' plans failed because the technocrats regarded themselves as scientists in action, and lacked an orientation towards production engineering. After 1941, the arrogance of military planners towards civilian engineers and scientists led the whole economy in the wrong direction. Instead of introducing new ideas into factories, the government boasted of steadily increasing production and bright prospects, giving the public the impression that armaments production was forging ahead. In fact, the lack of adequate machinery, poor quality of labour and inefficient distribution of raw materials resulted in a rapid decrease in production. After the war, one:

> found evidence of an amazing lack of coordination or even sympathy between military authorities and civilian scientists or manufacturers. Even when requested by military officials to undertake certain investigations, scientists were not sufficiently informed as to the ultimate objects [of their research] to enable them to attack the problems in an intelligent manner, and consequently could not make [an] important contribution to the war effort.
>
> (BIOS/JAP/PR 1283: 1)

So neither technocrats nor other bureaucratic engineers were leading efforts to introduce modern production methods into factories.

The assemblers' and designers' ignorance of modern production methods hampered production-engineering developments. Attempts to design an ideal aircraft without an awareness of the relationships between design and production, the lack of standardization, poor technical personnel and inadequate special machine tools, prevented the introduction of assembly-line production. It was the production-engineering-oriented engineers, though they were small in number, who made the first steps. They, too, often failed. But the problems of understanding production-engineering led to an 'intensive study of recent foreign production methods' (as a German engineer remarked; Information 141). This ultimately brought more awareness of the link between design and production, and between scientists and shop-floor engineers.

All of the propaganda on technological mobilization produced no satisfactory contribution to the war effort. But science and technology were widely propagated, building a consciousness of technology as a foundation for future prosperity. This seed, unintentionally planted in people's minds, helped create the basis for a technology-oriented society. It was on this foundation that technological development became possible after the war.

NOTE

1 The respective term 'economic general staff' used by economists like Rōyama Masamichi and Matsui Haruo stems from another source, namely Lewis Lorwin's book entitled *Advisory Economic Councils* which was translated into Japanese in 1933 as *Keizai sanbō honbu* (Economic General Staff) (see Gao 1994: 123–4). This translation could, of course, have also influenced the technocrats. The different sources both sides relied on were published, translated and read in the same period.

REFERENCES

Unpublished material

Information Related to Japanese Aeronautical Industrial Activities and to Japanese Military Aircraft as Reported by German Representatives Stationed in Japan. (Manuscript held in the National Air and Space Museum/Smithsonian Institution, Washington D.C., A 00 Japan/3.) (A crude translation of obviously original German material.)

BIOS/JAP/PR 1283 Magnetic Development in Japan during World War II, 1946.

BIOS/JAP/PR 1296 Japanese Navy Diesel Engines, 1945.

Journals

Kokusaku kenkyū-kai shūhō (Weekly Reports of the National Policy Association) (1944). Reprint: Kokusaku Kenkyū-kai, *Senji seiji keizai shiryō* (Materials on the politics and economy of the war period), 8 vols, 1983; Tōkyō: Hara Shobō.

Books and articles

Akazawa Shirō *et al.* (compiler) (1984) *Shiryō Nihon gendai-shi 12 – Taisei yokusan-kai* (Sources – Contemporary Japanese history, vol. 12 – Imperial Rule Assistance Association), Tōkyō: Ōtsuki Shoten.

Cohen, Jerome B. (1949) *Japan's Economy in War and Reconstruction*, Minneapolis: University of Minnesota Press.

Commission on the History of Science and Technology Policy (1991) *Historical Review of Japanese Science and Technology Policy*, Tōkyō: The Society of Non-Traditional Technology.

Department of Welfare (1939) 'Current Labour Measures', *Tokyo Gazette* 24: 17–26.

Gao, Bai (1994) 'Arisawa Hiromi and his theory for a managed economy', *Journal of Japanese Studies* Vol. 20, No. 1: 115–53.

Inamura Yasuo (1944) *Kenkyū to dōin* (Research and mobilization), Tōkyō: Nippon Hyōron-sha.

Itō Takashi (1987) 'Mōri Hideoto ron oboegaki', in Kindai Nihon kenkyū-kai, *Senji keizai* (Nenpō kindai Nihon kenkyū, vol. 9), pp. 129–50, Tōkyō: Yamakawa Shuppan-sha.

Iwasaki Minoru (1995) 'Poieeshisu-teki meta-shutai no yokubō – Miki Kiyoshi no gijutsu tetsugaku –' (The desire for a creative meta-subject – The philosophy of technology of Miki Kiyoshi), in Yamanouchi Yasushi *Sōryoku-sen to gendai-ka* (Total War and Modernization), Tōkyō: Kashiwa Shobo, pp. 185–209.

Kagaku gijutsu seisaku-shi kenkyū-kai (1990) *Nihon no kagaku gijutsu seisaku-shi* (History of Japanese science and technology policy), Tōkyō: Mitō Kagaku Gijutsu Kyōkai.

Kanda Fuhito (1981) *Shiryō Nihon gendai-shi 7 – Sangyō hōkoku undō* (Sources – Contemporary Japanese history, vol. 7 – Industrial Patriotic Association Movement); Tōkyō: Ōtsuki Shoten.

Katō Hiroo (1993) 'Rei-sen no sekkei: Shisaku katei to jinmei keishi no gijutsu shisō' (The process of the design of Zero-fighter and the technical thought that neglected the defense of the warplane crew's life), *Kagaku-shi kenkyū* (Journal of history of science, Japan), series II, vol. 32 (no. 187): 157–61.

Kinoshita Kenzō (1994) *Kiesareta himitsu-sen kenkyūsho* (The disappeared secret-war research institute), Nagano: Shinano Mainichi Shinbun-sha.

Kōseishō (Ministry of Welfare) (1988) *Kōseishō 50-nen shi* (50-year history of the Ministry of Welfare), Tōkyō.

Kyōchōkai (1983) *Senji-ka seisan-ryoku kakuju to kagaku to kōgyō* (The expansion of productive capacity in wartime and the science-based industry), (Kyōchokai shiryō/Kyōchōkai sources, vol. 3), Tōkyō: Kyōchōkai.

Maema Takanori (1993) *Man-mashin no Shōwa densetsu* (Men and machines, the tradition of the Shōwa period), Tōkyō: Kōdansha.

Matsumae Shigeyoshi (1941) *Tō-A gijutsu taisei ron* (On an East-Asian technological body), Tōkyō: Kagaku-shugi Kōgyō-sha.

—— (1944) *Senji seisan ron* (On war production), Tōkyō: Ōbun-sha (1943).

—— (1981) *The Second World War: A Tragedy for Japan*, Tōkyō: Tōkai University Press.

Miyamoto Takenosuke (1941) *Kagaku no dōin* (Scientific mobilization), Tōkyō: Kaizō-sha.

Morris-Suzuki, Tessa (1994) *The Technological Transformation of Japan from the Seventeenth to the Twenty-first Century*, Cambridge: Cambridge University Press.

Nihon kōkū gakujutsu-shi henshū iinkai (1990) *Nihon kōkū gakujutsu shi 1910–1945* (History of aeronautical research in Japan 1910–1945), Tōkyō: Maruzen.

Okamura Jun (1953) *Kōkū gijutsu no zenbō* (The full story of aeronautical technology), Tōkyō: Kōyōsha.

Ōkōchi Masatoshi (1938) *Shihon-shugi kōgyō to kagaku-shugi kōgyō* (Capitalistic industry and scientific industry), Tōkyō: Kagaku-shugi Kōgyō–sha.

Ōyodo Shōichi (1989) *Miyamoto Takenosuke to kagaku gijutsu gyōsei* (Miyamoto Takenosuke and science and technology administration), Tōkyō: Tōkyō Daigaku Shuppan-kai.

Samuels, Richard J. (1994) *'Rich Nation, Strong Army' National Security and the*

Technological Transformation of Japan, Ithaca: Cornell University Press.
Sumiya Mikio (1977) *Nihon shokugyō kunren hatten-shi* (History of vocational training in Japan), 2. vols, Tōkyō: Nihon Rōdō Kyōkai (1971).
Takahashi Yasutaka (1988) *Nakajima hikōki no kenkyū* (Studies on Nakajima aircraft), Tōkyō: Nihon Keizai Shinpō-sha.
Veblen, Thorstein (1994) *The Vested Interests and the Common Man and The Engineers and the Price System*, London: Routledge/Thoemmes Press (reprint).
Willeke, Stefan (1995a) *Die Technokratiebewegung in Nordamerika und Deutschland zwischen den Weltkriegen*, Frankfurt: Peter Lang.
—— (1995b) 'Die Technokratiebewegung in Deutschland zwischen den Weltkriegen', *Technikgeschichte,* vol. 62, 3: 221–46.
Yamazaki Masakatsu (1995) 'The Mobilization of Science and Technology during the Second World War in Japan – A Historical Study of the Activities of the Technology Board Based upon the Files of Tadashiro Inoue', *Historia Scientiarum – International Journal of the History of Science Society of Japan* (second series), vol. 5, no. 2, (consecutive no. 56), pp. 167–81.
Yoshida Hideaki (1990) 'Tsūshin kiki kigyō no musen heiki bumon shinshutsu' (The advance of the wireless arms departments of the communications equipment industry), in Shimotani Masahiro (ed.) *Senji keizai to Nihon kigyō* (War economy and the Japanese companies), Tōkyō: Shōwa-dō, pp. 95–124.

4

WOMEN AND THE WAR ECONOMY IN JAPAN

Regine Mathias

INTRODUCTION

Global warfare requires the total mobilization of not only a country's military strength, but also of its labour force and material resources. Production, especially in war industries, has to be increased. At the same time, the expansion of military conscription substantially reduces the number of male workers available. In order to cope with this, new reservoirs of labour have to be exploited. In times of national crisis, many countries have mobilized, and even drafted, women into the workforce.

In Japan, however, we observe a great reluctance to employ women, except at the lowest level of the economy. In a February 1942 speech to the Diet, the Japanese Minister of Health and Welfare, Koizumi Chikahiko, proudly stated that in order to secure its labour force, the enemy was drafting women, but in Japan, out of consideration for the family system, the Japanese would not draft them (cited in Havens 1975: 919–20).

Throughout the war, Japanese women were never forcefully drafted into the labour force, unlike the case in the United States and Great Britain. Nevertheless, as the war dragged on, the rapidly growing demand for labour forced the Japanese government to make various attempts to tap the underutilized reservoir of female labour. These attempts, which emphasized voluntary action and relied on the patriotic spirit of the women, were, on the whole, not very successful.

Why was a country like Japan, even in such times of emergency, so hesitant to fully use the reservoir of female labour? Koizumi's statement would suggest that ideological considerations about protecting the family system were given priority over economic needs. But were there other reasons as well? Was the ideological argument unanimously accepted, or were alternatives discussed? What concepts were developed to integrate women into the war economy?

Answers to these questions cannot be found by using a simple historical analysis of the political and economic development in those years alone. One also needs to scrutinize the motivations and goals which led to certain policy decisions. Therefore, this chapter focuses upon the discussions on female employment in government and industrial circles, which were supported to some degree by scientific institutions. Examining these discussions rather than the actual developments alone reveals ideas and concepts which for one reason or another never materialized.

DEVELOPMENT OF THE LABOUR MARKET AND THE MOBILIZATION OF LABOUR

The labour market situation after 1937 and government measures to ensure an adequate labour supply have been described in detail by, e.g., Cohen 1949, Havens 1975 and Hunter 1992. This chapter confines itself to a short summary of the most important points.

First, when the Sino–Japanese War started in 1937, women already accounted for a very considerable part of the Japanese labour force. No doubt the largest numbers were engaged in agriculture, but they also played a substantial role in commercial activities, services and light industries such as textiles and food. So the idea of women taking on paid labour outside the home was nothing new.

Nevertheless, this kind of work was largely related to two groups:

- Young, unmarried women, mostly from rural families, who were temporarily employed in textile mills and service industries, and
- Married women from lower- or lower-middle-class urban families, who would seek employment in small neighbourhood factories or took in piecework in order to supplement the family income.

Besides these groups, however, there remained a large proportion of women who were 'unoccupied or idle' as some reports called it, because they were married and either had given up paid employment or had never been employed. Therefore, all policies concerning the mobilization of women's labour, especially since 1943, had two targets. The first was to use women already in the labour force more effectively, especially to fill war production needs. The second target was to tap the currently under-utilized reservoir of unemployed women, including married women.

How, and to what extent, these policies were to be, and could be, realized, was of great concern, not only for groups in government and labour administration, but also for personnel managers in the large companies. They all participated in discussions on women's labour and their proper role in a war economy.

DISCUSSIONS ON FEMALE EMPLOYMENT IN TIMES OF EMERGENCY

The question of how and to what extent women should take up paid work has been the topic of many debates throughout Japan's industrialization process. During the 1920s, when even the middle class encountered economic difficulties, many women took up an occupation in order to supplement the family income. The appearance of the so-called *shokugyō fujin* (female white-collar employees), and their advancement into the labour market provoked strong reactions and became a favourite theme of discussion in newspapers and journals.

Due to the growing influence of the nationalistic ideology in the 1930s, strong emphasis was placed upon the special virtue of Japanese women and their supposed special role in maintaining the family system. But the increasing need to use women for the war economy clearly contradicted the traditional family ideology.[1] After the outbreak of the war with China in 1937, the awareness of a possible conflict between the goals of preserving the family system and ensuring the necessary workforce grew. But on the whole, politicians and officials of the ministries involved in labour policies seem to have been quite reluctant to address this topic until around 1943.

On the other hand, academia dealt with the problem quite early. The Japan Institute for the Science of Labour (JISL),[2] an institution with a long tradition of research on female workers, announced a comprehensive survey on the capabilities of working women as early as 1938. This survey was part of a proposed 'emergency programme' to ensure the labour force of all industries and to maintain the working ability of the whole nation. It was to cover not only the usual investigations into physical strength, intellect and technical skills of women, but also included a study of the changes in working methods and conditions brought about by employing women (Teruoka 1938: 15).

In November 1942, the JISL started a series of what were to be eleven volumes dealing exclusively with the labour management of female workers (for details see below). Only four of the volumes actually appeared. But the plan to publish such a comprehensive, research-based work reveals the growing interest in this topic.

In 1943 the discussion of whether and how to mobilize women reached a new stage. 'In September 1943 the Conference of Vice-Ministers passed a resolution recognizing that women were an under-utilized workforce, and urging that means of tapping the supply should be investigated' (Hunter 1992: 61). After this date, women's mobilization was a frequent topic of articles in journals and newspapers.

Administrative organizations as well as semi-official or private think tanks and institutions like the *Kokusaku Kenkyū-kai* (Group for the Study of National Policy) took up the topic in publications and round-table discussions. This study group, established in 1937 by high-ranking politicians, bureaucrats, diplomats and people close to the financial world, aimed at formulating a new 'national policy' (*kokusaku*). It tried to formulate a policy for the mobilization of additional workers from among the unemployed (including married) women, as well as for the efficient use of women already in the labour force.

The debate culminated in 1944, when the acute shortage of labour led to suggestions for mobilizing, and even forcibly drafting, married women. But there was still reluctance to go so far, and quickly it became too late to realize most of the plans.

Central points of the discussion

We can discern three major lines of reasoning, relating to the family system, gender and motherhood. Of course, there are a lot of overlap and interrelationships among these. But we treat them separately here for the sake of analysis.

In these lines of reasoning we can find different kinds of arguments: political-ideological, biological, and economic-functional. For a better understanding of the motives influencing the government's mobilization policy, we should distinguish between these arguments.

Family system

The preservation of the family system seems to have been by far the most important argument against a fully fledged mobilization of women. This is clearly expressed in the following statement made by Prime Minister Tōjō Hideki in 1942:

> That warm fountainhead which protects the household, assumes responsibility for rearing children, and causes women, children, brothers, and sisters to act as support for the front lines is based on the family system. This is the natural mission of the women in our empire and must be preserved far into the future.
>
> (Havens 1975: 920)

This statement contains all three aspects of the argument. It elevates the family system as being of great political importance; it links the system to the natural mission of women, thereby highlighting the biological relationship; and it elaborates on the function of women as responsible for the household, the raising of children, etc.

In conjunction with the quotation by Koizumi Chikahiko at the beginning of this chapter, this statement shows that in 1942 the government clearly gave priority to the preservation of the family system. In this respect, it had the backing of other influential groups such as the National Federation of Women's Associations, which in 1939 had launched campaigns urging women to go back to the home (Havens 1975: 921).

This attitude was criticized by authors in 'progressive' journals such as *Kakushin* (Reform). These authors pressed strongly for a recognition of the real situation, where Japanese women had to adjust and harmonize their domestic duties with outside work.

As far as industry was concerned, engineers and executives of large enterprises directly confronted with labour shortage cautiously demanded an expansion of women's employment. But at the same time they were clearly reluctant to question the importance of the family system.

What arguments were raised against women's mobilization? Why was paid labour thought to be so detrimental to the family system? Clearly, it was not so much the work itself. Minoguchi Tokijirō, an official in the Ministry of Health and Welfare (and later professor at Hitotsubashi University), stressed in a round-table discussion in 1944 that Japanese women had always worked hard. However, they mostly worked at home, in a family-owned shop, in agriculture or in a small workshop. It was the work outside the home that seemed dangerous to the family and would lead to the destruction of the family system. In his opinion, which was obviously shared by many of his contemporaries, mobilizing women in general, and married women in particular, was definitely in contradiction to the family system (see Kokusaku Kenkyū-kai 1944a: 2).

From a functional point of view, this argument carries some weight. Wartime restrictions meant that even the simple daily routine of running a household had become troublesome and time-consuming (see the chapter by Pauer on 'New Order for Japanese Society' in this volume). It is understandable why married women, responsible for a family, should be excluded from being drafted. Many advocates of women's employment also understood this; they therefore pressed for the reorganization and rationalization of the distribution system as one important precondition for the employment of (married) women.

As the war dragged on, these functional problems may have been the most important reasons for the decision against a full-fledged mobilization of women. In the debate, however, ideological arguments were clearly dominant. This is especially clear in the discussions about the mobilization of younger, unmarried women. Even though work outside the home had become customary for many in this age group (female textile workers and others), and though most participants in the discussions agreed upon the necessity of using this labour reservoir, there was still considerable reluctance to do so.

The damage done by outside work to young women is painted in dark colours on various occasions. Young, unmarried women were said to be in constant danger of 'losing their womanliness' (*onnarashisa o ushinau*

[*Daiyamondo* 21/12/1944: 9], *onna no seikaku ga kuzureru* [Kokusaku Kenkyū-kai 1944a: 5]). It was feared that they would become pretentious and lazy, and that they would have great difficulty in re-adapting to their native environment on leaving the work force. They would lack the proper education for a bride, and would therefore have difficulty getting married. Minoguchi summarized it thus: 'Everyone is worried that paid labour might weaken the customary preparedness of women to strongly uphold the family system' (Kokusaku Kenkyū-kai 1944a: 5). One point of concern obviously was that, under the strain of wartime economy, many factories were no longer able or willing to provide their female workforce with what was called 'training for married life' (*seikatsu no shitsuke*). As a result, an important part of discussions on mobilizing women focused on 'how to aid the development of the special character of women and womanly virtues,' as Hunter (1992: 65) remarks, citing the 'Outline Measures for the Receipt of Women's Volunteers Corps' of June 1944. At first sight, this seems strange: instead of considering ways to train unskilled women to improve the labour situation in factories, the debate focused on how to adjust the production system and working and living conditions in factories to the supposed needs of female workers.

But if we concede the general priority of the family system and its underlying ideology, then the demands for 'proper work' and measures to prepare young women for returning to the family become extremely important. To the ardent advocates of the family system, the fulfilment of these conditions probably offered the only way to bridge the contradiction between domestic duties and outside work. It eventually allowed them to tap this reservoir of labour.

The dominance of these ideological arguments, however, does not mean that there were no other views. Especially in the later years of the war, as the need to use women workers increased, the number of people and publications arguing in favour of women's employment grew.

The writings of JISL researchers probably carried the greatest weight. In 1942 JISL started the series of books (mentioned above) on working women and their role in a wartime economy. These were written by Japan's most experienced experts on the women's labour situation.[3] The first volume, originally to be called *Joshi rōmu* (Female labour), came out in 1944 under the title *Joshi Kinrō* (Women's labour service). This change was symptomatic of the attitude of JISL staff, who argued that in times of emergency, labour should be seen as a service to the country rather than a means to earn money, so should be carried out by men and women alike (Maki 1943: 80).

The author of *Joshi kinrō* was Kirihara Shigemi, who had worked at the institute since 1921. Kirihara maintained close connections with government agencies (as did most institute staff). He had been director of the Welfare Department of the Imperial Rule Assistance Association (*Taisei yokusan-kai*) during 1942–3. Nevertheless, in *Joshi kinrō* he strongly rejects the idea that outside work would damage the family system and motherhood. Instead, he argued that employment constituted an important experience for women in general, as it strengthened their will and abilities, and therefore would be useful in later life (Kirihara 1944: i–iv, 3). Furthermore, he argued that joining the workforce during the current emergency would implant in the women's minds a new patriotism and would educate them to be real 'mothers of the (militaristic) nation' (*gunkoku no haha*). Therefore, he wrote, 'it is not necessary to be concerned about how to harmonize women's life and outside work. One should rather think about how outside work could improve women's abilities, help educate them and shape the character of women and their culture' (Kirihara 1944: ii). Based upon the results of his research, he developed a set of conditions that would provide an optimum environment for working women. Other JISL authors presented similar views.

The mixture of scientific analysis with moral and patriotic imperatives appears strange, though it was not new: there are other traditions linking outside work with moral education. But the opinions voiced in the book series are interesting, inasmuch as they differ greatly from the mainstream ideas described above. If these ideas had been followed, a full-scale mobilization of women could have been possible, even within the framework of the traditional family system. But, as the series started only in 1944, it was too late for any changes.

Gender

Gender-related problems form another field of argument, and they were discussed in both biological and social terms. On the whole, this field of argument was less salient than the one concerning the family system, but its implications also exerted considerable influence on the mobilization policy.

Discussions on gender-related problems in the social context focused mainly on such themes as working restrictions by protective labour laws, government requirements for special facilities for women (such as separate washrooms and toilets), and the problem of commuting. Most of the participants in the discourse agree upon the need to provide special facilities and services for women, but they also make clear the additional efforts and costs involved. On the whole, however, social restrictions and the inflexibility of the female workforce are not directly mentioned as an obstacle to employing women. Only a short note in the *Oriental Economist* (a journal published in English even in wartime Japan) in April 1943 cites protective labour legislation as one cause for the limited use of female labour, although most such laws had been at least partly suspended during the war (cited in Cohen 1949: 320).

The physiological and psychological features of women also became a focus of debate. To many of those building their arguments on the family system, these features were of minor importance. Minoguchi, for example, did not consider women's physiology as a major problem because housework was often more physically demanding and difficult than factory work (Kokusaku Kenkyū-kai 1944a: 2). So there was no question that women were able to cope with the hardships of factory work, as long as health and safety measures were adequate.

In the various contributions to this debate, we can find all the well-known biological arguments about women being especially well-suited for light, simple, repetitive, dull, routine work; about women being enduring, patient, good with their fingertips, etc. These characteristics were mostly regarded as a matter of fact, and they determined the kind of work in which women were employed. The allotment of suitable work (*shokuba no haichi*) to female workers, especially in industries which so far had employed few or no women, posed considerable problems; these were addressed in numerous articles and books.

Motherhood

Arguments concerning motherhood were of central importance in the debate about the expansion of the female workforce (see Nakajima 1978, and also Miyake 1991). As motherhood was seen as an implicit part of a woman's family role, it was often discussed in connection with the family system. But the importance of these questions reached beyond the problem of maintaining the family.

The motherhood debate of the Taishō period (1912–26) in the women's movement focused on women's rights, including the right to choose about childbearing. In contrast, the state now took up this issue in the context of a national policy aiming at population growth. The preface to an 'Outline of the Establishment of a Population Policy' (*Jinkō seisaku kakuritsu yōkō*, cited in Akazawa *et al.*, 1984: 357–8), issued in January 1941, stated that rapid population growth was necessary to 'plan the sound development of the Greater East Asian Co-prosperity Sphere' and 'to strengthen (Japan as) the leading power in East Asia'. So the question of motherhood was directly linked to the future strength of the Japanese empire and hegemony in East Asia. Consequently, arguments related to motherhood carried great political weight in the debate about the expansion of labour service for women.

The 'Outline' set a target population of 100 million people in 1960, proposed that the marriage age for women should be lowered, and that each family should at least have five children. Furthermore, it demanded restrictions on employment possibilities for women older than twenty. This last demand, especially, shows that the authors regarded women's employment as an obstacle to marriage, and thereby also as detrimental to the state's pro-natalist policy. This attitude is even more clearly expressed in a December 1941 announcement by the leader of the Saitama branch office of the Imperial Rule Assistance Association (*Taisei yokusan-kai*), 'About the encouragement of marriage' (*Kekkon shōrei ni kansuru ken*, cited in Akazawa *et al.*, 1984: 366–7). This explicitly mentions the *shokugyō fujin* (female employees) as one group to be included in special measures to promote marriage, because 'if women are employed, they are said to miss a chance of marriage. And in times like this, when *shokugyō fujin* will rapidly increase in numbers, we must especially think about their marriage and devise suitable methods (to bring about marriage)' (Akazawa *et al.*, 1984: 368).

Embedded in the pro-natalist policy, motherhood-related arguments became a strong impediment to recruitment of women into the labour force on a larger scale. Nakajima (1979: *passim*) even describes it as the most important factor preventing the drafting of women. Opponents of drafting stressed the incompatibility of employment with marriage and motherhood, not only because of lost or deferred opportunities for marriage, but also because of fears of harm to women's health and minds, thereby obstructing their potential for motherhood. Even authors in (semi-official) business magazines like *Kōgyō kokusaku* (Industrial National Policy) put population policy above economic needs. Seki Jirō, an official in charge of labour affairs in Ōsaka, for example, wrote a lengthy article about labour policy and female workers in 1941. He concluded that the future hegemonic role of the Japanese empire meant that protecting mothers and children should be the most important condition in any labour policy concerning women (Seki 1941: 26).

As the war dragged on, however, the growing need for labour led to a shift in priorities. In general, there was no disagreement about the importance of motherhood and the state's pro-natalist policies. But in the rapidly worsening economic situation, the voices of those arguing for the compatibility of motherhood, family and productive work became louder. Among them, JISL researchers probably had the greatest influence. Making use of their prominent positions in the Imperial Rule Assistance Association and their scientific standing, they saw their task as reconciling motherhood and family life with productive work. 'With regard to present Japan and with regard to future Japan, the planning of how to guarantee labour service and motherhood, and the complete harmonization of both matters, is a very important responsibility' (Maki 1943: 69).

For the JISL researchers the question was not whether to bring more women into the labour force, but how to do so. Drawing extensively upon their numerous surveys, they tried to prove that work was not necessarily detrimental to women's health (e.g., Kano 1943: 116–55; Maki 1943: 80–90). But they also closely linked their concept of 'harmonization' to demands for changes in the workplace, suitable and more highly qualified jobs for women, better opportunities for women to acquire knowledge and technical skills, and revolutionary changes in society as a whole (see the following section). Such changes, they argued, would mean that work could positively support or influence motherhood, since work experience outside the household and workplace training could help women to broaden their knowledge and obtain a better, science-based education (*kagaku-teki kyōyō*). This, in turn, would enable them to educate their children better, thus improving their role and potential as mothers.

Such improvements in the science-based education of women was one of the main demands of a campaign aiming at 'training and education for motherhood' (*bosei no kyōyō kunren*). This was started in 1942 by the *Monbushō shakai kyōiku kyoku* (Bureau of Social Education of the Ministry of Education) as part of a programme for 'affairs concerning the guidance of education in families during war times' (*Senji katei kyōiku shidō ni kansuru ken*) (Nakajima 1979: 66; Nagahara 1990: 211–12). Overall, the JISL researchers' arguments fitted quite well into efforts to create a 'technology-oriented state' (*gijutsu rikkoku*) (see also Pauer's chapter on 'Technical Mobilization' in this volume).

Throughout the war, motherhood and its protection remained a topic of debate, and the conflict between the divergent aims of population policy and economic needs could not be solved. Those addressed in this debate, namely women, did not respond to either side: they had quite different concerns in trying to survive with their families. Although most of the JISL ideas were not realized, some of the ways proposed for integrating women into the labour force were quite revolutionary. The following section examines them more closely.

WAYS OF INTEGRATING FEMALE LABOUR

Many arguments advanced in the debate on women's employment posed considerable restraints on their possible roles. Nevertheless, over time even those against drafting women came to feel the need to tap the supply of female workers more efficiently. This resulted in a shift within the discourse, from whether employment was detrimental to women, to how to bring about the integration of female labour into the war economy. As already mentioned, ideological concerns were partly overcome by trying to prove that work was a better way to prepare for marriage and family life. But most probably, practical problems occurring in connection with women's work posed greater obstacles to women's employment. Therefore, ideas and concepts must have existed about how to solve these problems as well. What concepts existed, what ideas were pursued, and were there any new ideas?

We can detect a growing number of such ideas and concepts in the debate after 1941. Most deal with improvements of overall working conditions, like working hours, shift systems, the provision of dormitories, motherhood protection, and supervision and guidance in both work and related to future married life. All of these were seen as basic conditions necessary to employ more women. Among these improvements, one was hardly ever mentioned: attractive wages, which would have been one way to lure more women into factories and offices. Instead, low wages for women were regarded as an advantage, and were linked to short working periods and high turnover rates of female workers. Women were said to lack interest in wages, as they were usually not the breadwinners in the family (*Daiyamondo* 01/10/1943: 13–14; *Daiyamondo* 21/06/1944: 6). There were, however, some people, who obviously looked for new ways. One example is a proposition made in the journal *Daiyamondo* in July 1944. In a comment on the state of the economy, the author notes that there were two kinds of wage systems: the life-stage system (*seikatsu chingin*) and the efficiency system (*nōritsu chingin*). He states that Japan had so far used the former, thereby paying women considerably less since they were not the breadwinners in the family. He argues, however, that because an increase in productivity was urgently needed, Japan should switch to the efficiency system. As a consequence, women should be paid the same wages as men if they performed the same kind of work, regardless of their family role (*Daiyamondo* 11/07/1944: 2). For Japan, this was quite a revolutionary idea, but proposed as late as 1944, there were small chances for its realization.

One of the key words in the debate on women's employment was 'suitable work'. Suitable work for women was described by an official of the Ministry of Health and Welfare as being appropriate to women's physical and spiritual or psychological strength, which did not exert any bad influence on the body or the spirit, and which contributed to the production process (cited in Aoyama 1987: 45). It had to be suitable in terms of general circumstances as well as special working conditions.

Science-based education

Women workers were mostly unskilled. Therefore, most of the concepts centred around the question of how to employ them efficiently. One way was to train them so that they would become skilled.

Some labour scientists and technocrats voiced ideas for this. Kirihara (1944: 251–2), for example, proposed that women (including married women and mothers) should be trained thoroughly to be able to cope with qualified work, and should be employed as skilled workers and in the future even as supervisors, technicians, and engineers. Similar ideas were proposed by Kano Hiroyuki, an engineer and high-ranking Ministry of Health and Welfare official (Kano 1943: 3). He even suggested overcoming the rigid division between male and female labour, and allotting work according to individual abilities (Kano 1943: 5). Based on survey results, he argued that giving up the rather inflexible way of distributing work according to gender would allow a more efficient use of the female work force.

Other JISL staff, such as the physician Furusawa Yoshio, and the Home Ministry official and technocrat Miyamoto Takenosuke, viewed the problem more generally. They also proposed the better education of women in technology and science, especially as far as daily life was concerned. But even more important to them was the spread of a positive attitude towards a science-based lifestyle (*kagaku-tekina seikatsu taido*), which would enable women to rationalize daily routines, avoid waste of resources and act economically. This would improve living conditions, help the state save resources, and at the same time lay the foundations for further development towards the envisioned 'science-oriented state' (Miyamoto 1941: 358–9). Both Miyamoto and Furusawa use the terms *seikatsu no kagaku* (scientification of life) or *kagaku-sareta seikatsu* (lifestyle based upon sciences) frequently in connection with phrases like *seikatsu kaizen* (life improvement) and *seikatsu sasshin* (life reform), which belong to the vocabulary of the life-reform movement, of the 1920s (e.g., Miyamoto 1941: 368; Furusawa 1943: 181). The efforts to save as many resources as possible in times of emergency apparently led to a revival of certain goals and demands of the former life-reform movement, which, in turn, fitted well into attempts to turn Japan into a more 'scientifically minded nation' (*Kagaku Nihon no kensetsu*).

Though the underlying idea of these concepts was to serve wartime production, their realization could have changed the social and economic position of women on a long-term basis. And although they were based on scientific research and put forward by 'loyal' scientists, their nearly revolutionary character could not have been easily accepted by the conservative mainstream.

Mass production or neighbourhood factories?

Adapting the labour force to the needs of production by improving women's knowledge and skills would have been one way to overcome the labour shortage. Another was to change the production system to suit the unskilled labour force. Solutions to this problem were sought as early as in 1938. In August of this year, Dr Awaji of the Aeronautical Institute of Tōkyō Imperial University (*Tōkyō teikoku daigaku kōkū kenkyū-jo*) undertook a survey on suitable work for women in an aeroplane factory. He analysed different parts of the working process, such as drawing, casting, press- and lathe-work, and divided them into tasks suitable for both men and women on one hand, and unsuitable for women on the other. For the second category, he proposed several ways of adjusting this work to women's needs (*Kōkū kōgyō ni okeru joshi no shiyō ni tsuite*; cited in Shokugyō kyōkai 1943: 11–17).

In November of the same year, the semi-governmental organization *Kyōchōkai* (Harmonization Society; inaugurated already in 1919 for the purpose of promoting harmony between labour and management) sponsored a meeting about creating a 'new scientific plant' (*kagaku-shugi kōjō*). At this meeting, the engineer Ōkōchi Masatoshi, president of the *Ri-kagaku Kenkyūjo* (Institute of Physical and Chemical Research) suggested that, since the lack of skilled labour could not be overcome easily and quickly, the obvious solution was to change the production process. Production could be divided into small, easily learned, segments, which unskilled labour could easily handle with up to one month's training. In Ōkōchi's eyes, large-scale production, with its routine and repetitious work, was best suited to the employment of unskilled labour, i.e., women (Kyōchōkai 1938: 11–12). A similar idea was contained in the first labour mobilization plan in 1939, which also stressed that 'all articles and manufacturing methods were to be simplified and standardized' (cited in Cohen 1949: 309).

So, shortly after the outbreak of the Sino–Japanese War, substantial changes in production through rationalization and simplification of the work process were proposed as a way of using unskilled workers on a large scale. In the following years, demands for such a transformation surfaced repeatedly. But they were doomed to fail because of the insufficient degree of mechanization in many Japanese industries. As late as 1944, the personnel bureau chief of the machinery-industry control association complained that Japanese industry rated far below US factories in that respect, and that this severely hampered changes in production necessary for employing women efficiently (Ōkōchi Seiichi in Kokusaku Kenkyū-kai 1944a: 9–10). By that time the lack of raw materials and machinery, wartime production priorities, had eliminated the chances for such a comprehensive change in production methods. The lack of technically advanced production methods was thus one important reason for the dilatory, hesitant mobilization of women workers.

While leading managers of large industries tried to use the emergency as a lever to modernize Japanese industry, more conservative circles (mostly Ministry of Health and Welfare officials) held the opposite opinion. They were quite critical of what they called 'large-scale small production plants' that did not cope adequately with the national emergency (Kokusaku Kenkyū-kai 1944a: 4). Instead, Ministry officials envisaged decentralizing production by establishing a network of small, neighbourhood factories (*tonarigumi kōjō*) or family factories (*katei kōjō*) all over the country. Additionally, women were urged to take on work they could do at home. To the bureaucrats such 'small-scale mass production' seemed more appropriate for exploiting the national labour service, and especially well-suited for married women (Kokusaku Kenkyū-kai 1944a: 3). By working at home or in family or neighbourhood factories, women would be able to use certain hours of the day for work and still remain close to home, so that they could fulfil their domestic duties as well. In a round-table discussion in April 1944, Kano Hiroyuki, Ministry of Health and Welfare official, postulated that '(domestic) life and labour (service) should be one' (*seikatsu to kinrō to no itchi*), and that production processes should be restructured to allow this (Kokusaku Kenkyū-kai 1944a: 4).

Although some bureaucrats praised these ideas, most managers of large-scale war industries viewed them sceptically and considered them backwards and inefficient. More than just a hammer was needed to manufacture things. They feared that distribution to thousands of small factories would cause even more waste in the midst of raw material shortages. And inadequate transport facilities could not cope with the increased demand from a fragmented distribution network.

It seems that even those who supported decentralizing production were well aware of such a system's inefficiency. In July 1944 an article on mobilizing married women in the weekly journal *Kokusaku kenkyū-kai shūhō* stressed the importance of decentralized production. But noting experiences in Tōkyō's existing 4000-plus small, neighbourhood factories, the article also stated the need to organize the system more efficiently. It proposed establishing one or more independent administrative institutions to guide small factories and serve as a central control association (*chūō no tōsei kikan*) (Kokusaku Kenkyū-kai 1944b: 3–4). Thus, although a decentralized production system was realized at least in part (in contrast to efforts to develop modern mass production), it never developed into the efficient instrument its protagonists hoped.

Visions of a 'new productive society'

The adaptations discussed so far aimed mainly to partially improve production processes or labour conditions. But other concepts went much further, demanding changes in society as a whole.

In November 1942 the Imperial Rule Assistance Association issued an 'Outline for People's Movements' (*Kokumin undō yōkō*), aimed to mobilize all kinds of resources (Akazawa *et al.*, 1984: 336–43). These movements were regarded as an additional effort to strengthen and increase production, and to disseminate ideas of a wartime lifestyle. A major demand was for an 'All People's Working Movement' (*Kokumin kaidō undō*), which specifically included an 'All Women's Working Movement' (*Joshi kaidō undō*) (Akazawa *et al.*, 1984: 338–40). In order to enable all women to work, the Outline demanded the establishment of day-care centres in factories, flexible working times and other measures, to ensure that the women's movement would pose no obstacle for female workers to 'accomplish their family role as Japanese women' (Akazawa *et al.*, 1984: 339).

At first sight, the 'Outline' does not go beyond the demands discussed above. But at least in the minds of its drafters (who included Kirihara Shigemi, the JISL staff member and author of *Joshi kinrō* cited earlier), its intentions went further. Kirihara regarded the All People's Working Movement as a lever to bring about fundamental social change. He aimed at nothing less than turning Japanese society into one based on the ideal of 'the productive person' (*seisan-jin*). His vision is clear from a January

1943 interview with Hani Setsuko (daughter of the liberal educator Hani Motoko) in the magazine her mother had founded, *Fujin no tomo*. The separation of family and work in women's life was to be abolished. Work was to become an integral part of women's life, even after marriage and while raising children (Hani and Kirihara 1943: 43–4). In order to achieve this goal, Kirihara demanded that state and employers provide the necessary conditions at the workplace. But society as a whole also had to adapt. Kirihara developed detailed plans, ranging from the establishment of such communal facilities as joint kitchens, to the reorganization of the retail and traffic systems. Art, literature and the mass media were to support the movement by taking up the topic of working people. School education was also to be incorporated into the movement. The curriculum was to become more practically oriented, and classes were to spend part of their time at a workplace, which was to be regarded as another classroom. In short, every man and woman, and every organization was called upon to support working people (Hani and Kirihara 1943: 46–9). Here at least, Kirihara's vision is unmasked as a rather totalitarian utopia in which every single aspect of social life is submitted to work and to working people.

Kirihara's goals in trying to initiate these social changes reached far beyond the need to increase the workforce. He used not only the well-known argument that women would be better mothers with improved education and broader knowledge of life outside the home. He also viewed the 'All people working movement' as a means to unite the people. In his opinion, the goal of the motto 'one million (people), one heart' (*ichi oku, isshin*) could only be attained if people shared the experience of working together (Hani and Kirihara 1943: 46). 'If one puts the All People's Working Movement and the All Women's Working Movement in the centre of wartime life, then the whole life begins to move seriously in that direction' (Hani and Kirihara 1943: 45).

One could argue that this 'new society' was the vision of just one man. But his ideas may have reached his target: he could, after all, discuss it in one of the oldest and best-known women's magazines, with its mainly middle-class readers organized in the *Tomo no kai*. Moreover, the enthusiastic support of Hani Setsuko, herself a renowned social critic, shows that she saw many similarities between his vision and her and her mother's efforts to reform and modernize women's life. Like Kirihara, Hani evidently tried to use the wartime situation to implement her ideas to modernize society. These ideas were based upon the ideals of the life-reform movement of the 1920s. Her main goals, namely to rationalize and simplify daily life and to base it on science, seemed to fit perfectly into the wartime economy's needs. And for Kirihara and Hani, the wartime restrictions provided an ideal framework to implement their goals:

> If a woman stays at home 24 hours a day, the simplification of daily life becomes a life reform just for the sake of the life reform. But if one has to reform one's way of life to save time in order to go out working, then the real strength will appear.
>
> (Hani and Kirihara 1943: 45)

The wartime economy seemed to offer a chance for changes they had long striven for. This was apparently a reason that 'progressive' women like Hani co-operated closely with the war regime. As Suzuki Yūkō shows in her book on feminism and war (Suzuki 1988: chapters 2 and 3), this willingness to cooperate, or at least sympathize, with the war regime was not limited to Hani. It also applied in varying degrees to other outstanding women activists, such as the Japan Women's University professor, Takayoshi Tomi. Even the famous feminist and consumer activist Oku Mumeo regarded the war as a chance to realize her ideas, which were quite similar to those of Hani and Kirihara (see Narita 1995: 174–7).

Needless to say, the hoped-for social changes did not occur. Nor did the support of women like Hani Motoko substantially help overcome the difficulties in wartime production. Their attempts to realize their visions of a new society failed in part because the wartime conditions they thought would support their ideals severely hampered efforts to change the society and the economy.

CONCLUSION

The debate on women's employment in the Japanese war economy clearly shows that there were several reasons hampering the mobilization of women on a larger scale.

A major reason was the great importance attached by all sides to the preservation of the Japanese family system. Its alleged historical importance is stressed by attributes like 'precious', 'special', 'of ancient beauty', and so on. The high priority given to the family system can only be understood considering the current political framework. For the mainstream, there was more at stake than just the family, more than the assurance of birth rates, even more than social stability. The nationalistic ideology of the 1930s strongly emphasized the family state (*kazoku kokka*) which, in turn, rested on the family system. Therefore, anything detrimental to the family system could be seen as a potential danger to the political system as a whole.

The fear of weakening the whole political system as well as the credibility of the ideological framework supporting it forced the elite to uphold a certain ideal of womanhood, namely the Confucian ideal of good daughters, who in turn would then become 'good wives and wise mothers' (*ryōsai kenbo*). To ensure this ideal, which had always been closely linked to the modern Japanese state (see e.g., Nolte and Hastings 1991), factories had to comply with various restrictions concerning their female labour force.

Another reason for the hesitant mobilization of women was the conflicting goals between the state's population policy, which stressed motherhood, and the demands of the economy, which called for an expanded productive role for women. While conservatives thought it impossible to reconcile the two goals, groups like labour scientists, technocrats and feminists offered quite different ideas for combining women's employment with their role in the family.

These groups' proposals were as diverse as their backgrounds and goals. They ranged from merely adapting the production system to the needs of unskilled women, to a new view of women, and even to visions of a new society. Not all of the ideas were new. Some, like the proposal to disperse production to small workshops, were rather backwards-oriented. Others, like the demands to rationalize and simplify life and work, and to base them on science, can be traced back to the life-reform movement of the 1920s. But there also were new, quite revolutionary ideas, like the proposition to change the wage system, and the suggestion that men and women were not so different at all, and that therefore the gender-related distribution of work should be replaced by a system related to individual abilities.

An interesting common feature of many of the ideas is the underlying pursuit of a science-oriented society, in which daily life and production were thoroughly planned. The ideas thus picked up threads from the modernization movements of the Taishō period. Although these proposals had little chance to be realized, the mere hope for changes in women's status and in society doubtless led progressives (including certain feminists) to support the wartime regime in its efforts to mobilize resources to strengthen Japan's economic power.[4]

All of these efforts ultimately failed. Besides the conceptual difficulties, other, more practical, reasons may also account for the hesitant mobilization of women workers. Employers were confronted with technically backward production methods, raw material shortages, deteriorating transport and food distribution, and the additional costs these entailed. They were hemmed in with government restrictions and obstacles. So they were probably not keen to take on the additional costs and headaches of employing women. Women, for their part, had little to gain by entering the workforce, because to the very last they were seen as temporary, cheap labour.

Did wartime developments influence the economic or social position of women in the long term? With regard to the ideas discussed in this chapter, women's employment scarcely changed in the first decades after the war. The introduction of an efficiency-based wage system, which would have given women a better chance, was discussed, but it was rejected in favour of a life-stage system based upon seniority. The new educational system gave women the chance to acquire a solid education in sciences and technology, but very few women rose to the position of manager. Instead, technical progress promoted large-scale mass production, thereby increasing the demand for unskilled and semi-skilled workers. The conservative ideal of womanhood, emphasizing the importance of women's family role, survived long after the war, reducing the wartime productive role of women to a temporary interlude.

NOTES

1 The ideology regarded the traditional family system (*ie seido*) as the basis of society and state. The 'family' or 'household', as the term *ie* is also translated, consisted not only of the members living in the contemporary household, but also of their deceased ancestors and unborn generations to come. Under the patriarchal power of the household head, personal relations in the *ie* were strictly hierarchical, making women and younger members subordinate to men and older members. Women's role in the *ie* was that of a 'good wife and wise mother' (*ryōsai kenbo*).

2 The JISL was founded in Kurashiki, Okayama Prefecture, as part of the (private) *Ōhara Shakai Mondai Kenkyū-jo* in 1919. It became a separate entity in 1921 under the name *Ōhara Rōdō Kagaku Kenkyū-jo*. In 1937, the institute moved to Tōkyō and became a national research institute named *Nihon Rōdō Kagaku Kenkyū-jo*. During the war the JISL maintained strong institutional and personal ties to government organizations like *Dai Nihon Sangyō Hōkoku-kai* (Great Japan Industrial Patriotic Association) and *Taisei Yokusan-kai* (Imperial Rule Assistance Association).

3 The titles of the planned series show the wide range of topics studied by JISL researchers: vol. 1 (published in 1944): *Joshi rōmu* (Female labour); vol. 2: *Joshi no tairyoku to rōdō* (Women's physical strength and work); vol. 3 (1942): *Joshi no shokuba haichi* (The distribution of workplaces for women); vol. 4: *Joshi no ginō yōsei* (The training of women's technical skills); vol. 5: *Joshi no rōdō jōken* (The labour conditions of female workers); vol. 6: *Joshi rōmusha kyōiku* (The education of female workers); vol. 7 (1943): *Kinrō bōsei hogo* (Work and motherhood protection); vol. 8: *Joshi kishukusha kanri* (Administration of women's dormitories); vol. 9: *Joshi rōmusha no rensei* (The training of female workers); vol. 10: *Joshi no shokugyō byō* (Women's occupational diseases); vol. 11: *Nachizu joshi rōmu dōin kenkyū* (Study of the labour service of women in Nazi Germany).

4 The question as to how far hopes for improved social position for women motivated certain feminists to adopt an affirmative role in wartime politics has been raised frequently in recent times. An outline of the debate is given in Narita 1995.

REFERENCES

Journals

Daiyamondo, publ. by Dayamondo-sha.

Books and articles

Akazawa Shirō *et al.* (eds) (1984) *Shiryō Nihon gendai-shi 12: Taisei yokusan-kai* (Sources: Japanese contemporary history 12, The Imperial Rule Assistance Association), Tōkyō: Ōtsuki Shoten; especially source no. 99.

Aoyama Etsuko (1987) '"Senjiki" ni okeru joshi rōdō' (Women's work in wartime), *Rōdō shi kenkyū* 4, July 1987, pp. 39–55.

Cohen, Jerome B. (1949) *Japan in War and Reconstruction*, Minneapolis: University of Minnesota Press.

Furusawa Yoshio (1943) *Fujin rōmusha hogo* (Protection of female workers), Tōkyō: Tōyō Shokan.

Hani Setsuko and Kirihara Shigemi (1943) 'Josei no atarashii hatarakikata ni tsuite. Joshi kaidō undō no teishō' (New ways of work for women. Explication of the All Women's Working Movement), *Fujin no tomo*, 17, 1: 43–50 (January 1943).

Havens, Thomas R. (1975) 'Women and war in Japan 1937–1945', *American Historical Review* 80, 4: 913–34 (October 1975).

Hunter, Janet (1992) 'An absence of change: Women in the Japanese labour force 1937–1945', in T. G. Frazer and Peter Lowe (eds) *Conflict and Amity in East Asia. Essays in Honour of Ian Nish*, Basingstoke and London: Macmillan, pp. 59–76.

Kano Hiroyuki (1943) *Joshi no shokuba haichi* (The distribution of work places for women), Tōkyō: Tōyō Shokan.

Kirihara Shigemi (1944) *Joshi kinrō* (Women's labour service), Tōkyō: Tōyō Shokan.

Kokusaku Kenkyū-kai (1944a) '(Zadankai) Joshi kinrō dōin no shinten to sono tokusei o monogataru' (Round-table discussion: Talking about the development of the mobilization of women's labour service and its special character), *Kokusaku kenkyū-kai shūhō*, 6, 19: 1–16. Reprint: Kokusaku Kenkyū-kai, *Senji seiji keizai shiryō* (Materials on politics and economy of the war period), 8: 211–8, 1983; Tōkyō: Hara Shobō.

Kokusaku Kenkyū-kai (1944b) 'Katei fujin no dōin to tonarigumi kōba' (The mobilization of housewives and neighbourhood factories), *Kokusaku kenkyū-kai shūhō*, 6, 28: 2–12. Reprint: Kokusaku Kenkyū-kai, *Senji seiji keizai shiryō* (Materials on politics and economy of the war period), 8: 284–305, 1983; Tōkyō: Hara Shobō.

Kyōchōkai (1983) *Senji-ka seisan ryoku kakuju to kagaku kōgyō* (The expansion of productive capacity in wartime and the science-based industry), (Kyōchōkai shiryō/ Kyōchōkai sources vol. 3), Tōkyō: Kyōchōkai.

Maki Kenichi (1943) *Kinrō bosei hogo* (Motherhood protection in the labour service), Tōkyō: Tōyō Shokan.

Miyake Yoshiko (1991) 'Doubling expectations: Motherhood and women's factory work under state management in Japan in the 1930s and 1940s', in Gail Lee Bernstein (ed.) *Recreating Japanese Women, 1600–1945*, Berkeley/Los Angeles/ Oxford: University of California Press, pp. 267–95.

Miyamoto Takenosuke (1941) *Kagaku no dōin* (The mobilization of science), Tōkyo: Kaizō-sha.

Nagahara Kazuko (1990) 'Josei tōgo to bosei' (The integration of women and motherhood), in Wakita Haruko (ed.) *Bosei o tou* (Questioning motherhood), 2: 192–218.

Nakajima Kuni (1978) 'Senjika no boseiron: Joshi kinrō-dōin to no kanren de' (The motherhood debate in wartime period. In relation to the womens' labour service), in Namae Yoshio sensei kanreki kinen rekishi ronshū henshū iinkai, *Namae Yoshio sensei kanreki kinen rekishi ronshū kankōkai*, Tōkyō: Chōfu Doho Gakuen Hōjin Honbu, 113–27.

Nakajima Kuni (1979), 'Bosei-ron no keifu' (Genealogy of the motherhood debate), in *Rekishi kōron* (special issue: Kindai Nihon no josei-tachi), 12: 61–8.

Narita Ryūichi (1995) 'Haha no kuni no onnatachi – Oku Mumeo no "senji" to "sengo"' (Women of the motherland – Oku Mumeo in war- and postwar time), in Yamanouchi Yasushi, J. Victor Koschmann, Narita Ryūichi (eds) *Sōryoku-sen to gendaika* (Total war and the modernization after the war), Tōkyō: Kashiwa Shobō, pp. 163–84.

Nolte, Sharon H. and Sally Ann Hastings (1991) 'The Meiji state's policy towards women, 1890–1910', in Gail Lee Bernstein (ed.) *Recreating Japanese Women, 1600–1945*, Berkeley/Los Angeles/Oxford: University of California Press, pp. 151–73.

Seki Jirō (1941) 'Senji rōmu taisaku to joshi rōdō no tokusei. Jinko seisaku daiichi' (Wartime labour policies and the speciality of women's work. Population policy first), *Kōgyō kokusaku* 4, 10: 2–26.

Shokugyō kyōkai (1943) *Joshi kinrō no jūyōsei to kono kanri* (The importance of the labour service of women and its management), Tōkyō.

Suzuki Yūko (1988) *Fueminizumu to sensō* (Feminism and war), Tōkyō: Maruju (1st edn, 1986).

Teruoka Gitō (1938) *Annual Report of the Director of the Japan Institute for Science of Labour for 1937*, Tōkyō.

5

A NEW ORDER FOR JAPANESE SOCIETY

Planned economy, neighbourhood associations and food distribution in Japanese cities in the Second World War

Erich Pauer

INTRODUCTION

The Japanese military, especially the army and its planning staff stationed in the Manchurian State (Manchukuo) after 1931, tried to develop the economy and industry there according to their needs. They saw Manchuria as a kind of testing ground for their plans for industrial development. Influenced by economic ideas then seen as 'modern', the military favoured a 'controlled economy' for development on the continent. In Japan, too, the military supported the establishment of a control network based on various laws during the 'quasi-war economy' of 1932–7. During these years, there evolved the features of a 'planned economy'. The term 'planned economy' was quite common. In some ways it was connected with a Marxian view of the economy and early experiences in the Soviet Union, which the army's planners eagerly observed. But most non-military economists in the Japanese administration later based their views of a planned economy on those of German economists. (For these ideas, see the chapters by Nakamura and Kerde in this volume.)

'Planning' became a buzz-word in the 1930s in Japan in other fields too. But in the second half of the decade, the word 'plan' was gradually replaced by 'control': thus 'planned economy' (*keikaku keizai*) became 'controlled economy' (*tōsei keizai*). After the establishment of the New Order in 1940 and the Planning Board Incident (*Kikaku-in jiken*) in early 1941, the term 'planned economy' lost currency, but the goal of planning economic life in its entirety was still pursued. After 1940, 'planning' was often replaced by 'New Order' (*shintaisei*), which connoted dynamic change. Thus emerged

'New Economic Order' (*keizai shintaisei*), 'New Technological Order' (*gijutsu shintaisei*), and others.

This was more than just a shift in vocabulary. Another factor forced Japanese officials to avoid the term 'planning'. Although huge numbers of 'plans' were made nearly everywhere within the Japanese administration and military, these 'plans', and the ideas that lay behind them, differed from planning in other countries. In the West, including the Soviet Union and Germany, planning meant establishing concrete goals with specific targets, and determining how the target was to be achieved. This principle-oriented way of thinking fixes targets in advance, defines rules and actions, and arouses expectations on what is likely to be found in the target area.

The Japanese approach is different. In its rule-oriented thinking, the future cannot simply be extrapolated from factors known here and now. What will be found on arriving at the goal should emerge in good time. The direction to be taken is found by relying on information that reflects changing conditions, leading in turn to a constant re-formulation of the rules and actions to be followed. This is why in the Japanese way of thinking, rules of action formulated today to arrive at a goal must not exclude certain other kinds of action. Whereas Western thinking concentrates on a pin-point target, the Japanese idea of a goal is diffuse, broad and lacking in any order that is recognizable in advance (for a more detailed discussion see Pauer 1996). This fundamental difference in looking at targets and governing actions must have contributed to the Japanese change in terminology.

Detailed plans did not exist either for the war economy, nor for its constituent parts, such as the organization of consumers and distribution of staple foods. Plans were developed to respond to specific needs and overcome obstacles arising in the wartime economy. They certainly reflect the incrementalist approach.

The 'New Order' is the major set of plans developed in the 1930s and 1940s. But it also lacks detail, generally aiming at broad, diffuse goals. It indicates the direction of change, but does not specify how to enact the change or what society or the economy would look like at the end.

At the company level, the government requested firms to cooperate and coordinate with each other, and for company leaders to develop a 'joint responsibility' (*kyōdō shugi*). The various ordinances, laws and acts promulgated under the umbrella of the 'Economic Law' (*Keizai-hō*) during the war were intended to replace an economic system hitherto based on the Commercial Code (*Shō-hō*, adopted in the late nineteenth century) and the Civil Code (*Minpō*). It thereby aimed to create an entirely new economic system. (The chapter by Otto in this volume describes attempts to create a new type of firm as part of this system.) The efforts started with the proclamation of the New Economic Order (*keizai shintaisei*) in 1940. But they did not progress very far during the war, even though the ever-growing bureaucracy established control associations and other mechanisms in its attempts to establish a 'controlled economy' and to concentrate industry towards war production. Although the government made huge efforts, economic leaders mostly opposed these, usually not openly, but by their actions.

The industrial structure of wartime Japan never progressed further than a 'controlled economy'. This was mainly because of the failure of the various control associations and their structure. This structure had no central guiding body, and the *zaibatsu*-dominated control associations rarely accepted the government's wishes, usually making decisions in their own interest.

Most research into the Japanese wartime economy has centred upon manufacturing industry. Until recently, it has not been realized that in other economic sectors, the 'planned economy' (unannounced and often under a different name) advanced considerably. This was possible because of the lack of strong opposition from the *zaibatsu* or other powerful organizations.

'Joint responsibility' should not only be established among company leaders, but also in the minds of the population as a whole. Unlike industry leaders, the masses lacked organization and specific goals. They were subject to official propaganda and to the Imperial Rule Assistance Association (a political mass organization) in nearly every aspect of their lives, and had few possibilities of escape. Nevertheless, the New Social Order had a very broad and diffuse goal; its structure was not given in detail because a detailed blueprint did not exist. 'Joint responsibility' was to be established, and all other efforts should concentrate on this goal. Actions were to be determined according to the needs at the time.

Behind the economic policy of the 'New Order' after 1940 is a vision of an 'economy in equilibrium'. This means an economic state where raw materials, capital and labour are distributed according to conditions that are known, fixed, or to be determined, for various purposes for the greatest benefit of the population. An 'economy in equilibrium' does not mean absolute immobility of the economy, but implies that certain movements are quickly counterbalanced by other movements. This economic policy cannot be called anti-capitalistic; it merely rejects unrestricted competition, replacing it with state planning, guidance and control. It is therefore aimed at overcoming shortcomings of the capitalist economy. Although this policy had little effect on the manufacturing sector, its effects on other areas of the economy are not to be overlooked.

Taking a brief look at the distribution of staple foods and other essential commodities, one can find a number of measures on the supply side aiming to reduce the number of small shops and replace them with dealers' cooperatives, and then by state-controlled distribution stations. A similar process occurred on the consumption side. At the beginning of the Pacific War, the individual was still accepted as the consumer. But later on, the right to act as a consumer shifted to the family and then to neighbourhood associations, with staple foods and commodities being regulated by ration-cards, purchase-permits and other restrictive measures.

In both supply and demand can be seen a trend towards replacing traditional distribution systems by measures leading to a more planned economy (and a New Order). The shop was to be replaced by the state distribution station; the individual consumer by the neighbourhood association. But the war hampered government and local authority measures to transform the distribution of staple foods and essential commodities. They were implemented completely only in large cities.

In line with the Japanese rules-based approach, measures were taken based on information about the situation and to overcome obstacles. There were no overall plans or descriptions of the structure of a new consumer society. The overall goal was to distribute staple foods and commodities exactly where they were needed, thereby minimizing losses of these scarce commodities.

Individual measures varied as circumstances changed. But the goal to establish a loosely defined 'New Consumer Order' was not abandoned until the end of the war. It is remarkable how far traditional social relations and the distribution system were changed in this period – at least in the big cities.

BLOCK- AND NEIGHBOURHOOD ASSOCIATIONS: DEVELOPMENT AND STRUCTURE

Despite their similarities, only a few of the wartime neighbourhood associations (*tonarigumi*) and block associations (*chōnaikai*) can be traced back to nineteenth-century village associations. (These village associations themselves survived the dissolution of the Edo-period associations after the Meiji Restoration.) Most of the new associations developed during the Sino–Japanese War of 1894–5, the Russo–Japanese War of 1904–5, after the Kantō earthquake in 1923, and the administrative reorganization of Tōkyō in 1932. Most of these groups had self-help as their goal. Other associations developed out of organizations like shrine-, youth-, landlord- and self-administration groups (for a detailed description of neighbourhood associations, see Nakamura 1979, Kobayashi 1973, Ari 1973). The government and city administrations supported the establishment of such associations after 1936. In 1938, the mobilization campaign during the Sino–Japanese War boosted the establishment of new associations. By November 1939, 82 per cent of all households in Tōkyō had been organized in block- and neighbourhood associations (Akimoto 1974a: 104).

At this early stage, the associations' functions lay merely in the political and psychological mobilization of the people; their economic activities were not very important. In September 1940, an administrative memorandum issued by the Ministry of Home Affairs (Ordinance no. 17: 2–4) led to the spread of neighbourhood associations as an officially recognized system throughout the entire country. This was part of the nationalist movement to unify the people spiritually. Only two years later, block- and neighbourhood associations were incorporated into the political mass organization, the Imperial Rule Assistance Association (*Taisei yokusan-kai*), led by the Prime Minister. Shortly thereafter, the war led to changes in the associations' role. With the growing importance of various economic activities, they became involved in distributing staple foods and essential commodities. Another administrative change in 1944 shows the associations as 'cogwheels' in a general socio-economic reorganization within the goals of a new economic system.

According to a Ministry of Home Affairs memorandum, all cities, towns and villages were to be divided into block- and neighbourhood associations. The smallest unit, the neighbourhood association, usually covered ten to twenty households, but in the cities much larger associations were established. A block association consisted of an average of twenty neighbourhood associations. In large cities, groups of block associations were organized into 'leagues' (*rengō-kai*). According to the memorandum, every household was required to become a member of a specific neighbourhood association. All households belonging to a given neighbourhood association had to meet once a month at the association leader's house. The leader himself received his instructions from the head of the block association. The food-rationing system, the collection and distribution of staple foods and other commodities, as well as the distribution of food ration-cards and purchase-permits (which became a labour-intensive duty) led the neighbourhood associations to play an increasingly important role in the economic life of the Japanese people.

THE DISTRIBUTION SYSTEM

At the beginning of the Sino–Japanese War in 1937 and Japan's entry into a war economy, the first restrictions were introduced on goods to secure the supply of staple foods and other essential commodities for the population. Import controls for cotton were the first. The number of rationed and controlled commodities rose rapidly. A system of food ration-cards and purchase-permits soon followed, and the block- and neighbourhood associations became involved in distributing them.

The distribution system (*haikyū seido*) was supervised by the Ministries of Commerce and Industry and of Agriculture, together with the equivalent departments in the prefectural and city governments, and the control associations. Between 1937 and 1941, nearly every commodity was rationed, and a distribution system established for it. The distribution of staple foods can roughly be divided into two: for rice (and several other grains), and for other staple foods.

Strict controls on rice distribution started shortly after the Sino–Japanese War began. The military draft of young men from rural areas, and the shift of such workers from farming to industry, soon resulted in lower rice production. Rice shortages could not be made up fast enough by imports from the colonies. Various rice control laws were issued in 1938–9 and afterwards, but these laws and a rice-saving campaign at the same time did not bring relief. The supply situation worsened until the beginning of 1941, when people had to queue for rice at shops.

The government was sure that the complicated rice distribution system, with its huge number of small dealers, was to blame for the rice shortages. It first tried integrating small dealers into cooperatives, aiming to reduce the number of shops. In Tōkyō, the free rice trade was abolished: 9,000 independent rice shops were closed, and 1,200 distribution stations took over their role. From April 1941, the rationing and distribution of rice with ration-cards was begun (Akimoto 1974b: 103; TKKK 1975: 169–70). Much more comprehensive controls were enforced through the Food Administration Law (*Shokuryō kanri-hō*), introduced in 1942. This was the basis for the establishment of the Central Food Corporation (*Chūō shokuryō-eidan*) and the Regional Food Corporation (*Chihō shokuryō-eidan*). These public utilities imported and bought up rice, stored and processed it, and then distributed it and other cereals via distribution stations, which they directly controlled (TKKK 1975: 170, ŌSMK 1964: 138). (Figure 1 shows a simplified diagram of the rice distribution system). The distribution of other staple foods was rather more complex; free trade in other foodstuffs continued for some time.

Special distribution and rationing systems began in Tōkyō in June 1940. The first commodities to be rationed were sugar and matches. At the same time, the government called on shopkeepers in these trades to group themselves into cooperatives, as with rice (Tōkyō-to 1979: 144). The government assumed that buying and storing jointly would reduce costs. Establishing cooperatives (through the cooperative law) would give the government the right to intervene and provide additional control methods. This latter assumption went unspoken. The encouragement of cooperatives did not completely eliminate the free market as the government had hoped, but the number of cooperatives grew.

A huge bureaucratic machine was necessary to manage the distribution system. This included official departments and other administrative units. It also engaged others not employed by the government, such as the members of block- and neighbourhood associations. These non-officials were not necessarily paid for their work. The distribution of sugar is a good example of such a system (Figure 2).

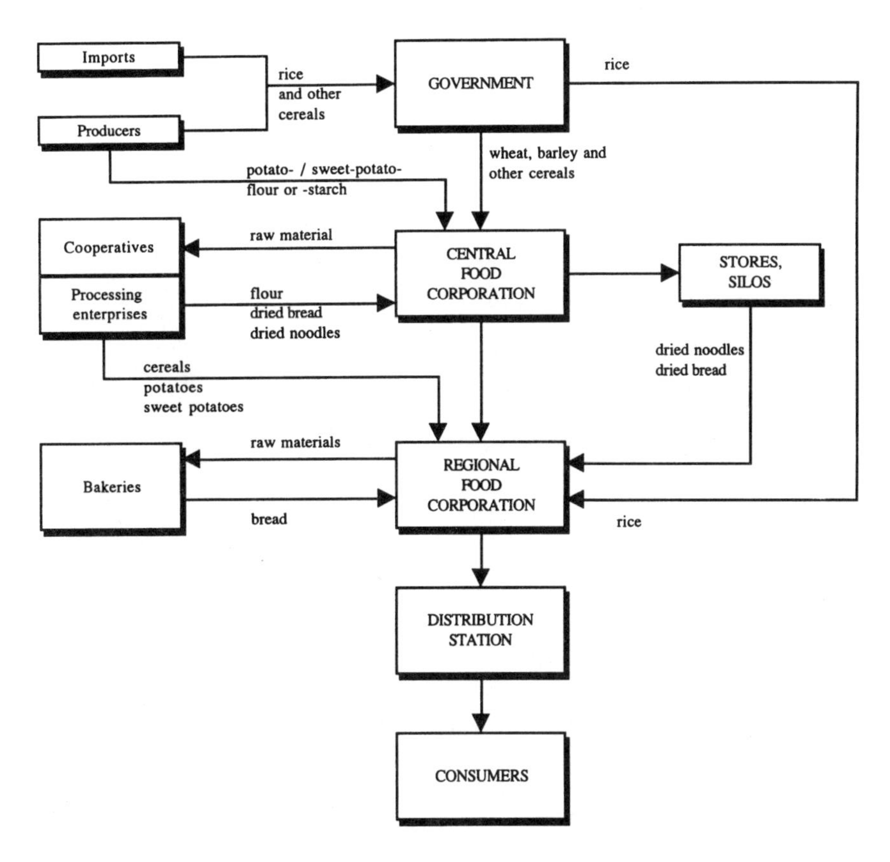

Figure 1 Simplified diagram of rice distribution by means of the central and regional food agencies after 1942 (based on Shōkō Kumiai 1943, table after p. 8).

Food ration-cards and purchase-permits

The purchase-permit system was introduced at New Year 1939–40, when, for the first time, rice for *mochi* rice-cakes could be purchased only with a permit. A few months later, in April 1940, this rationing system was extended to other staple commodities: sugar, *miso* (fermented bean paste), soy-sauce, ordinary rice, beer, oil and others. Ration-cards for rice were distributed from April 1941 on. At first, this system was used only in large cities, but it was soon expanded throughout the country. There was no standardization of food ration-cards and purchase-permits; the distribution system also differed from prefecture to prefecture (ŌSMK 1964: 134; Izeki 1943: 17–18).

A huge bureaucratic machine issued and distributed the cards and permits, and it planned details of the distribution of staple commodities. Despite

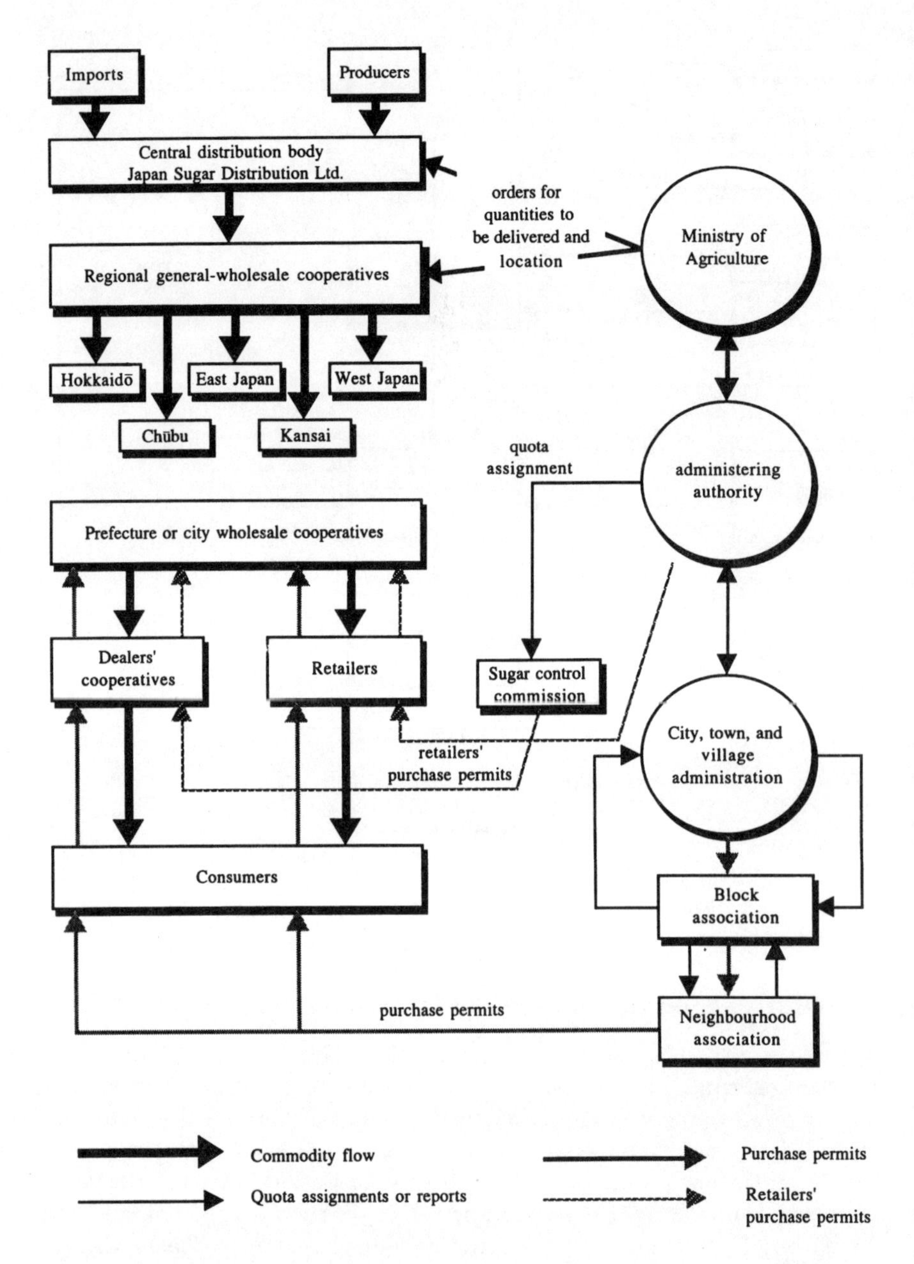

Figure 2 An example of staple food distribution after 1940: sugar distribution (simplified) (Tochigi-ken 1942).

this, food shortages were quite common. It was often not possible to meet consumer demand, even for those with purchase-permits. Owing to price controls and price-fixing, coupled with the lack of transportation facilities, distributors often preferred to sell commodities on the black market. The first remedial measure taken by the small shopkeepers was to take orders in advance from their customers. Similar measures were applied in some large cities, where official advance-order cards were issued. In other places, police were ordered to supervise food distribution. In many cases, the gap between individual demand and the official distribution quota of certain commodities could not be easily filled. As a result, the (forbidden) exchange of purchase-permits within block- and neighbourhood associations soon began to appear (Izeki 1943: 44–5). Various complaints about the system led to some changes in 1943; other changes became necessary during the following years because of the war – particularly the air raids – which also caused confusion within the planned distribution system.

Rationing and food distribution

Shortly after the outbreak of the Sino–Japanese War in 1937, a campaign for cutting down rice consumption was initiated. Measures like mixing rice and barley (70:30 per cent), the use of poor-quality rice, and the use of rice substitutes, were introduced (ŌSMK 1964: 138). In April 1941, rice was included in the rationing system, as previously mentioned, and was distributed via ration-cards according to the sex and occupation of the individual. Early in the Pacific War, the use of white rice was reduced and unpolished 'black' rice was distributed. More and more 'substitutes' like wheat, barley, soybeans, poor-quality rice and maize were mixed with the rice. People often called it 'five colour rice' because it was a mixture of white rice, yellow (old) rice, green beans, red grains and brown insects (TKKK 1975: 172).

Beginning in the autumn of 1942, it was impossible to meet the demand for rice, and the substitutes were no longer merely mixed with rice, but sometimes replaced it entirely (TKKK 1975: 172; ŌSMK 1964: 138–9). In 1943, between 10 and 20 per cent of the rice quota was distributed as substitute foodstuffs. In 1944, the overall rate rose to 20 and 30 per cent, but in the cities it was even higher. In 1944, imports of staple commodities from Southeast Asia almost ceased, and the food crisis became more acute. In mid-1945, between 50 and 70 per cent of the rice ration was distributed as substitute foodstuffs (ŌSMK 1964: 140).

In the last years of the war, the Ministry of Agriculture started a campaign to increase the use of buckwheat, millet, potato leaves and sweet potatoes, and foods like acorns (ŌSMK 1964: 141). Until then, these had been used only in remote areas. Not only was rice scarce; so were nearly all other staples supposedly available with purchase-permits. Research by the Tōkyō city government in 1943 shows that the amount actually distributed was usually much lower than the amount people were entitled to buy. Sugar supplies fell short by an average of 6 per cent, soy-sauce by 7 per cent, *miso* by 20 per cent, fish by 27 per cent, vegetables by 30 per cent, eggs by 40 per cent and fruit by 60 per cent (TSKK 1943: 15–16).

The food situation rapidly worsened during the Pacific War. The lack of labour in agriculture, import difficulties, the rationing system and its bloated bureaucracy, price controls and price fixing were all important reasons for the lack of staple commodities on the official market. Some staples were obtainable only on the black market.

INCORPORATION OF ASSOCIATIONS INTO THE DISTRIBUTION SYSTEM

Various factors led to the incorporation of the block- and neighbourhood associations into the food distribution system. The process was multi-layered and complex. First, distribution was transferred to the associations – the reason the block- and neighbourhood associations changed from social and political groups to economic units. Difficulties in the supply of meat, fish and vegetables produced a demand that the associations also take on the provision of daily needs. This resulted in activities such as the joint purchase of staple foods, joint cooking, and so on. At the same time, the government began to establish a new distribution system, which gradually replaced the traditional trade- and distribution structures, thereby pursuing a new economic system.

Neighbourhood associations as distribution units

The early function of block- and neighbourhood associations was political. They were also referred to as local control units for the economic life of the people, but their activities were not itemized. This later led to various problems. Their economic activities included the distribution of staple foods and essential commodities, saving and buying war bonds, collecting scrap metals, and labour organization.

Shortly after the beginning of the Pacific War, their increasing economic responsibilities became a heavy burden for the neighbourhood association leaders, as is shown by many of their reports (for example TYS 1980: 118–19). Officially, the individual or the family was the smallest unit of consumption, especially in terms of staple foods. But by 1940, the first indications of a change could be observed, when a block association in Tōkyō started to call upon neighbourhood associations to organize the joint purchase of certain staple commodities. These commodities were not distributed through local dealers, but directly by the leaders of neighbourhood associations (TYS 1942: 8). Shortly afterwards, joint purchase by one responsible person elected by the members of the neighbourhood association became more common (Izeki 1943: 50). It started with rice, because after the dissolution of the small rice shops and the establishment of rice distribution stations, it became more difficult for people to procure their rice allotments.

The person was elected to act as procurer for one month (*tsuki-tōban*), after which he was replaced. As it was troublesome for the procurers to collect all of the food ration-cards, get them stamped, and return them after buying rice at the distribution station, it was not long before joint purchase-permits for the whole neighbourhood association appeared (Izeki 1943: 58–9). This was a sign that neighbourhood associations were gradually becoming an integrated economic unit, at least in the field of rice distribution.

Generally, the food rationing system proved less than ideal, because with their purchase-permits, the individual or the family bought in one shop on one occasion, and in another shop the next. This was because shops had more stock on hand than necessary for the population in its area. The scarcity of staple foods and decreasing production in the war years made it even more difficult to distribute these commodities according to demand. To avoid unsold surpluses and thus waste of certain staples, the customers' choice of shops was restricted. Every household was required to select one shop for each staple; this, the government hoped, would allow the right amounts of commodities to be distributed for the number of people living in a particular area. Excessive stocks at one dealer meant shortages at another. This distribution method was meant to prevent this – another step towards a new economic order.

Such a 'registration system' or 'distribution-registration system' (*tōroku-sei* or *tōroku haikyū seido*) began in Tōkyō in 1941 (TKKK 1975: 187); other cities such as Ōsaka soon followed suit (ŌSMK 1964: 114). As the retail system was extremely ramified, and each shop sold a different type of goods, households had to be registered at many shops in order to obtain all the commodities they needed.

In Ōsaka, the registration system began in February 1942 for the fish trade. Five hundred households were assigned to one fishmonger. There were already cases where an entire neighbourhood association, rather than its individual members, registered at a certain fishmonger. In Tōkyō in November 1942, registering a neighbourhood association (called *tonarigumi tōroku-seido*) as a single unit became possible in the vegetable trade. Such cases were rather rare at the time, but it was quickly adopted by other cities during 1943. In Tōkyō itself, where this method of registration and distribution began in a single trade, the system was expanded, and from May 1944 on, nearly all staple foods and other commodities were included in a similar registration system (Akimoto 1974b: 64).

It must be mentioned, however, that written sources from the neighbourhood association level show regional differences. In some areas, the registration system was quickly adopted, whereas in other areas, block associations had to call upon the neighbourhood associations as late as July 1944 to register as a single unit (Ebato 1978: 46). The wartime conditions evidently made it difficult to enforce the new order.

Neighbourhood associations as self-contained units

Difficulties with the distribution of meat and vegetables led to plans to transform the neighbourhood associations into self-contained units. Plans were introduced to raise at least one or two chickens, fed with kitchen refuse, in each association. Instructions for raising rabbits and pigs were distributed by the neighbourhood associations (SSK 1941: 102–3). These plans for self-sufficiency produced limited results. Vegetable-growing was more successful. In 1940, gardening campaigns were begun in the larger cities, with neighbourhood associations deeply involved. The associations leased uncultivated areas outside the cities; the association members cultivated them jointly, and harvested and ate the vegetables (SSK 1941: 102). These beginnings were taken up by the Ministry of Agriculture in late 1941 and, in the following year, a five-year plan for the whole country was established. Plans drawn up for Tōkyō were used as a basis for other cities.

The supply of vegetables worsened in 1943, and the registration system proved of no help. The plans were extended, and vegetable growing was also allowed in urban areas. Schools, factories and neighbourhood associations were ordered to cultivate areas within their boundaries – mainly school grounds, factory yards, river banks and parks. By July 1944, an area of 1,700 hectares had been cultivated, 1,000 hectares of it by neighbourhood associations (TKKK 1975: 189). Government departments supported these campaigns. Block associations were able to invite government lecturers on vegetable growing, and the radio broadcast gardening instructions (Ebato 1978: 36–7). Seeds were distributed not to individuals or families, but to the neighbourhood associations, which were thus also expected to act as an economic unit in such activities.

Joint purchases and cooperative cooking

Problems in the distribution system often made it necessary for consumers to rush from one shop to another to find things to buy. To simplify this time-consuming and inefficient purchasing, consumer cooperatives were established in Tōkyō and other cities in 1940 and 1941. Sometimes such cooperatives were established at the block-association level, but most were at the neighbourhood level. Sometimes all members of a neighbourhood association were members of the cooperative, but voluntary membership was more usual (Izeki 1943: 63–4). Some cooperatives' activities reached beyond joint purchasing; they jointly bought staples on the wholesale market, deciding what to buy ahead of time based on what was available. They then distributed the food to their members together with a recipe. During the war, this system improved, and nutrition experts at government-controlled distribution stations taught the associations how to cook (especially with the unfamiliar substitute foodstuffs) and conserve food (SSK 1941: 92; Izeki 1943: 63–4; Tōkyō-to 1979: 995).

It was not a big jump from cooperatives that made joint purchases, to more specialized cooperatives that produced and distributed whole meals, to cooperative kitchens. The neighbourhood associations were designated as the base unit for establishing these kitchens. (Usually) five housewives took turns to cook for the whole association. In some cases, meals were not distributed to members' houses; instead, the members' families ate together in a special dining room near the cooperative kitchen (Izeki 1943: 67). The attractions of such kitchens were reduced because all the food bought using purchase-permits and ration-cards went to the cooperative kitchen. As a result, it became impossible to prepare even light meals at home – unless the food was bought on the black market.

Consumer divisions in block associations

These developments raised the importance of neighbourhood associations. The block associations, which grouped the neighbourhood associations, had to adjust to meet these new economic functions. Shortly after food rationing and the new distribution system began, people began to complain about food shortages and irregularities in distribution. Most of these irregularities were caused by swindlers involved in distribution; in some cases these involved the leaders of neighbourhood or block associations. Usually, the people holding such offices assumed a powerful function because they distributed or issued the ration-cards and purchase-permits. They signed the cards, granted special favours to some persons, and supervised purchase and distribution; they were thus able to profiteer. Some association leaders were shopkeepers themselves, so had the opportunity to hoard commodities to sell later on the black market. Shopkeepers and small industrialists were appointed by their association members as leaders because after 1940, the associations' economic functions increased quickly; for people unacquainted with business matters, such a position became a heavy burden.

In 1942, the government decided to reorganize the block associations. It added a consumer division (*Shōhi keizai-bu*) to each association (Ordinance no. 250: 14–16) to make contracts with shopkeepers, cooperatives and food distribution stations, as well as with consumers. The consumer division was also to supervise the food rationing system, study the level of demand for staple foods and essentials, and report this to the relevant ministry – which would, in turn, use these figures to plan distribution. The consumer divisions consisted of people selected from the supply side (shopkeepers and others involved in distribution), as well as selected consumers. In most cases, they were representatives from the block or neighbourhood associations. The consumer division was also to take up some control functions within the distribution system.

The order to establish such divisions was issued in October 1942. It was sent to all prefectures and smaller administrative units, where it was sometimes expanded and made more specific. An order in Hiroshima in 1944 added a slight but significant change. The consumer division was to consist not only of representatives of suppliers and consumers, but also several 'distribution leaders' who represented neither side (Hiroshima-*ken* 1944). This could be seen as another attempt by the government to interfere in distribution and to supervise it more closely.

The break with the associations' earlier political and social functions became clearer in the following years, as they became burdened with additional economic activities such as tax collection (Nakagawa 1980: 156–7). The target to establish block associations and neighbourhood associations as new economic units at the lowest level of distribution and consumption thus came nearer.

THE 'GENERAL DISTRIBUTION SYSTEM'

Food rationing, ration-cards and purchase-permits, as well as changes in the distribution system, were all caused by the difficulties in distributing scarce staples to consumers in a way that would please everyone. However, these measures did not make shopping easier. On the contrary, buying food became much more difficult, because nearly every staple was rationed, and had to be bought from many different shops – if an item was available at all. It was not uncommon for people to queue for hours to get food. In cities, 'it took one member of the family five full days out of seven to produce food' (Braibanti 1948: 151).

Neither the registration system nor the establishment of consumer divisions solved the problems. Moreover, the establishment of retail cooperatives (voluntarily or under compulsion) often led to the demise of stores. An example in Nagoya in 1943 (Figure 3) shows that in order to procure the necessary items, a consumer had to go to thirteen different shops between one-half and six blocks apart (Tōkyō Shiyaku-sho 1943: 55). In such circumstances, it is not surprising that joint purchase of the necessary staple foods and commodities found willing ears.

Research on the collection and distribution of rationed foods and commodities was done shortly after the rationing system was established. In contrast to the earlier Nagoya example shown in Figure 3, now,

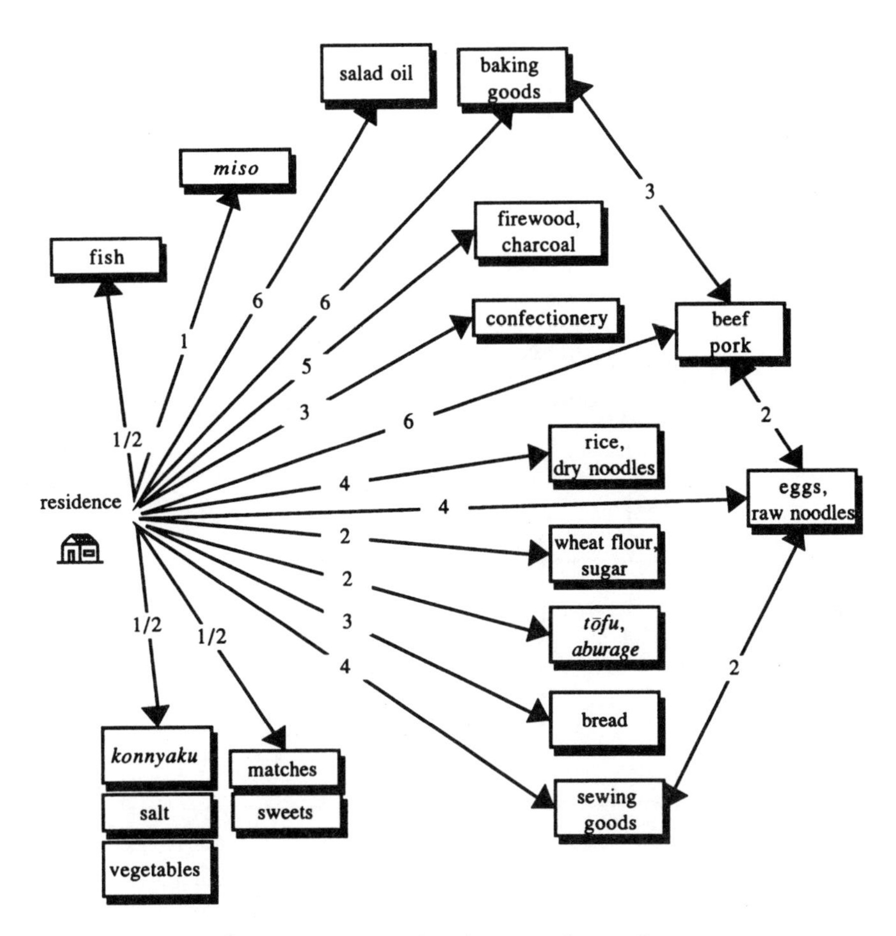

Figure 3 Layout of the various sites for obtaining foodstuffs and other commodities in Nagoya (Nagoya-*shi*, Nakamura-*ku*, Nakashima-*chō* 1–3963) in 1943. The figures give the distance in *chō* (1 *chō* = about 110 metres) from the consumer's residence to the shops (Tōkyō Shiyaku-sho 1943: 55).

consumers could buy the whole range of commodities in three places or less (Figure 4) (Tōkyō Shiyaku-sho 1943: 55).

Government planners developed programmes to reorganize the distribution system with such an idea in mind. Introducing a new 'General Distribution System' (*sōgō haikyū seido*), the government expected to make the distribution procedure easier for suppliers as well as for consumers. To ensure a better and quicker supply, 'General Distribution Stations' (*sōgō haikyū-sho*) with a wide range of items for sale were to be installed. These stations would also replace the traditional shops. As a first step, it was decreed that shops should form dealers' cooperatives in order to manage the newly built general distribution stations.

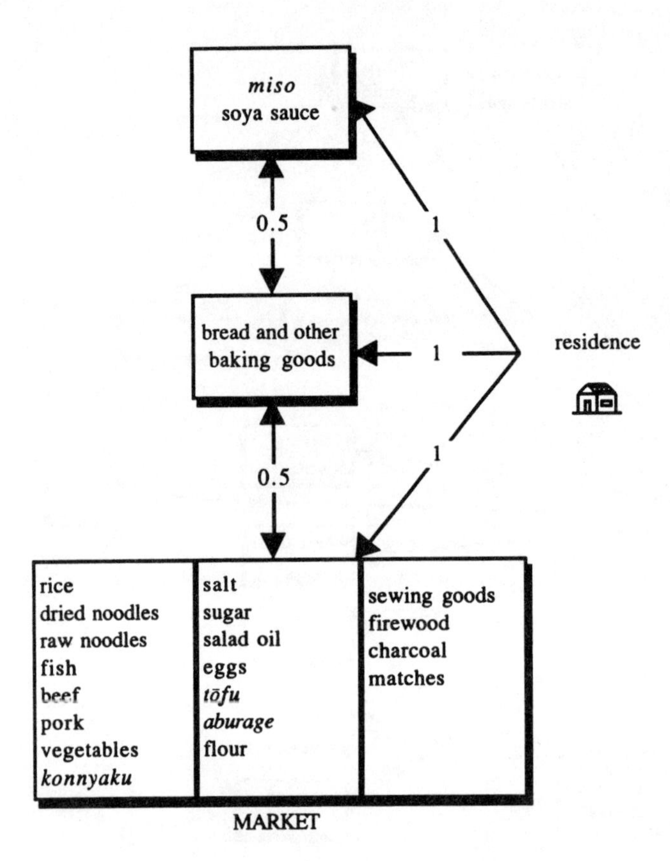

Figure 4 Layout of the market situation in Nagoya (Nagoya-*shi*, Chikusa-*ku*, Kanda-*chō* 4–54) in the wartime. The figures give the distance in *chō* (1 *chō* = about 110 metres) from the consumer's residence to the shops (Tōkyō Shiyaku-sho 1943: 55).

The plan called for the new stations to allow consumers to purchase all necessary commodities in one place. Distribution was to be simplified by issuing new 'general food ration-cards', replacing the earlier ration-cards and purchase-permits, which were usually used for one commodity each (Izeki 1943: 130–2; Tōkyō Shiyaku-sho 1943: 45). The registration system would support the introduction of the new system and ration-cards. The new distribution system allowed *only* the neighbourhood association to register at general distribution stations, thereby making neighbourhood associations the smallest unit of consumption.

The city of Ōsaka was the first to establish this system. In February 1942, the forced merger of small shops dealt a severe blow to free trade, and the number of shops fell by an average of over 25 per cent. Three thousand such general distribution stations were planned, often making use of existing shops, markets and other sites. By mid-1943, nearly 400 such associations had been founded, 90 of them newly built (Tōkyō Shiyaku-sho 1943: 42–4).

The distribution procedure started in the station. Commodities were divided according to the number and size of the neighbourhood associations, and the leaders of the neighbourhood associations were called on to collect the commodities. Other cities, especially in Hokkaidō, were nearly as quick as Ōsaka in establishing the new system. In March 1942, one general distribution station was established for every block association league in Hokkaidō. Ordering, distribution and purchasing were done within the neighbourhood association, which served as the basic unit of consumption (Tōkyō Shiyaku-sho 1943: 30–31). In Hokkaidō, the former rice distribution stations were also integrated into the new general distribution stations. This was done in Tōkyō much later, in 1945.

A slightly different system was established in Hiroshima, where the retailers' cooperatives founded a general distribution system themselves. One station covered one block association. Except sake, beer, meat, fish and baking goods, all staple foods and commodities had to be distributed by the new station (Tōkyō Shiyaku-sho 1943: 32).

On the basis of such examples, in 1944 the Tōkyō government planned to establish a general distribution system (TKKK 1975: 152–6). As in the examples already mentioned, the government delineated certain areas for supply by a single distribution station. The neighbourhood associations became the basic units of consumption. There was no free choice of distribution station: registration was possible only at the distribution station of the respective block association area. In the middle of 1944, block associations informed the retailers that they would soon be transferred to new distribution stations, and that the distribution procedure would change. They were informed that the distribution of almost all commodities would have to be made via neighbourhood associations, and not to families and individuals. New general food ration-cards were to be distributed soon thereafter (Ebato 1978: 47; TKKK 1975: 155).

The Tōkyō plans meant building a general distribution station for each block association (approximately 600 households or 3,000 residents). Commodities to be sold included fruits and vegetables, seafood, meat and meat products, spices and seasonings, as well as preserved foods. Over the long term, the complete replacement of shops by the new system was planned. But in the early stages, shopkeepers would manage the stations on a cooperative basis. Moreover, the merger of many small shops into large, general distribution stations was delayed, and the stations were used instead as central supply depots. Instead of acting as a single distribution station, stations were allowed to manage five 'sub-stations', one for each of the commodity groups listed at the beginning of this paragraph (TKKK 1975: 150, 153–4). The changeover to a single distribution station was often not carried out. Because of the air raids on the city in late 1944, it was impossible to build new stations. Newspapers reported differences from one part of Tōkyō to another. In some areas of the city, not even the beginnings of a new station could be seen. But despite these reports, by mid-1945 452 new general distribution stations had been opened (TKKK 1975: 150). Tōkyō also lagged behind in issuing general ration-cards, and continued to use the single-commodity cards.

The new distribution stations and distribution system added to the already heavy burden on the neighbourhood association leader, or the person responsible for buying rations. He had to go to the station twice or three times a week, spending perhaps the whole day there getting the rations, stamping the cards, paying and counting change. He had to deliver the rations he had bought to each household. In some cases, household members picked up their rations from his home. Other variations in the distribution procedure were introduced in different areas. The new stations in no way made it easier to get food and other necessities. It was often necessary to travel nearly a day to get to the station, and a day to return (Braibanti 1948: 152).

The last change in the distribution system occurred in July 1945 in Tōkyō, when rice was integrated into the general distribution system (TKKK 1975: 150). With this, the new general system, with its goal of having every staple food and essential supply distributed by the new stations, was completed – at least on paper.

The new system aimed to reduce distribution and consumption to quantities and units easy to survey. For this purpose, retailers (on the supply side) and individuals and families (on the consumer side) would be replaced by other basic units: general distribution stations and neighbourhood associations. A new socio-economic order was thus established. The plans had been laid down, the aims were to be followed: but their realization was hampered by the complications of war.

SUMMARY

Totalitarian states always strive to integrate the whole of society into political organizations – for the purpose of political indoctrination and to keep society under control. In Japan from the 1930s on, block- and neighbourhood associations were the tools for indoctrination and supervision. They aimed to establish a 'joint responsibility' (*kyōdō shugi*) within the population. After the whole society had been incorporated into these associations – a process completed in early 1941 – the changing wartime situation altered the associations' functions. Economic functions quickly replaced their original political ones. With food rationing, the associations became involved in distributing staple foods and other essentials. After late 1942, they were ordered to play an active role in distribution. An impending dramatic change in socio-economic structure was evident.

The propagation of the 'New Order' (*shintaisei*) in 1940, with its vision of a complete reorganization of state and society, is also reflected in the state's efforts to plan and control distribution, especially of staple commodities.

Within the 'planned economy', consumers would each get the amount of food and supplies they were entitled to, but in a 'planned' and 'controlled' way. The allocation and distribution procedures were planned and controlled in detail at all levels: production, wholesale, retail, consumption and bureaucratic controllers checking commodity flows. Price controls and price fixing gradually eliminated the free market and competition. The retailer was degraded to a mere organ of distribution. The tendency towards the replacement of retailers proceeded in 1941 with the elimination of rice shops in Tōkyō. Afterwards, the government introduced the integration of retailers into cooperatives.

At the consumer level, too, the government changed the distribution of staple foods and other commodities. After rationing began, individual demand was replaced by fixed quotas. Distribution was controlled via food ration-cards and purchase-permits, which at first entitled the individual or the family to buy commodities. But soon individuals began to be replaced as consumption units by neighbourhood associations. Various campaigns, as well as the establishment of a registration system for the distribution of rationed goods, reflect this trend.

After a 'General Distribution System' was introduced, both the supply and consumer side were rapidly affected. The establishment of cooperatives was only the first step. The integration of retailers and cooperatives into general distribution stations threatened the supply side further. The new system aimed at a complete replacement of free trade and went beyond a mere 'controlled' economy to a 'planned' economy. In 1944 the trend towards adding 'distribution leaders' grew stronger, meaning that both suppliers and consumers were to be guided by these persons with their aim of achieving the planned economy and the New Order.

The family was replaced as the basic consumption unit by the neighbourhood association. Under the registration system, this was the only entity allowed to register at the general distribution station. Rations were distributed from the general distribution station to the neighbourhood associations. The distribution station had to be supplied with only the amount of goods corresponding to the rations for the neighbourhood association members. The free market was replaced by planned distribution.

Details of the prospective New Order of society and the economy were never published – because no such details could have been developed under the Japanese way of thinking. Only buzz-words like 'joint responsibility' gave the basis for actions. The very diffuse and broad goal of a 'New Society' led to the implementation of these extensive socio-economic changes, which were to impact the entire society.

REFERENCES

Official documents

Ordinance no. 17, entitled *Buroku-kai chōnaikai to seibi yōkō* (Outline of the reorganization of block and neighbourhood associations); text cited in Chihō-jichi Kenkyū Shiryō Sentaa (1977) *Sengo jichi-shi* (History of self-government after the war), vol. 1, Tōkyō: Bunsei Shoin.

Ordinance no. 250 (29 October 1942), text cited in Chihō-jichi Kenkyū Shiryō Sentaa (1977) *Sengo jichi-shi* (History of self-government after the war), vol. 1, Tōkyō: Bunsei Shoin.

Books and articles

Akimoto Ritsuo (1974a) 'Senji-ka no toshi ni okeru chōnaikai-tonarigumi soshiki' (Block- and neighbourhood associations system in wartime cities), in Waseda Daigaku Shakai Kagaku Kenkyū-sho, *Nihon no fuashizumu* (Japanese fascism), vol. 2, Tōkyō: Waseda Daigaku Shuppan, pp. 87–120.

—— (1974b) *Sensō to minshū* (The war and the people), Tōkyō: Gakuyo Shobō.

Ari Bakuji (1973) 'Chihō seido' (The local administration system), in *Kōza Nihon kindai-hō hattatsu-shi* (The history of the development of modern Japanese law), vol. 6, Tōkyō: Keisō Shobō, pp. 165–208.

Braibanti, Ralph J. D. (1948) 'Neighbourhood associations in Japan and their democratic potentialities', *The Far Eastern Quarterly* 7, 2: 136–64.

Ebato Akira (1978) *Denen-Chōfu no senji kairanban (The neighbourhood association's newsletters in wartime Denen-Chōfu)*, Tōkyō.

—— (1980) 'Senji tonarigumi ni kansuru futatsu no shiryō' (Two documents on wartime neighbourhood associations), *Meiji daigaku kyōyō ronshū (Jinbun kagaku)* 133: 93–150.

Hiroshima-ken (1944) *Shibu chōnaikai, tonarigumi unei kyōka yōkō / Chōsen jōkai buraku-kai sasatsu shidō yōryō* (Programme for the strengthening of block and neighbourhood associations/Outlines for leading the meetings of the block associations), Hiroshima.

Izeki Jun (1943) *Tonarigumi haikyū no chishiki* (Understanding the neighbourhood association distribution system), Tōkyō: Dōbunkan.

Kobayashi Ryūkichi (1973) 'Tōkyō ni okeru chōnaikai no hensen ni tsuite' (The changes in the block associations of Tōkyō), *Nihon rekishi* 297: 81–96.

Nakagawa Go (1980) *Chōnaikai* (Block associations), (Chūkō shinsho 591), Tōkyō: Chūō Kōron-sha.

Nakamura Hachirō (1979) *Senzen no Tōkyō ni okeru chōnaikai* (Block associations in pre-war Tōkyō), Tōkyō: United Nations University Publications UNUP–23.

ŌSMK (Ōhara Shakai Mondai Kenkyū-sho) (1964) *Taiheiyō sensō-ka no rōdōsha jōtai* (Living condition of workers during the Pacific War), Tōkyō: Tōyō Keizai Shinpō-sha.

Pauer, Erich (1996) 'Rules, Goals, Information – A Key to the Question of Continuity and Change in Japan', in Sarah Metzger-Court and Werner Pascha (eds) *Japan's socio-economic evolution: Continuity and Change*, Sandgate, Folkestone, Kent: Japan Library (Curzon Press), pp. 1–26.

Shōkō Kumiai (1943) *Saihensei-ka no haikyū-kikō I* (Distributing organization after the reorganization), Tōkyō: Shōkō Kumiai Chūo-kinko.

SSK (Senji Seikatsu Kenkyū-sho) (ed.) (1941) *Tonarigumi dōin no sho* (Writings on the mobilization of neighbourhood associations), Tōkyō: Bōki Shobō.

TKKK (Tōkyō Kōshū o Kiroku suru Kai) (ed.) (1975) *Tōkyō dai-kōshū sensai-shi* (The history of the big air-raid and the war damages in Tōkyō), vol. 5, Tōkyō: Kōdan-sha.

TSKK (Tōkyō-to Shōkō Keizai Kyoku) (ed.) (1943) *Senji-ka no haikyū to katei shōhi no jitsu-jō / Maru-hi* (Current conditions of family consumption and wartime distribution/Secret), Tōkyō.

Tochigi-ken (1942) *Keizai tōsei jitsu-mu yōran* (Manual for the practical operation of economic control), Utsunomiya.

Tōkyō Shiyaku-sho (1943) *Sōgō haikyū seido ni kansuru chōsa* (Research on the General Distribution System), Tōkyō.

Tōkyō-to (1979) *Tōkyō hyaku-nen-shi* (Tōkyō: 100 Years), vol. 5, Tōkyō.

TYS (Taisei Yokusan-kai Senden-bu) (1942) *Watashi no tonarigumi* (My neighbourhood association), Tōkyō.

6

DRAWBACKS TO CONTROLS ON FOOD DISTRIBUTION

Food shortages, the black market and economic crime

Anke Scherer

INTRODUCTION

During the Second World War in Great Britain there was a daily radio feature right after the eight-o'clock morning news called 'The Kitchen Front'. It told how to make the best of those items that were still available despite the widespread food shortage. Not only did the British Ministry of Food sponsor this radio programme, it also campaigned nationwide for people to husband scarce resources to support the British war effort. One of the campaign slogans was: 'Food is a munition of war. Don't waste it' (Longmate 1973: 153).

The Second World War also had an enormous impact on the food supply in Japan, especially after 1939. When Japan first started its aggression in Manchuria in 1931, a virtual war fever swept through the media. Manchuria was called a '"bottomless treasurehouse", "unlimited land", "inexhaustible resources" – in short the "key to the national economy"' (Young 1996: 77). The Japanese people were expecting riches and wealth from the Asian continent to better their standard of living. However, towards the end of the 1930s, people started realizing that the mainland victories constantly featured in government propaganda affected their lives only in that further sacrifices were required in the name of the national goal of winning the war (Havens 1978: 99). Daily life in Japan in the last five years or so of the Second World War became more and more difficult due to the rationing of most staple foods, textiles, and other daily necessities. Demand exceeded supply, an official price freeze kept prices artificially low, and the food market was regulated and monitored by the government. A second, unofficial, channel developed alongside the highly controlled official market.

All rationed goods were somehow available in the black market, albeit at a much higher price.

This chapter looks into this unofficial channel and its impact on the lives of the average Japanese citizen during the later years of the war. Starting from the assumption that the official food rations were often not sufficient, this chapter asks how the Japanese war economy affected one of the most basic functions of everyday life: the procuring of food. We know how the government regulated the distribution and purchase of basic supplies (see Pauer's article on 'A New Order for Japanese Society' in this volume), but this official distribution system was merely normative stipulation. Since reality tends to deviate from the norm, it is interesting to look at the strategies people used to circumvent the rules during the early 1940s. How did farmers, shopkeepers, housewives, etc., react to circumstances that forced otherwise law-abiding citizens to resort to illegal methods to secure their livelihood, or offered previously unavailable ways to make extra money by exploiting one's privileged position in the government's distribution scheme? How did the rationing, food shortages and the black market change not only people's lives, but also their morality? Since sufficient food is indispensable, the failure of Japan's war economy to provide enough food through official channels changed people's lifestyle drastically. How did citizens try to make ends meet, and how did the government react to attempts to undermine the carefully orchestrated control of the food market? What did people think about the government measures that deprived them of daily necessities and made petty crime a feature of everyday life?

There is not much material on topics like the black market in wartime Japan. Although it is often mentioned that people relied on it for certain goods (e.g., Matsudaira 1985: 8–9), there is hardly any information on its scope and the way it worked. By their very nature, black-market activities are evasive and hard to document. However, one way to access this topic is to look for government actions against profiteering and other illegal transactions. The series *Shiryō Nihon gendai-shi* (Materials on modern Japanese history) (Akazawa *et al.*, 1990) contains a chapter called *Keizai hanzai* (Economic crimes), which is a collection of edited files from the public prosecutor's office in Tōkyō from 1941 to 1944. The material was first edited for publication in the journal *Keizai geppō* (Monthly reports on the economy), which was run by the Criminal Affairs Department of the Ministry of Justice from July 1941 to September 1944. The purpose of this journal was to explain economic aspects of the New Order as well as to combat economic crimes (Akazawa *et al.*, 1990: 578). Since it was addressed especially to those fighting economic crimes, the articles contain rather detailed descriptions on how shopkeepers manipulated their accounts, how people doctored their ration-cards, etc., in order to provide information for prosecutors. Thus, we can say that these articles summarize the scope and shape of the problem as it was known to the prosecutors.

We should keep in mind, however, that this official picture does not describe the black market as it really was, since such documentation, like all statistics on crime rates, cannot give any information about undetected cases. It does, however, provide an insight into what was considered illegal as well as into general tendencies in a field where the expression 'economic crimes' can only vaguely describe what was going on. Regardless of the absolute figures, it provides in itself a revealing insight into the state of the economy and of society as a whole.

The range of materials collected under the label 'economic crimes' shows that one of the primary concerns of the collecting agency was the link between the recorded crimes and public morality. A significant portion of the published files consists of rumours about the scarcity of rice, the black market and corruption in the food-distribution agencies. This indicates that the government recognized the connections between the state of the economy, the food-supply shortage and public opinion of the government's ability to secure a supply of staple food and daily necessities. Therefore this chapter treats the black market not only as a criminal problem, but also as a psychological phenomenon affecting people's outlook on society and their value system.

Before going into the details, however, let us step back and look at people's living conditions, since the food shortages that ensued from the government's food-control system form the background to the economic crimes described later.

THE KITCHEN FRONT

Japan's military actions on the Asian continent had been influencing the Japanese economy for some time, but from 1937 on the economy turned into a real war economy. Production shifted towards steel and heavy industry in general. The government tightened its control over economic transactions such as the distribution of raw materials and consumer goods. Laws and regulations were supposed to ensure an optimum balance between supply and demand, so that the smallest possible amount of resources could have the best effect possible. The idea was to put anything that was not immediately necessary for the survival of the people into the war effort.

In order to achieve this goal, the government set out to regulate all aspects of the economy. On 19 September 1939, a sudden price freeze for general consumer prices, rents and wages was proclaimed. Rationing of staple food items followed in 1940. Shopkeepers were organized in cooperatives to rationalize the storage and distribution process; the free rice market was abolished in 1941 and replaced by state-run distribution centres; and in 1942 the distribution of rations was handed over to the neighbourhood associations. The government thus intended to ensure a basic supply of staple food and daily necessities for everyone, and at the same time to exercise utmost control over prices and the distribution process.

However, daily rations of 300–400g of rice for adults (who were ranked according to sex, age and kind of labour) and 120–200g for children, were far from enough in a country where people ate rice for breakfast, lunch and dinner. According to a survey of 10,421 Yokohama households in 1943, a ten-day ration of rice lasted for nine days in 4,403 households, eight days in 1,646 households, seven days in 447 households, six days in 72 households and only five days in 31 households (Shiryō 8: 89). This means that more than half of the households surveyed had to get more rice or some other staple from elsewhere, or else cut down their daily rations. In some cases rice distribution centres could not supply everybody with their rice entitlement, since the amounts delivered gradually declined. In such cases people were to receive 'substitute food' – a mixture of grains and beans – but often even this ersatz was not available. As a result, people had to reduce their daily food intake. Pupils came to school with smaller-than-normal lunches; some had no lunch or only some bread; and lunch boxes were stolen. Only a minority of pupils – around 3 per cent – had to skip one meal altogether, but the majority had to make do with rice gruel instead of rice. In some cases, the food shortage had adverse effects on pupils' health: some fainted during the morning roll-call or physical education lessons; others were not allowed to participate in physically taxing activities such as sports or school outings because of their weakened health (Shiryō 8: 92–3). Records of pupils' weights in the state-run Muromachi Elementary School in Sakyō Ward of Kyōto from 1938 to 1941 show a sharp drop in average weight gain in 1941 (Shiryō 8: 93). Parts of fruits and vegetables normally considered inedible (e.g., the skin or stem) were recommended for consumption in an effort to change 'eating habits to win the war' (*kessen shoku-seikatsu kufū*). But the average calorie intake in 1945 had dwindled to 85 per cent of the 1941 figure (Kinbara and Takemae 1995: 168).

Government agencies were well aware not only of the food shortage but also of its effect on public morality:

> In a situation of general discontent resulting from a feeling of insecurity among workers and their families, all kinds of strange things are occurring. Especially numerous are rumours; however, theft and other crimes as well as the distribution of inflammatory pamphlets are (also) on the rise. *So we have to admit that the rice shortage is causing more and more complicated ideological problems in society.*
>
> (Shiryō 8: 91 [emphasis added])

Complaints collected from different parts of the country show that people were not satisfied with the official rations of rice. Adolescents and manual labourers such as miners, especially, needed more rice than they were allotted. This general feeling of not receiving enough through the official channels led to a general perception that everybody else was receiving more than oneself, and that the whole process of allocation was somehow unjust. People in Nagasaki thought that their rations were smaller than those elsewhere; people in Tōkyō complained about workers receiving lunch in their factory on top of a rice ration for three meals a day; workers in Gifu complained about not receiving extra rations like workers in Nagoya; and everybody seemed convinced that families involved in the distribution of rice got more than their fair share anyway (Shiryō 8: 87–8).

Besides an atmosphere of mutual jealousy the food shortage also led to absenteeism at work. A survey in Kanagawa Prefecture showed a decline in attendance from 90 per cent in November 1941 to 84 per cent in February 1942. In common with a similar survey in Nagasaki, it attributed this decline to the rice shortage, since the majority of absentees were busy 'shopping' for food somewhere in the countryside. Some workers left their workplace altogether to move to rural areas where there was more food available, and munitions plants and other heavy industries asked for higher rations as an incentive to retain their workforce (Shiryō 8: 91–2). Some businesses like mines and dockyards as well as small private sweatshops even started paying 'black market wages' (*yami chingin*) to attract day-labourers to alleviate their shortage of workers (Shiryō 9: 112).

So, we can see that the food shortage was not a marginal problem, and people were very conscious about the worsening situation. It influenced all walks of life, affecting schoolchildren as well as workers, and disrupted the production process. In such circumstances, using the black market to buy food or paying 'black market wages' to keep workers was less of an option and more of a necessity.

THE BLACK MARKET

Even before the war, the Japanese government had tried to control the production and distribution of rice through various laws and regulations, and had initiated a rice-saving campaign with the intention of ensuring a sufficient supply of rice for everyone in the long run. However, the more the government tried to control, the bigger the gap between supply and demand grew.

The farmers' role

The free rice market was abolished in 1941, and on 1 July 1942 the so-called Food Control Law (*Shokuryō kanrihō*) was promulgated, further restricting the food market. Under this law only the government was entitled to buy rice and a certain amount of other crops from farmers, and to distribute it to the shopkeepers' cooperatives. Since the government paid relatively low, fixed prices, farmers had a further incentive to sell crops on the black market. For many families in the countryside making a living was not easy during the war, since the draft as well as labour service had taken most adult males away from the fields, leaving women, children and the elderly behind. So when city people came to the villages and offered substantially higher prices than the government for vegetables and rice, most farmers did not think twice. Farmers from Nara Prefecture, for example, received four or five times the official price for rice on the black market in Ōsaka. In this city, they could sell 1 *shō* (1.8 litres) of rice to a middleman for ¥10; the middleman then resold it on the black market for ¥20. After subtracting ¥1 or ¥1.5 for the train fare, the farmer had earned more than ¥8 per *shō* instead of the miserly government price. When rumours spread that the black market was paying ¥50 in Nagoya for a sack of rice, or even ¥80 to ¥100 in Tōkyō, some enterprising farmers from Toyama are said to have gone all the way to Tōkyō, sold their rice, and enjoyed some sightseeing with their new fortunes before returning home (Shiryō 8: 101).

This shows that farmers did not suffer from the worsening food supply conditions as much as the city populations. Although country life might not have been as comfortable as city life, farmers were able to profit from the general supply crisis: their role as suppliers of products with a high black-market value suddenly made it possible for them to earn some money and even spend it on luxury.

The consumers' situation

However, the usual direction of traffic was from the city to the countryside. A report from the summer of 1941 about bulk-buying in the countryside stated that due to exaggerated rumours in the big cities about food shortages, many families used the trip back to their ancestors' home during the Bon-festival holiday to stock up on food. They bought not only vegetables, but also canned and dried food. They used their relatively high city incomes to buy up the countryside's resources. A factory producing canned food in Hyōgō Prefecture reported a rapid rise in demand for its products, as did some shopkeepers. Some shopkeepers resisted selling all their canned and dried food to visitors from the city, arguing that in the hard times to come they had a responsibility to serve their regular customers. This tendency in turn led to quarrels between shopkeepers and customers, who accused the shopkeepers of preferential treatment (Shiryō 6: 80–2).

Most families just bought for their own use when they went to the countryside, but some who could afford to do so bought all they could get and resold it on the black market. Those who were not fortunate enough to have enough money began trading, for instance swapping sugar or textile coupons for rice, or applying various tricks and theft. The head of a neighbourhood association in Ōsaka 'adjusted' some of the ages in the ration-books to get higher rations for adolescents and senior citizens. The organizers of a theatre production tried to claim extra rice by registering six more persons than really were in their play. Another method to put more rice on the table was to apply for 'special rations', sometimes for phoney reasons – like an Ōsaka family who received rice for twelve persons for a funeral reception that never took place. A woman in Kyōto applied for a 'special ration' on behalf of a neighbouring family, which she then duly kept for herself. Some people borrowed rice from others and failed to repay their debts. The wife of a neighbourhood association head misused the ration books kept in her house to obtain 18 kilos of rice, which she then kept for her own family (Shiryō 8: 95–6). Rice storage facilities reported break-ins and theft of rice as well as 'substitute food'. Rice and other food was also stolen from shops and even from private homes – as in the case of one Toyama family, whose rice ration was stolen from their doorstep after the person distributing the ration had left it there when the family was out. Some people in Nara were even desperate enough to hunt stray dogs to turn them into something edible (Shiryō 8: 97).

Official prices rose only slightly during the war years. The official price for 10 kilos of rice went up from ¥2.50 in 1935, to ¥2.87 in 1939, and ¥3.57 in 1945. Equivalent black-market prices were a rather moderate ¥3.50 to ¥5 in 1941, but they rose six-fold by 1943, and then another ten-fold by 1945. The same happened to black-market prices for meat, sugar, *sake*, etc. (Hayashi 1989: 164).

Consumers were in no position to bargain: they usually had no choice but to pay the constantly rising black-market prices. They had to employ all possible means to get something to eat, be it scouring the countryside for food, playing the black market in the city, cheating the bureaucracy and even stealing.

The shopkeepers' privileged position

The situation on the food market described above gave a whole new importance to the ordinary profession of the shopkeeper. Like the example about alleged favouritism shows, the humble shopkeeper's power increased significantly in the course of the war. Not everybody could resist the temptation to exploit their privileged position in handling the scarce food. Shopkeepers were indicted for asking for more than the fixed prices for goods, or for selling certain products only together with non-sellers. Another widespread accusation was the selective holding back of products for special customers in return for favours (Shiryō 7: 84). In the face of this situation it was only logical to exclude shopkeepers from the post of the head of the neighbourhood association, since starting in October 1942, this office also involved the distribution of food rations.

Some shopkeepers went further than just exploiting the consumers' desperate need for food in return for favours or extra money. Some cheated every customer by slightly reducing the amount or weight they sold – which most customers probably never realized. The resulting surplus did not appear on the books, so could be sold for black-market prices (Shiryō 9: 114).

Not all shopkeepers were corrupt, but the range of recorded offences shows that their privileged position gave them many opportunities for cheating that were unavailable to ordinary citizens. But they were also exposed to suspicions from customers and the police.

ECONOMIC CRIMES

The last section dealt mainly with the different participants and their role in black-market activities. This section shifts its focus from the actors to their actions and to the official reactions. A look into the activities of the various actors and the outcome of prosecutions can help to define the range and the meaning of the notion of 'economic crimes' in the context of the wartime black market.

Manifestations of illegal activities

Shopping in the later years of the war required not only the means to go to the countryside for vegetables or the patience to queue for hours in front of distribution centres. Customers also had to keep a watchful eye on what they bought, since a frequent complaint was the low quality of virtually all processed food. Due to a reduction of the Japanese fishing fleet and the ensuing shortage of fish on the market, the ingredients of food made from fish and seafood had to be changed sometimes. The same happened to bread, cake, pastries and sweets. Since prices were fixed, items tended to get smaller because of the problems of obtaining ingredients. There were cases of outright fraud as well, for instance when *sake* was mixed with water or even low-quality alcohol, which in one case poisoned the person who drank it. Some butchers sold meat from animals which had died of disease, or secretly mixed regular meat with offal (Shiryō 9: 109–11).

Such irregularities were hard to detect, as the police grudgingly acknowledged. The police were well aware of the methods used to conceal black-market activities, though. Shopkeepers did not record illegal or overpriced sales. They either entered the official price for black-market transactions in their books, or they entered nothing and burned the receipts. Communication was often by telephone, and payments were in cash so as to leave as few traces as possible (Shiryō 9: 114). The storage and transport of black-market goods had to be inconspicuous: black-market rice was sometimes mixed into bags of sawdust, high-quality textiles were hidden in rags, and gasoline cans were concealed in heaps of wastepaper. Black-market transactions tended to take place in rather conspiratorial locations like old warehouses, backyards and mountain temples. Dealers agreed to meet customers at small, rural rail stations, and most deals were completed without the customer knowing the real name or address of the dealer (Shiryō 9: 115).

The otherwise ordinary act of buying food by innocent housewives mutated into a camouflage operation, sometimes in adventurous conditions. These illegal activities in turn called for appropriate reactions from the monitoring agencies.

Countermeasures against economic crimes

A special 'economic police force' was established in July 1938, and in its first year of existence 96,907 police were assigned to it nationwide. Only after a large-scale black market was created by the price freeze of September 1939 did this force grow into the proportions it was to have during the first half of the 1940s. By 1941, 743,381 police were assigned to fight economic crimes – a figure which is even more stunning when we consider that this was about 1 per cent of the whole population (Akazawa *et al.*, 1990: 595).

Although the police knew about black-market activities, there was not much they could do. If shopkeepers who were trading illegally were clever enough, their books did not reveal their activities, and most transactions happened on such a small scale that the police hardly had a chance detecting them. Even the prosecutors themselves had to admit this:

> Due to a lack of personnel and technical shortcomings in the criminal investigation sector as well as due to a tendency of lacking thoroughness, we have a situation where the number of arrests is extremely low in relation to the widespread occurrence of violations [in the economic crime sector].
>
> (Shiryō 9: 111)

A report about so-called 'wholesale buyer groups' or 'food hunters' descending on Saitama, Tochigi and Yamanashi prefectures in December 1943 shows that the prosecutors were well aware of the train and bus routes people took to travel from Tōkyō to the countryside. This report estimates that 1,500–3,000 city 'shoppers' were using the four train lines to southern Saitama prefecture on an ordinary day. A raid in Saitama on 23 October 1943 (a Saturday) caught 2,684 persons carrying illegally bought foodstuff; the largest amounts of confiscated food were sweet potatoes (3,530 *kan* [1 *kan* = 3.75 kg]), green vegetables (2,590 *kan*) and rice (2,157 *shō*). Since the sale of rice on a private basis was prohibited, the possession of this rice was illegal.

Prefectural governments tried to prevent the bulk-buying of vegetables and other farm products by banning the private transportation of large amounts of food beyond prefectural boundaries. An example of such a ban was Saitama's 'Prefectural announcement number 585 of September 10, Shōwa 18 (1943)'. These bans could be used against the 'wholesale buyer groups' from Tōkyō, without the need to prove a violation of the Food Control Law. However, such controls could not keep the starving city population from trips to the countryside. They merely led people to take precautions, like taking the last train back to the city, or staying with relatives or acquaintances and taking the first train in the morning, since those were the times when control was least likely (Shiryō 11: 124–5).

Most countermeasures seem to have been rather ineffective, and an exercise in frustration for the police involved. When laws were created to regulate the food market further, people soon found ways to circumvent them.

Corruption in the food control and distribution system

Besides ordinary city people making 'shopping trips' to the countryside and hot-spring tourists using their stay in country inns to stock up on rice and vegetables, the prosecutors had to watch another group carefully. These were people involved in the distribution of food rations, either as heads of neighbourhood associations, or employees of food-distribution centres. Some of these people could not resist the temptation to exploit their privileged position. Neighbourhood association heads were apprehended for adding non-existing persons to the ration cards they kept for each family in their group. Some did not redistribute the association's rations fairly, keeping more for themselves than their share. Others used their position to favour relatives and friends, and to blackmail people they disliked. Workers at rice-distribution centres were caught stealing rice or reducing the amounts bagged, keeping the remainder for themselves or for sale on the black market. Food was not the only target of criminal employees: blank ration-cards disappeared, and cards were counterfeited (Shiryō 10: 119–21).

These activities both weakened the food distribution system from within and tainted its public image. The food administration and distribution system gained a reputation for corruption, and the police in charge of preventing such crimes were also tarnished. There were stubborn rumours about policemen who kept confiscated food for themselves, accepted bribes from black-market dealers, and enjoyed white rice and other luxuries they could not possibly have bought legally from their meagre salary (Shiryō 15: 154–5). One likely result of this alleged or real corruption was the deterioration of public morality. If even government employees broke the law to get food, average citizens felt they did not have to have a particularly bad conscience when doing the same.

Criminal prosecution

Conscience is a private matter, though, and so cannot be used as an indicator of the proliferation of petty crime in mainstream society. However, there are more tangible indices of criminal behaviour. The number of people arrested for economic crimes rose sharply after 1939, when the price freeze created the black market (Table 1).

A look at the reasons for the arrests is also revealing. Nearly 75 per cent of those apprehended in 1943 offended against the price-control law, i.e., they were selling goods for higher prices than officially allowed. The overwhelming majority of such offences committed in the first nine months of 1943 can be found in the food sector (Table 2). Other daily necessities like textiles and fuel were also involved, but on a much smaller scale. More than 40 per cent of the offenders in the food sector were retailers; nearly 30 per cent were producers (i.e., farmers), less than 20 per cent were wholesalers, and only about 7 per cent were classed as private persons.

These figures support the supposition that such economic crimes were generally where people exploited their privileged positions in food production

Table 1 Number of persons arrested for economic crimes nationwide, 1938–43

Year	*1938 (July–December)*	*1939*	*1940*	*1941*	*1942*	*1943*
Number of arrests	11,294	28,637	127,761	129,110	142,152	165,945

Source: Shiryō 12: 131

Table 2 Offenders against the price control law according to profession and sector of offence, January–September 1943

	Producers	*Wholesalers*	*Retailers*	*Private persons*	*Total*
Iron, steel	331	856	642	278	2,107
Other metals	79	457	186	101	823
Machinery	60	204	361	53	678
Textiles	640	783	861	222	2,506
Fuel	671	230	672	522	2,095
Chemical products	182	298	402	143	1,025
Food	6,340	4,190	9,173	1,644	21,347
Wood	230	183	157	67	637
Leather	192	132	233	34	593
Rubber	114	217	361	105	797
Other	3,346	1,110	1,876	865	7,197
Total	12,185	8,660	14,926	4,034	39,805

Source: Shiryō 12: 137

and distribution to make some money on the side. The compilers of the records on economic crimes in 1943 describe the general situation as one where:

> it seems that large-scale organized crime has decreased. However, in the period of transition to the set-up of control laws and regulations as well as control organs, due to the existence of profiteers and immoral, greedy producers, there is spread and diffusion of crime among consumers who desperately need [certain] goods.
>
> (Shiryō 9: 107)

This tends to exonerate the consumers and blame the surge of criminal activities on the lower instincts of some greedy individuals.

The pettiness of these crimes is shown by the way the judicial system dealt with the offenders. Of the 162,540 persons arrested for economic crimes in 1943, only 82,928 (51 per cent) were put on trial. Although this figure is not high, it was higher than in any year from 1938 to 1942, where between 27 and 44 per cent of cases were sent to trial (Shiryō 12: 137). Nor did offenders need to fear a long trial or harsh punishment. In March 1943 the system of judicial proceedings had to be changed to deal with a flood of trials pushed through a fast-track process for small offences (Shiryō 9: 108). Of the 82,928 persons prosecuted in 1943, 93 per cent were sentenced through a new 'summary court'; less than 7 per cent underwent a full trial (Shiryō 12: 138). Most of these, however, had not been trading merely a few vegetables or kilos of rice, since most regular trials involved something other than food (Table 3). That full trials were more common in cases involving metals than for food indicates that this two-tier system of prosecution was used to separate the serious, large-scale crime committed mainly in the industrial sector from the overwhelming majority of petty offences. Food-related crimes alone accounted for more than ten times the total number of full trials; without the summary court procedures, they would have clogged up the judicial system.

Punishment was not particularly harsh either. Most offenders got away with a fine. Only 2.4 per cent of those sentenced in 1943 had to go to jail, and 3 per cent received a combination of imprisonment plus fine (Shiryō 12: 139). The prison sentences were seldom longer than one year, the average being about six months (Shiryō 12: 140).

From the point of view of the prosecution, the black market produced a sudden surge of criminal activities but shifted the emphasis from serious, large-scale crimes to petty offences, mainly in the food sector. The judicial system had to be adapted to this sudden impact, but the low number of full trials and the relatively lenient punishments show that although black-market activities were widespread, a single offence was usually not serious enough to call for harsh treatment. Thus a paradoxical situation arose:

Table 3 The kinds of trials according to the sector of offence against the price control law, January–September 1943

	Total number of defendants	*Summary court trials*	*Pre-trial hearing*	*Full trial*	*Percentage of full trials*
Iron, steel	2,107	1,773		334	15.9
Other metals	823	626	3	194	23.6
Machinery	679	617	2	59	8.6
Textiles	2,506	2,234	1	271	10.8
Fuel	2,095	1,967	11	117	5.6
Chemical products	1,025	944		81	7.9
Food	21,347	20,807	5	535	2.5
Wood	637	617	7	13	2
Leather	593	528		65	11
Rubber	797	727		70	8.8
Other	7,197	7,037	2	158	2.2
Total	39,805	37,877	31	1,897	4.8

Source: Shiryō 12: 136

a surge of crimes on the one side, but on the other side too many small offenders to enable economic crime to be combated effectively.

RUMOURS ABOUT THE BLACK MARKET

The police recorded another interesting phenomenon: the prosecutors' files contain a considerable collection of rumours about all kinds of illegal activities connected with food. This demonstrates the interest of government agencies in the mood of the people on the street.

According to the classic definition of Allport and Postman, a rumour is 'a specific (or topical) proposition for belief, passed along from person to person, usually by word of mouth, without secure standards of evidence being present' (cited in Fine and Severance 1987: 1102). Although rumours are not necessarily true, they contain elements that mirror social norms, collective values and the fears and worries of the environment in which they develop. When official information channels break down or become unreliable (e.g., during crises such as wars or in totalitarian societies), rumours develop as a way to explain what is going on (Fine and Severance 1987: 1103–6). Rumours are similar to another form of narrative studied by folklorists: the 'urban legend', 'belief legend' or 'foaftale' (meaning 'friend of a friend's tale', since their origins are mostly too removed from the narrator to be verified on the spot). These legends usually reflect the social, political and economic situation of the community where they circulate. Most are exaggerated or border on the unbelievable, but cannot be denied outright as sheer fantasies. Some contain a kernel of truth, and most also carry a clear message about the society and circumstances of their origin (Brednich 1994: 5–29).

The rumours from all over Japan collected in the public prosecutor's files offer rare insights into the social norms and collective fears revolving around food supply and the black market during the later years of the war. Most of the rumours follow a certain plot structure and can be grouped together with similar stories – showing they belong in the realm of 'urban legends' or 'foaftales'.

The bad policeman and his innocent victim

Stories about policemen who kept or resold confiscated rice appear more than once in the records. A related group of stories emphasizes the tragic effect being caught had on the offender and his or her family. The person caught buying food on the black market is usually portrayed either as the father of a large family or as the mother of a small infant. After being 'robbed' of their last food by merciless policemen, they see no other solution but the murder of the family they can no longer support, and finally suicide. The sympathy of the narrator of these stories clearly lies with the person carrying the black-market goods, since there is no other way to feed the family. The real culprit is always the policeman who enforces an absurd law without thinking about its consequences on his 'victim'. In some stories the policeman realizes his 'wrongdoing' after hearing about the deaths, and commits suicide himself. However, there is also the motif of the policeman who prosecutes the old and weak without mercy, but succumbs to the power of the rich and mighty when he lets some rice smuggler off the hook after learning that he is a manager at Mitsubishi (Shiryō 8: 98–9).

This class of rumours shows how the people's version of what is right and wrong differed from the state's version. The members of the economic police, the guardians of the New Order, turned into villains in the eyes of the consumers. The consequence, however, was not open opposition to the system: 'there were few cases of revolt and resistance, while unchallenging remonstrance was common in all facets of life' (Tsurumi 1986: 18). Rather, it was the mass participation in black-market activities which weakened the official supply system by draining more and more resources from it, and the creation of a tacit understanding that doing so was morally correct.

The spread of criminal behaviour in mainstream society

Suicide as a result of desperation or shame is a distinctive feature of many of the rumours recorded, and can also be interpreted as a form of remonstrance. Another plot that contains this element revolves around a person, usually a child or housewife, who steals rice out of desperation, is caught, and commits suicide out of shame. Such thieves are usually portrayed as essentially 'innocent' – hence children or housewives trying to feed their family. The crime is committed out of desperation when the opportunity arises, not in a cold-blooded manner or according to some plan. This kind of rumour does not condemn a special group like the police, but puts the responsibility for the tragedy on the general situation (Shiryō 8: 99–100). Rumours credit the situation with causing other tragic incidents: for example, starvation (especially of infants) and collective suicides by families after running out of things to eat. Another motif is a quarrel in the family about food, which ends with one family member murdering another – followed perhaps by suicide as well (Shiryō 8: 101–2). Such rumours show that the food shortages affected the very centre of the family, since it forced mothers and children to steal, cheat or murder.

Another class of rumours concerned people being cheated out of some foodstuff. One topic is the old lady from the countryside visiting her children in the city. She brings a big bundle of rice or vegetables for the children, and falls prey to some smart young man who offers to help her carry the heavy burden. The young man disappears with her food, and all the old lady is left with is some money she finds in her sleeves or in the luggage the young man has left behind. Another motif is the farmer who is cheated on the black market by being paid with counterfeit money (Shiryō 8: 100–1). Both stories show the danger of the city, especially for naive country folk, and the extent to which people would go to get hold of food. The broader context is the general deterioration of trustworthiness. The clear message of such rumours is that crime had spread through society to such an extent that it made it impossible to trust anybody.

On the whole, these rumours show how people perceived the food situation. Buying on the black market was unavoidable. The fact that those activities were outlawed led to such tragedies as suicide or murder. The real culprits of those stories are not the citizens, who had no choice but to bend the rules to rescue their families from starvation, but the merciless policemen, enforcing laws that made no sense. This in turn must have severely damaged the reputation of the police force and led to a gradual change in people's consciousness, so that certain illegal activities were no longer perceived as immoral but as justifiable under the given circumstances.

CONCLUSION

To sum up the contents of the prosecutors' files, one could say that the food control system implemented by the Japanese government in the early 1940s, together with the worsening food shortage due to the war, created a whole new field of criminal activities and mobilized criminal energies in otherwise law-abiding citizens. Petty crime became a feature of people's everyday lives and affected their outlook on society. Since most economic crimes were committed when the necessity to secure some food or the opportunity to cheat the system arose, certain criminal behaviour left the realm of the underworld and dissipated into mainstream society. Stories about offenders committing suicide after being caught show that people felt ashamed for what they were forced to do, but at the same time clearly identified the distribution system and its monitoring agencies as the real culprits. Since their daily lives were dominated by hunting and queuing for food, they were not particularly elated by the government propaganda praising overseas victories that did not result in food on their plates at home.

The procuring of food required not only a considerable amount of money, energy and wit; it also affected the highly valued human relations (*ningen kankei*). Good relations with shopkeepers, with the head of the neighbourhood association, and with local policemen, became vital for housewives. On the other hand they also had to cultivate a healthy amount of distrust for anybody related to the sale of food, since some obviously used their privileged positions for their own profit.

When the government started to remodel the free market into a planned distribution of most consumer goods and daily necessities, one of its goals was to make people's lives easier. The food distribution system was designed in a way to match supply and demand, so that everybody would receive enough to eat at a fair price. But there is no such thing as total control. The very moment the government pressed free-market flows into a rigid cast of fixed prices and controlled distribution, new channels circumventing the official ones evolved. The evidence collected by the prosecutor's office in Tōkyō shows that the attempt to create a planned economy and a New Order had some very unexpected and serious consequences. Since the new economic design deprived people of items necessary for survival, and at the same time created opportunities for profiteers, it led to an explosion of petty economic crime and the spread of all kinds of criminal activities into mainstream society. It changed everybody's daily life and influenced public morality. The black market was not only an economic phenomenon; it also had psychological implications. It caused considerable stress in people's lives, reminded them of their precarious situation every day, and reduced their trust in the government's ability to secure their livelihoods. This problem should not be underestimated, since economic security is also a basic psychological need, not merely a goal to be achieved in economic planning.

REFERENCES

Documents

(The abbreviation *Shiryō* (Material) and the following numbers correspond to the system used by the Japanese editors of the documents.)

Shiryō 6 'Rinsenji ka ni okeru busshi baigyo jōkyō chōsa, 1941 nen 11 gatsu' (Report on the situation of bulk-buying in the wartime, November 1941), in Akazawa Shirō, Kitagawa Kenzō and Yui Masaomi (eds) (1990, first edition 1985), *Shiryō Nihon gendaishi* (Materials on modern Japanese history), vol. 13, Tōkyō: Ōtsuki Shoten, pp. 80–2.

Shiryō 7 'Jikyokka no keizai kankei ryūgen higo ni kan suru chōsa, 1941 nen 11 gatsu' (Report on rumours about the present economic situation, November 1941), in Akazawa *et al.*, 1990, pp. 83–6.

Shiryō 8 'Kinji ni okeru hammai busoku no jōkyō oyobi kore ni tomonau ryūgen nado hassei jōkyō, 1942 nen 3 gatsu' (On the situation of the recent rice shortage as well as the accompanying rise of rumours etc., March 1942), in Akazawa *et al.*, 1990, pp. 86–105.

Shiryō 9 'Shōwa junana nendo keizai hanzai gaisetsu, 1943 nen 4 gatsu' (General outline of economic crimes in Shōwa 17, April 1943), in Akazawa *et al.*, 1990, pp. 106–18.

Shiryō 10 'Tōsei shodantai nado no yakushokuin no busshi haikyūjō no fusei kōi sono hoka shokumu ihai kōi no jitsujō oyobi kore ga gendai hōjō ni okeru hōteki sochi no gaiyō no chōsa, 1943 nen 8 gatsu' (General report on the actual state of wrongdoings committed by officials of the various control organizations in the food distribution process and other irregularities in official functions as well as legal countermeasures in accordance with the present laws, August 1943), in Akazawa *et al.*, 1990, pp. 118–23.

Shiryō 11 'Saitama, Tochigi, Yamanashi-ken ka ni okeru iwayuru kaidashi butai torishimari jōkyō, 1943 nen 12 gatsu' (Report on the control of so-called food hunting groups in Saitama, Tochigi and Yamanashi, December 1943), in Akazawa *et al.*, 1990, pp. 124–31.

Shiryō 12 'Shōwa juhachinen ni okeru keizai jiken no tōkeiteki chōsa, 1944 nen 3 gatsu' (Statistical report on economic incidents in Shōwa 18, March 1944), in Akazawa *et al.*, 1990, pp. 131–42.

Shiryō 15 'Shokuryō kyūhaku wo meguri keisatsukan wo hihan suru ryūgen higo no omo naru mono' (The main rumours criticizing the police force in connection with the severe food shortage), in Akazawa *et al.*, 1990, pp. 154–5.

Books and articles

Akazawa Shirō, Kitagawa Kenzō and Yui Masaomi (eds) (1990), *Shiryō Nihon gendaishi* (Materials on modern Japanese history), vol. 13, Tōkyō: Ōtsuki Shoten (first edition 1985).

Brednich, Rolf Wilhelm (1994), *Sagenhafte Geschichten von heute* (Modern fairy tales), Munich: C. H. Beck.

Fine, Alan Gary, and Janet S. Severance (1987) 'Gerücht' (Rumours), in Rolf Wilhelm Brednich *et al.* (eds) *Enzyklopädie des Märchens* (Encyclopedia of fairy tales), vol. 5, Berlin, New York: de Gruyter, pp. 1102–9.

Havens, Thomas (1978), *Valley of Darkness: The Japanese People and World War Two*, New York: Norton and Company.

Hayashi Kentarō (ed.) (1989) *Jitsuroku Shōwashi: gekidō to kiseki* (The true record of the Shōwa period: Tracks and motion), vol. 2, Tōkyō: Gyōsei (first edition 1987).

Kinbara Samon, Takemae Eiji (1995), *Shōwa-shi (zōhoban): Kokumin no naka no haran to gekidō no han-seiki* (Supplement to the history of the Shōwa period: Half a century of violent shake-ups and commotion among the people), Tōkyō: Yūhikaku (first edition 1989).

Longmate, Norman (1973), *How we lived then: A history of everyday life during the Second World War*, London: Arrow Books.

Matsudaira Makoto (1985), *Yami-ichi* (The black market), Tōkyō: Domesu shuppan.

Tsurumi Shunsuke (1986), *An Intellectual History of Wartime Japan 1931–1945*, London, New York, Sidney, Henley: KPI.

Young, Louise (1996) 'Imagined Empire: The Cultural Construction of Manchukuo', in Peter Duus, Ramon H. Myers and Mark R. Peattie (eds) *The Japanese Wartime Empire, 1931–1945*, Princeton: Princeton University Press, pp. 71–96.

7

NATIONAL POLICY COMPANIES AND THEIR ROLE IN JAPAN'S WARTIME ECONOMY

Silke-Susann Otto

EMERGENCE OF NATIONAL POLICY COMPANIES

Japan's wartime economic system has been characterized as a planned economy (e.g., Nakamura 1989 and Chapter 1 in this volume, Okazaki 1987, 1988, 1994). In fact, the Japanese business world had experienced centralization and state controls even before government intervention increased after the outbreak of the Sino–Japanese War in 1937. Numerous industry associations and more than 100 cartels already existed (Hirschmeier and Yui 1981: 188, Momose 1990: 135–8), providing a basis for further implementation of controls during the wartime. State controls were further strengthened by the foundation of 'Control Associations' (*tōsei-kai*), starting in 1941. Thus the National Policy Companies (*kokusaku-gaisha*) were but one characteristic means of realizing state control. Yet little is known about these companies outside Japan, and publications in Western languages are scarce.

Only a few modern Japanese scholars have raised the issue of National Policy Companies as a special type of business. Among these, Okazaki's contributions (see above) stand out for embedding the issue of Japanese firms under wartime conditions (including the National Policy Companies) in a wider framework of an economic theory on the evolution of the Japanese firm. Others, including Nakamura (see above) and Hara (1977, 1989), relate primarily to the overall subject of the Japanese wartime economic system as a planned economy.

Most accessible Japanese sources and data on the National Policy Companies date back to the 1930s and 1940s. This paper is based largely on these contemporary sources. They comprise such scholarly works as Rōyama (1939), Takenaka (1942) and Takata (1942, 1943), as well as semi-official publications initiated by the Japanese government, including e.g., Kikaku-in kenkyū-kai (1944) and Takahashi (1930) (Takahashi was a staff member of the *Kikaku-in* Planning Board). A third group is made up of contributions by journalists, e.g., Matsuzawa (1941).

In discussing the National Policy Companies, this chapter attempts to contribute to a deeper understanding of the Japanese wartime economic system from a micro-economic viewpoint. Okazaki (1994: 351) points to the Second World War as being the major transition in the evolution of the Japanese firm. Bearing that in mind, the analysis focusses on (a) the formation and characteristics of National Policy Companies as a specific type of firm developed during the war, and (b) their functions during a time of drastic change and controls. For the latter task, the overall economic and political development in prewar and wartime Japan must also be considered.

The chapter first outlines the economic and political background for the National Policy Companies. It then compares their legal basis with other forms of business and groups them into categories. The main focus will then be on the National Policy Companies' relationship with the state. The level of state ownership was a major determinant of their financial structure. Privileges granted to these companies stand in sharp contrast to state control and influence in management matters. This section attempts to answer questions such as: Did the managers of the National Policy Companies voluntarily submit to the public interest, or did they perceive the privileges as incentives? Was state control the price for the privileges? To what extent did the state actually exercise control, either through direct investment or participation in management? Finally, the implications of the National Policy Companies for Japan's wartime economic system will be summarized.

Japan's National Policy in the 1930s and 1940s

Informal gatherings in military circles in the early years of the Shōwa era (1925–88) laid the foundations for Japan's National Policy (*kokusaku*), which strongly influenced wartime economic and political thought and became the key to establishing National Policy Companies. High-ranking army officers formed a Research Association on National Defence (*Kokubō seisaku kenkyū-kai*). In 1928, a Research Association on National Policy (*Kokusaku kenkyū-kai*) was established (Seki 1984: 145–7). The Shōwa Research Association (*Shōwa kenkyū-kai*) was established in 1933; this became known as Prime Minister Konoe Fumimaro's (1937–41) think tank.

These associations became the central institutions where innovative national policies were designed. Besides academics and politicians, they included many of the same high-ranking army officers who had earlier started discussions on national policy. This paved the way for a growing political influence of both the army and navy.

At the core of Japan's National Policy had long been the nation's lack of natural resources. A growing population and the rapid development of industries in Japan caused shortages of agricultural products and raw materials. This was a major driving force behind Japan's expansion on the Asian continent and later in the South Pacific, leading to the colonization of Korea and Taiwan. Colonization efforts in turn led to Japan's mission to dominate Asia, which included the idea of *Lebensraum* – influenced heavily by Nazi Germany's self-sufficiency policies and ideology (Hirschmeier and Yui 1981: 236) – and the idea of an economic empire, the East Asian Co-prosperity Sphere, comprising most of Asia under Japanese hegemony.

Another characteristic of Japan's National Policy of the 1930s became the military's incessant call for setting up a national defence state (*kokubō kokka*) as a response to the general armament movement in other states, e.g., Germany, the Balkan states and China (Matsuzawa 1941: 277, Takenaka 1942: 236–8). Preparing for national defence meant sharp rises in production and the mobilization of natural and human resources. Failing to act this way, Army and Navy circles reasoned, would endanger Japan's existence as a nation. After the outbreak of the Sino–Japanese War in 1937, the military conflict and its settlement became another focus of Japan's National Policy (NKK 1940: 11, Bee 1985: 12, 31–2).

The liberal, capitalistic economic system that had emerged in Japan after the 1860s in general, and private corporations in particular, came under criticism since they would not enable National Policy goals to be achieved (e.g., Takahashi 1930). Accordingly, the economic and political systems had to be changed; the state needed to gain direct control of the economy to ensure that all activities concentrated on public welfare (which was equated with state interest) rather than private interest. The members of the research associations mentioned above became proponents of the resulting changes and of Japan's expansionist policies.

Ideas on the separation of ownership and management as well as the nationalization of industries were clearly expressed by Ryū Shintarō (1900–67, editor of the newspaper *Asahi shinbun* and member of the Shōwa Research Association) in 1939 in his publication *Nihon keizai no saihensei* (Reorganizing the Japanese economy) (Nakamura 1974: 72). His function as member of the Shōwa Research Association was to supervise research into implementing the state-planned economy. He strongly advocated complete government control of companies' economic activities to ensure that they, and whole industries, submitted to the public interest instead of pursuing profit. His ideas significantly influenced the 'New Economic Order' (*Keizai shintaisei*) prepared by the Planning Board (*Kikaku-in*) and announced in 1940 (Nakamura and Hara 1972), although the reforms put into effect were less drastic than he had suggested. The less radical approach was also reflected in the attempted revision of the Commercial Code in 1940: the draft called for state control over management, but was rejected because of strong opposition from the business community. As a consequence, the Shōwa Research Association was dissolved in November 1940.

As Nakamura points out in his article in this volume, the profit principle, which originates in the liberal, capitalistic business environment, remained intact in Japan during the whole wartime period. This contrasts with the Japanese government's steady attempt to gain control over the economy by restricting free-market mechanisms and by influencing private companies' behavior to support government policies.

The government had realized that political – and concurrent with the Army's growing political influence after 1936, also military – goals could not be achieved without a steady supply of essential raw materials and goods. Provision, production, distribution and consumption of these materials and commodities became crucial due to the worsening situation after the outbreak of the Sino–Japanese War in 1937. The government was urged to find means to coordinate supply and demand, the latter caused mainly by military actions. Policy makers finally decided that – given a certain degree of state influence and control – the business community's adherence to the proclaimed national policy could be secured without total nationalization. The state had neither the funds nor the expertise to run by itself all businesses needed in an expanding war economy. Using private capital and managerial expertise was a way around this dilemma.

The National Policy Companies became a characteristic feature of Japan's wartime economic system. They were basically private (only partially government-owned) companies whose purpose was to support Japan's national policy. From the 1930s to 1945, this focussed on expanding Japan's influence in Manchuria, north and central China and the South Pacific. Accordingly, the National Policy Companies were primarily expected to promote industrial control, increase productivity, and facilitate the economic and political development of the occupied territories.

CLASSIFICATION OF NATIONAL POLICY COMPANIES

How were the National Policy Companies organized to fulfil this mission? Under the legal framework in force in the 1930s, the Commercial Code (Law no. 48, 1899) provided for three types of enterprise besides individual entrepreneurship: unlimited partnership (*gōmei-gaisha*), limited partnership (*gōshi-gaisha*), and joint stock (*kabushiki-gaisha*). In 1938, the Limited Company Law (Law no. 74, 1938) added the limited company (*yūgen-gaisha*) to this list.

Business type and legal status of National Policy Companies

The National Policy Companies were without exception incorporated as joint stock companies. This type was chosen as best suiting the purpose of combining state interests with private capital and managerial expertise. In joint stock companies, the basic principle of division between capital ownership and management control was given; the state could become a shareholder or participate in the management to ensure that public rather than private interests were pursued.

Contemporary scholars such as Rōyama Masamichi (Professor of Political Science at Tōkyō University, who headed the Shōwa Research Association), and Takenaka Tatsuo (Professor of Business Administration at Kōbe University) discussed the National Policy Companies' status. They came to the conclusion that although the National Policy Companies were organized as joint stock companies, they certainly did not belong to the private category (Rōyama 1939, 1981; Takenaka 1942). A subgroup of the National Policy Companies, the special-purpose companies (see below) showed many similarities with mixed and public enterprises. Takenaka (1942: 224–6) argued that under wartime conditions, mixed companies were subsumed under public companies; mixed and public enterprises therefore came to be treated as a single group.

Both National Policy Companies and public enterprises pursued the public interest, but National Policy Companies raised capital by issuing shares, while public companies were financed through bonds. Both Rōyama and Takenaka argued that the special-purpose companies should be regarded as a new, separate form of administrative organization (*shin gyōsei soshiki*) rather than be subsumed under any of the categories mentioned above. Their existence depended heavily on the political and economic circumstances during the war; changing conditions could easily lead to a different view of the National Policy Companies' status, and therefore to a different way of categorizing them.

Categories of National Policy Companies

National Policy Companies varied considerably in the nature of their business. Some were founded specifically as National Policy Companies; others were existing companies later designated as such.

First came the 'colonization companies' (*takushoku (kokusaku)-gaisha*), established around the turn of the century. After 1931 (and especially after 1937) an increasing number of National Policy Companies were founded or designated: the 'national defence companies' (*kokubō (kokusaku)-gaisha*) between 1931 and 1937, and 'control companies' (*tōsei (kokusaku)-gaisha*) after 1937. These three stages correspond with the political and economic development of Japan (Matsuzawa 1941: 277, Takenaka 1942: 236–8).

Colonization companies

Many colonization companies existed long before the Second World War; most were founded after the Sino–Japanese War of 1894–5 and the Russo–Japanese War of 1904–5. These companies were the government's means to expand its influence on the continent, focussing on Japan's colonies and occupied territories. The giant South Manchurian Railways Co. (*Minami-Manshū Tetsudō KK*, founded in 1906) and the Tōyō Colonization Co. (*Tōyō Takushoku KK*, founded in 1908) are two of the best-known examples.

In economic terms, the colonies and occupied territories served primarily to secure Japan's supply of natural resources and raw materials for industrial use. They thus helped to reduce the country's dependence on expensive imports that had to be paid in foreign currencies. A number of the colonization companies eventually became semi-official economic promotion bodies; they developed infrastructure and provided financial and technological assistance to private companies that could not be supplied adequately by the private sector itself (Ōhara 1939: 94). Through the colonization companies, the central government gained control over large parts of local industries outside Japan.

National defence companies and control companies

Because the military had successfully promoted the idea of a national defence state, national defence companies soon grew considerably in number, especially after 1931. Heavy industries and fuel supplies were at the core of the state's interest. Production capacities had to be increased and large-scale production introduced to meet the army's potential demand (Ōhara 1939: 94–5, Matsuzawa 1941: 32). About half of the national defence companies were established in Manchuria, where raw material supplies were easier and cheaper. Examples of such national defence companies were the Nippon Steel Co. (*Nippon Seitetsu KK*) and the Teikoku Fuel Co. (*Teikoku Nenryō Kōgyō KK*).

National defence companies were soon followed by 'control companies', which were established mainly in the distribution sector of the Japanese economy around 1940, after the idea of the Planned Economy had materialized. At the time demand grew steadily, continuously reaching new peaks, whereas most essential commodities were in short supply. The control companies were accordingly concerned with transportation, the generation and transmission of electricity, and the supply of natural resources, coal and petroleum (Matsuzawa 1941: 41). They resembled industry associations and controlled distribution in major business sectors. The government granted explicit monopoly rights to some (see below). They controlled numerous subsidiaries throughout Japan and in the colonies and occupied territories (Takata 1943: 195).

Companies responsible for general economic assistance to industry (*kyūsai kokusaku-gaisha*) in defined regions were also subsumed under the category of control companies (Matsuzawa 1941: 41). Nippon Coal Co. (*Nippon Sekitan KK*), Nippon Rice Co. (*Nippon Beikoku KK*) and Nippon Fertilizer Co. (*Nippon Hiryō KK*) are examples of control companies.

Financing and holding companies

Two more important groups of National Policy Companies must be mentioned: financing companies (*yūshi-gaisha*, mainly banks) and holding companies (*mochikabu-gaisha*). Although many could be classified as colonization, national defence or control companies, they differed from these in that they did not engage in physical production or distribution, but concentrated on financial functions.

Banks were some of the oldest National Policy Companies. As early as the 1880s, the government relied on companies such as the Bank of Japan (*Nihon Ginkō*, founded in 1882) and the Yokohama Foreign Exchange Bank (*Yokohama Shōkin Ginkō*, founded in 1887 and later renamed the Bank of Tōkyō). These banks supplied capital to private enterprises, especially those engaged in international trade, in order to promote the country's industrialization (Shimizu 1984: 2286). Both banks functioned during the war as a 'national policy bank' (*kokusaku ginkō*). The Bank of Japan is said to be Japan's first quasi-national policy bank (*jun kokusaku ginkō*) (NKK 1940: 6), responsible for issuing banknotes, it was central to Japan's wartime monetary system.

During the war, the government's main institutions to provide funds to business were the Japan Hypothec Bank (*Nippon Kangyō Ginkō*, founded in 1897) and the Industrial Bank of Japan (*Nippon Kōgyō Ginkō*, 1902). The latter was the first institution to be established through a special company act – the type of legislation generally introduced as legal framework for National Policy Companies after 1937 (see below). The 1938 National Mobilization Law (*Kokka sōdōin-hō*) provided for the Japan Industrial Bank to take over the responsibility for granting credits to industries, and to a degree even guaranteed compensation for losses occurring in certain companies (Ōhara 1939: 94). Funds for industry and trading companies were to be handled exclusively by National Policy Banks; private financial institutions, including the city banks, were not given permission for such transactions (Ōhara 1939: 94).

Financing companies or National Policy Banks were not confined to Japan itself (NKK 1940: 6–7; Hirschmeier and Yui 1981: 194). With the prospect of gaining further influence and control over local industries, such institutions were soon established in Taiwan (Bank of Taiwan, *Taiwan Ginkō*) and Korea (Bank of Korea, *Chōsen Ginkō*). Both banks were expected to cooperate with the Japanese central government in its efforts to develop industry and infrastructure in the colonies.

Holding companies emerged as National Policy Companies only after 1937. Examples are rare; they include the Teikoku Fuel Co. and the Manchurian Heavy Industries Development Co. (*Manshū Jūkōgyō Kaihatsu KK*). The investment function was emphasized instead of physical production or distribution (Kusumi 1941: 98–9). Holding companies invested in selected target companies and gained control over their management through their shareholding.

Changes in the legal framework: special-purpose companies

The basic legal provisions for private companies, such as the Commercial Code, were not revised, but remained intact during the wartime years (see also Nakamura's discussion on the planned economy in Chapter 1 of this volume). Still, under the wartime circumstances a new legal framework was created that changed the status of National Policy Companies. Special legislation was introduced to emphasize the importance of these companies for the state's policy.

Special-purpose companies

The early National Policy Companies (the colonization companies) were usually based on imperial ordinances (*chokurei*) that approved their establishment and provided regulations for their management. In contrast, the majority of the National Policy Companies founded after 1937 were administered as 'special-purpose companies' (*tokushu-gaisha*). They were considered to be an important means of implementing the principles of the planned economy, focussing as they did on increased production, overall mobilization and state control of the economy.

Special company acts (*tokushu-gaisha-hō*) formed the legal basis for the foundation or designation of new National Policy Companies during the wartime period. These acts changed the legal status of the National Policy Companies (*keizai hōjin*): they were exempt from civil legislation and put under the provisions of the new interventionist Economic Law (*Keizai-hō*).[1] Normal private businesses (*kaisha hōjin*) were left under civil law (Takata 1942).

The economic independence of the National Policy Companies was also influenced by the 1938 National Mobilization Law (*Kokka sōdōin-hō*). This did not mean the abolition of the existing system, but state influence became stronger. Article 11 of this Law opened the way for state intervention in private business affairs (Takata 1942: 68–9). The establishment of new businesses, capital increment, changes in the object or purpose of business and issuing of bonds were prohibited; the disposal of profit, repayment of credits or management personnel changes needed official approval.

Special company acts were passed only for individual companies, one act for each company (Rōyama 1939: 106, 115, Ōhara 1939: 99). The government or single ministries had to prepare a draft and justify why the company should become a National Policy Company. If state investment was intended, a budget had to be included. The draft was then passed to parliament, which decided each case separately. Major changes, for example in capital, articles of incorporation or bond issues, likewise required parliamentary approval. An increasing number of special company acts after 1937 reflect the growing weight put by the government on the National Policy Companies as its 'economic backbone'. In 1938–9, for instance, there was hardly a parliamentary session without at least one or two such acts being submitted (Rōyama 1939: 90, Ōhara 1939: 93). A look at the National Policy Company-related bills presented to parliament during the wartime years also reveals which industries attracted most government interest at what time – in other words, which were considered most important for national policy (electricity in 1938, food supply in 1939).

Establishment procedures and capitalization

Establishing a National Policy Company through a special company act required a founders' committee of seven members to be formed. These members included businessmen, government members, bureaucrats and military personnel. There was no need for them to sign any of the new company's shares, as was required by the Commercial Code for private corporations, and the committee members bore no liability for the company. Their main task was to draw up the articles of incorporation, which among others, had to include a detailed account of the company's business purpose to demonstrate its qualification as a National Policy Company.

Shares of National Policy Companies were issued only as name shares (*kimei kabushiki*); there were no shares to bearer (*mu-kimei kabushiki*). The minimum value of a share was set at ¥50; lower values (down to ¥25) were exceptionally permitted in case of full cash payment when the shares were signed. Shares held by the government were usually deferred shares (*kōhai kabu*), which meant that they were entitled to dividends only if a specified dividend had already been paid on privately held shares (Takata 1942: 100–4; see also below).

Existing private businesses could also be designated as National Policy Companies (Rōyama 1939: 105–6). The government made use of this alternative especially in the complex distribution sector. Instead of investing time and scarce resources in building up its own system, it took advantage of the existing sophisticated private network of distribution channels. The government had another reason to choose this alternative: National Policy Companies that had been designated as such generally worked more efficiently and successfully than those that were newly founded, as they did not face start-up costs, planning and operating problems. In some cases, several private companies in an industry were merged into new, large-scale National Policy Companies. In the steel industry, for instance, the Nippon Steel Corporation (*Nippon Seitetsu KK*) came into existence in 1934 through a merger between the state-run Yawata Iron and Steel Works and six private steel companies. (In 1950, the Nippon Steel Corporation was broken up into Yawata Steel [*Yawata Seitetsu KK*] and Fuji Steel [*Fuji Seitetsu KK*], only to be merged again in 1970 to form the giant [New] Nippon Steel Corporation [*Shin Nippon Seitetsu KK*]).

Another way of establishing National Policy Companies was for the government to make special agreements or contracts with private businesses (Rōyama 1939: 107). These agreements were not subject to parliamentary decision or approval. This last option, however, was hardly practiced.

RELATIONSHIPS WITH THE STATE

One major feature of the formal relation between the government and National Policy Companies has been dealt with above: National Policy Companies of the wartime period generally held a special legal status defined by special company acts. These laws provided a formal means for state influence in business matters. Furthermore, the relation between the state and National Policy Companies was characterized by the size of the state's equity share and its capital investment. Because the state to some extent depended on the companies to achieve its own goals, it on one hand strove for influence and control, but on the other hand granted these companies privileges not available to normal businesses.

Financial structure: state and private capital

Capital ownership is one way to maintain control over a business. The government's goal of controlling the economy therefore implies some equity ownership of the National Policy Companies. Considerable differences among companies in the amount of equity it owned, however, suggest that this was not the only way the state exercised control.

State equity share in National Policy Companies

That the state lacked the funds to own 100 per cent of all essential businesses in the war economy had long been acknowledged; this was one of the major factors contributing to the establishment of the National Policy Companies. Generally speaking, the government tried to become the principal shareholder of the National Policy Companies, holding more than 50 per cent of the shares (Matsuzawa 1941: 12–13, 62). In practice, even this could not be achieved because of the government's self-proclaimed policy of avoiding continuing debt financing through the issuing of government bonds, which in turn led to a lack of funds which could be invested. Most National Policy Companies, therefore, relied heavily upon self-financing. The special company acts facilitated their self-financing. For instance, whereas the Commercial Code restricted the amount of bonds issued by normal companies to the equivalent of their paid-in capital, the ceiling for bond issuing of the National Policy Companies was considerably higher (see also the section below on capitalization through bond issue).

Among the wartime National Policy Companies, only one National Policy Bank was 100 per cent state-owned: the People's Bank (*Shomin Kinko*). The state held the majority of shares in only a few National Policy Companies (e.g., Nippon Steel Co.). Many were founded with 50 per cent state investment, but this ratio sank gradually as a consequence of continuous capital increases without additional state funds. Some National Policy Companies, such as the East Asia Shipping Company (*Tō-A Kaiun KK*), never experienced any state equity ownership but remained 100 per cent privately owned.

In 1941, the state held stock directly in only thirty-two of the more than 150 National Policy Companies that existed at that time. The average quota of state equity reached only 30 per cent in these thirty-two companies (¥1.15 billion of ¥3.6 billion paid-in net capital) (Kusumi 1941: 94–6). These figures show only direct state investment. They do not reflect indirect investment, such as shareholding by government institutions, administrative bodies in the colonies or occupied territories, prefectural governments, or members of the imperial family. The last held shares – especially in banks – not personally, but through the head of the responsible section within the Imperial Household Ministry (*Kunai-shō, Uchi no kura no kami*) (Kusumi 1941: 92, Obama 1940: 70).

In 1941 the colonization companies had the highest proportion of state-owned equity, with almost 50 per cent (¥690 million of ¥1,38 billion paid-in net capital). They were followed by the control companies with 33 per cent (¥20 million of the comparatively low total of ¥60 million). National defence companies came last with 27 per cent equity being state-owned (¥380 million of ¥1.4 billion), reflecting private capital's continuing importance in the productive, industrial sector (Matsuzawa 1941: 64–73, 278).

Zaibatsu investment

One noteworthy thing about the National Policy Companies' capitalization is the amount of capital supplied by the *zaibatsu*, especially Mitsui, Mitsubishi and Sumitomo. An 'unwritten law' obliged them to invest heavily in National Policy Companies (Rōyama 1939: 53). Between 1937 and 1945, the *zaibatsu* banks' overall investment in heavy industries, steel, machinery and chemical industries expanded more than sevenfold, from ¥730 million to ¥5.53 billion (Bee 1985: 57). Still, the government made sure that more than one *zaibatsu* invested in the same National Policy Company to avoid any gaining control over an industry.

This strategy of equal *zaibatsu* shareholding was realized, for instance, in the following National Policy Companies in which Mitsui, Mitsubishi and Sumitomo held shares (percentage refers to privately owned shares only, Rōyama 1939: 54–5): Nippon Goldmining Co. (*Nippon Sankin Shinkō KK*) (Mitsui 15.6 per cent, Mitsubishi 15.6 per cent, Sumitomo 12 per cent); Teikoku Fuel Co. (*Teikoku Nenryō KK*) (Mitsui 6 per cent, Mitsubishi 5 per cent, Sumitomo 6 per cent); Nippon Steel Corporation (*Nippon Seitetsu KK*) (Mitsui 12 per cent, Mitsubishi 6 per cent, Sumitomo 2 per cent). It is interesting to note that the government avoided or restricted *zaibatsu* capital investment in the most important and prestigious National Policy Companies, such as the South Manchurian Railway Co. and the Tōyō Colonization Co.

Special account for government expenditures

Until 1939, state capital funds for investment in National Policy Companies were taken out of the government's general budget. In the 1940 fiscal year, the government established a 'special account for government expenditures' (*seifu shusshi tokubetsu kaikei*), intending to carry out all further state investment through it (Obama 1940: 68, 70). The account was attached to the Ministry of Finance. It was considered a way of coping with the increasing amounts of funds needed for investment in and rationalization of the National Policy Companies. Still, in 1941 only twelve of the thirty-two National Policy Companies with direct state equity ownership received funds through the account; the rest were still paid out of the general budget. Nevertheless, one effect of the establishment of the account was the increasing influence of the Ministry of Finance on the National Policy Companies (see the discussion on personnel below).

Similar special accounts had already been established in Manchuria and Mongolia to facilitate investment and financial transactions with National Policy Companies.

Monetary and non-monetary privileges

The government needed the National Policy Companies and their economic strength to achieve its political goals. If private business was not to be dissolved completely, but its cooperation sought, some kind of incentive had to be offered in return for the private sector's efforts. The earlier prospect of nationalizing industries had aroused vehement opposition among the business community. Political pressure alone could not suppress this, as business leaders (and especially the *zaibatsu*) knew about the state's dependence on their capital funds and managerial know-how. The government therefore complied with the demands of big business: it provided the National Policy Companies with various privileges. This was possible because the National Policy Companies were exempt from civil legislation. The other side of the game of give-and-take was the government's consolidation of its far-reaching influence and control on the National Policy Companies (see below). Both the privileges and the scope of state control in individual companies were fixed in detail in the underlying law or other regulations. Naturally, the government restricted the privileges while trying to keep provisions for state influence and control flexible.

Subsidies and loss compensation

Subsidies (*hojokin*) and other financial assistance (*joseikin*) were direct instruments to grant privileges to National Policy Companies (see Rōyama 1939: 42, Obama 1940: 70, Kusumi 1941: 89–90, Matsuzawa 1941: 99). These instruments were applied to avoid insolvencies of companies that under free market conditions would have gone bankrupt as a result of inefficiency or under-capitalization. Insolvencies are especially likely as a business starts up. Many National Policy Companies were newly founded, meaning that their risk of losses and of failure was comparatively high.

The appropriation of subsidies and financial assistance to National Policy Companies shows that under the wartime circumstances the government valued production of certain commodities and services (distribution and finance) higher than the potential monetary profit – which in a free market would have been crucial for a company's survival. The government even went as far as compensating for losses (see below).

Guaranteed dividends and loan repayments

Nevertheless, the profit principle was still valid. Private investors seek capital gain at minimum risk; they therefore needed a minimum dividend on capital invested in National Policy Companies. The government established a system of state-guaranteed dividends for privately held shares in these companies for a fixed period of up to ten years. Since they minimized capital risk, these guaranteed dividends were an incentive for private business and individuals to invest. The dividends were lower than those in the private sector, however. In the first half of 1940, the eighty-five most successful or profitable private companies showed an average profit ratio (*rieki ritsu*) of 22.4 per cent; most went to investors. By contrast, the National Policy Companies' profit ratio barely reached the 10 per cent mark, and was usually between 4 and 6 per cent (Matsuzawa 1941: 280). The guaranteed dividends were set at approximately the average net profit level, 4 to 6 per cent. In case of losses, dividends were paid out of subsidies (Rōyama 1939: 42,

111–13); the company's real profit or loss thus did not influence the income of private shareholders or their return on investment.

These figures are for privately owned shares only. As state-owned shares were generally deferred shares (see above), no dividends were paid, at least not for a fixed period or until profits exceeded the guaranteed dividend payments on private shares. In some cases, two different dividend levels were fixed: one for privately held and another for government-owned shares, the latter usually being lower. The South Manchurian Railway Co., for example, paid an 8 per cent dividend on private, but only 4.43 per cent on government shares.

Not only did the government guarantee dividends; it also guaranteed the repayment of loans or interest to creditors of National Policy Companies (Kusumi 1941: 89). Funds again came from the government's special expenditure account or the general account.

Tax reductions and exemptions

Tax reductions or even exemptions for National Policy Companies required legal provision in the special company acts. National Policy Companies were supposed to pursue public (i.e., state) interests. Taxation was therefore regarded as capital turnover rather than income that increased state funds (Obama 1940: 68, Kusumi 1941: 89). High taxes meant high expenditures that would reduce profits or even lead to losses, thereby requiring subsidies or compensation. Therefore, taxes were reduced or the companies made exempt from the start.

National Policy Companies could be (and usually were) exempt from real estate acquisition tax (*fudōsan shūtoku-zei*), corporate income tax (*shotoku-zei*) and business profit tax (*eigyō shūeki-zei*). Registration tax (*tōroku-zei*) was also considerably lower than that paid by private businesses.

Capitalization through bond issue

Permission to issue bonds to raise capital was given to National Policy Companies because the state itself did not have enough funds to guarantee sufficient capitalization, and did not want to increase its debt by issuing bonds. The Commercial Code restricted the issuing of bonds by private companies; the amount was not allowed to exceed the paid-in capital (*harai-komi shihon*). National Policy Companies, by contrast, were allowed to issue bonds up to three or five times their paid-in capital. In a few cases – especially in the case of financial institutions (such as the Japan Hypothec Bank) crucial for supplying industries with capital – the upper limit was set up to fifteen times the paid-in capital (Kusumi 1941: 88).

In addition, National Policy Companies could increase their capital with government approval – before the company's capital (equal to issued shares) was fully paid in. Under the Commercial Code, normal companies could do so only afterwards.

Monopoly rights

The government even went as far as granting monopoly rights (*dokusen ken*) to certain National Policy Companies (Rōyama 1939: 41), mostly in the distribution sector. If the company was not legally based on a special company act, other administrative and control acts provided sufficient regulations to guarantee the monopoly. The establishment of potential competitors was often restricted by introducing an authorizing system which enabled the government to enforce selective measures.

THE PRICE OF FAVOUR: STATE INFLUENCE AND CONTROL

National Policy Companies were subject to supervision by both the government and the ministry with jurisdiction over them. Such supervisory rights were included in the special company acts. The ministries were authorized to issue ordinances relating to National Policy Companies (Rōyama 1939. 114).

General supervision

Supervision was exercised through three major mechanisms. First, if managers neglected the public interest or if their decisions or behaviour violated legal provisions or the articles of incorporation, the decisions could be repealed and the managers dismissed (Takata 1942: 122). Second, many management decisions could not go into effect without the relevant minister's approval (Rōyama 1939: 114, Kusumi 1941: 90): examples are changes in the articles of incorporation, mergers, dissolution or liquidation, bond issues, credits and borrowings, and the disposal of profit. Third, business plans and budgets for the following fiscal year required prior government approval, as did changes in such plans (Kusumi 1941: 90).

Information necessary to control the National Policy Companies was thus passed directly to the government or ministry, giving them an opportunity to control or significantly influence management decisions.

Financial and management supervision and auditing

The Commercial Code provided that the shareholders' meeting elect a statutory auditor (*kansayaku*) to audit the company's accounting, financial statements and management. The auditor's report was submitted to the shareholders' meeting but was not addressed directly to the public.[2] This provision was applied to all companies, including the National Policy Companies, as long as no contrary provisions were maintained by the special company acts.

The government had a legitimate interest in the financial soundness of National Policy Companies. It placed supervisory government officials (*kanri kan*) into these companies, with the task of watching closely over the companies' business in general and of supervising and auditing their financial situation in particular (Rōyama 1939: 114, Kusumi 1941: 91). They were authorized to check cash and deposits, the company accounts and all business-related documents at any time. Despite being 'outsiders', they were entitled to take part in the general shareholders' meeting and diverse management meetings. They even had the right to speak in these panels, and could ask for delivery of special reports by managers and directors about the company's financial and business situation. They reported to the minister in charge, and it was mainly on their advice that the minister would dismiss executives or revise management decisions.

Eventually, the financial statements of certain National Policy Companies were audited by the government's Board of Audit (*Kaikei kensa-in*).

Personnel decisions

One direct way for the state to secure its interests in the National Policy Companies was by participating in management. Personnel matters, at least at the management level, were not left to the companies themselves. The government usually appointed the president (*sōsai* or *shachō*) and vice-president (*fuku sōsai* or *fuku shachō*), and most other directors and executives (*yakuin*) of a National Policy Company. The former were appointed directly; the latter were chosen from candidates elected at the general shareholders' meeting (*baisū no kōhosha*) and confirmed – or rejected – afterwards. Formally, an Imperial decision (*chokusai*) approved the Cabinet's decision (Takata 1942: 120–1).

While in private businesses only the general shareholders' meeting had the right to remove a director before the end of his term, in National Policy Companies the government also had the authority to dismiss executives under certain conditions (Takata 1942: 122; see above).

According to the Commercial Code, at least three directors had to be elected, and their tenure of office was fixed at three years. In case of the National Policy Companies, the special company acts determined the number of directors – a minimum of only two directors in the case of the Bank of Taiwan (*Taiwan Ginkō*), but five for the Japan Electric Power Generation and Transmission Company (*Nippon Hassōden*). The special acts also fixed the directors' tenure (between two and five years) and how they were to be elected (Takata 1942: 108–16).

Recruitment of managers: businessmen versus bureaucrats

The government had two alternatives in choosing managers for National Policy Companies. It could recruit suitable private businessmen, or appoint bureaucrats (see Obama 1940: 70–3, Matsuzawa 1941: 74–5). Recruiting businessmen had one enormous advantage: their experience and know-how in managing businesses. But it was difficult to recruit competent people, especially after 1937. As the number of National Policy Companies rose rapidly, many new positions had to be filled. Executives of private companies were generally reluctant to give up jobs they had worked for many years to reach. They had built strong, binding ties with their company. High salaries would have been an incentive for them to change jobs, but would have been incompatible with the goal of pursuing the public interest rather than profit. Although the government realized that higher pay could ease recruitment, the level of National Policy Company executives' remuneration was usually fixed by law or in the articles of incorporation, and could not be altered. There was therefore little motivation for businessmen to take such a position. This motivation was further reduced by the prospect of state influence and control restricting their managerial freedom.

One more factor might have contributed to private businessmen's reluctance to take over posts in National Policy Companies. Personnel changes in the ministry often led to personnel changes in the companies they oversaw. As a result, managers could be dismissed suddenly, without any wrongdoing. Later, with the enforcement of the New Economic Order (*Keizai shintaisei*) in 1940, the government implemented measures (Hirschmeier and Yui 1981: 249) that forced managers to work in National Policy Companies.

After 1938, to compensate for the lack of private managers and to secure state interests, the government appointed an increasing number of senior and retired bureaucrats as managers in National Policy Companies. Such bureaucrats could not be expected to have the skills essential to manage businesses in the wartime economy – businesses that faced a certain amount of competition in the home market. But they could be relied upon to support national policy goals. Most of these bureaucrats came from the Ministry of Finance, which gained influence over National Policy Companies after it was given control over the special account for government expenditures in 1940. They were followed in number by staff from the Ministry of Commerce and Industry. By 1939 there were hardly any National Policy Companies without at least one former bureaucrat in an executive position (Ōhara 1939: 70, 97–8); usually there were two: one from the Ministry of Finance and one from the functionally relevant ministry.

Staff of the ministries of Finance and of Commerce and Industry were mostly graduates from the Tōkyō Imperial University. They were (and still are) members of the highly respected elite. When they took over managerial positions, it was primarily to ensure smooth relations between government and company; they were rarely given real management or operational functions. The bureaucrats always kept close ties with 'their' ministry, and they were known not to compromise. A serious problem for National Policy Companies was thus the rivalry that could occur between different ministries or divisions. Political aspects were often overemphasized, to the neglect of managerial and economic sense. Bureaucrats in managerial positions therefore often came under criticism.

CONCLUSION: THE NATIONAL POLICY COMPANIES' ROLE IN JAPAN'S WARTIME ECONOMY

National Policy Companies were an important factor in Japan's wartime economic system. Under a planned economy, total control or even nationalization of industry would be expected, but this did not materialize in Japan. Through the establishment or designation of National Policy Companies in key sectors of the economy, the government succeeded in gaining control over large parts of the economy without completely renouncing capitalist principles such as private ownership or the profit principle. A group of businesses was formed that were responsive to the government's and military's needs in return for preferential treatment.

The fact that nationalization of industries did not occur in Japan was due mainly to the government's lack of funds, and to its lack of managerial expertise. The state held shares in some of the National Policy Companies, but acted as principal shareholder in only a few. The comparatively low level of state-owned equity in National Policy Companies during the late 1930s and early 1940s suggests that there were other means to maintain control than state capital investment.

The state exercised control over the economy in Japan and its colonies and occupied territories through a sophisticated system of give-and-take. The government provided economic, monetary and non-monetary incentives to National Policy Companies and gained control over most management matters in return. Special company acts formed the main legal basis for the government's fostering of these companies. These acts provided detailed regulations for the state's rights and liabilities on one hand, and private investors' and management's rights and responsibilities on the other.

Insufficient recruitment of competent managers and the appointment of retired bureaucrats, however, caused some serious managerial problems. These in turn led to inefficiencies that under normal circumstances would have caused business failure. The fact that the government created and used mechanisms such as subsidies, tax reduction or tax exemption to avoid insolvencies of National Policy Companies, and spared no effort to keep even troubled companies alive underscores their importance for Japan's wartime economy.

After the Second World War, most of the National Policy Companies were dissolved or transformed into government-chartered, public companies, e.g., Japan Airlines Co. (*Nihon Kōkū*) or the International Telegraph and Telephone Co. (*Kokusai Denshin Denwa*). Their legal status is still defined as special companies (*tokushu-gaisha*), but they otherwise differ completely from the wartime National Policy Companies – whose formation as a specific form of corporate organization and whose importance can be explained only by the extreme political and economic circumstances of the 1930s and 1940s.

NOTES

1 'Economic law' means government legislation to implement economic policies. There are two forms: that aimed at restoring market mechanisms distorted by monopoly tendencies, and that aiming to gain control over production and distribution in an economy. Before the end of the Second World War, the latter form was current in Japan. It was afterwards transformed into the former with the Anti-Monopoly Law at its core (*Shin hōgaku jiten* (1991), Tōkyō: Nihon Hyōron-sha, p. 238).

2 A compulsory audit of the financial statements by an independent and qualified certified public accountant (CPA, *kōnin kaikei-shi*) was introduced in Japan only in 1948, on the basis of the Securities Exchange Law (*Shōken torihiki-hō*, Law no. 25, 1948).

REFERENCES

Bee Bugiru (1985) *Nihon keiei shisō-shi* (History of Japanese business thought), Tōkyō: Maruju-sha (first published 1983).

Hara Akira (1977) 'Senji tōsei keizai no kaishi' (Introduction of wartime economic control), *Iwanami kōza Nihon rekishi 20 – kindai* 7 (Iwanami lectures on Japanese history vol. 20, Modern age 7), Tōkyō: Iwanami Shoten, pp. 217–68.

—— (1989) 'Senji tōsei' (Wartime control), in Nakamura Takafusa (ed.) *Keikaku-ka to minshū-ka* (Planning and democratization), Tōkyō: Iwanami Shoten, pp. 69–106.

Hirschmeier, Johannes and Yui Tsunehiko (1981) *The Development of Japanese Business 1600–1980* (2nd ed.), London: Allen and Unwin (first published 1975).

Kikaku-in kenkyū-kai (1944) *Kokusaku-gaisha no honshitsu to kinō* (The essence and functions of National Policy Companies), Tōkyō: Dōmei Tsūshin-sha.

Kusumi Issei (1941) 'Kokusaku-gaisha to kokka shihon' (National Policy Companies and state capital), *Keizaigaku zasshi* 7: 81–106.

Matsuzawa Isao (1941) *Kokusaku-gaisha ron* (National Policy Companies), Tōkyō: Daiyamondo-sha.

Momose Takashi (1990) *Shōwa senzen-ki no Nihon – seido to jittai* (Japan in the pre-war period: System and reality), Tōkyō: Yoshikawa Kōbun-kan.

Nakamura Takafusa (1974) 'Ryū Shintarō to tōsei keizai' (Ryū Shintarō and the control economy), *Rekishi to jinbutsu* 32: 66–74.

—— (1989) 'Gaisetsu' (Summary), in Nakamura Takafusa (ed.) *Keikaku-ka to minshū-ka* (Planning and democratization), Tōkyō: Iwanami Shoten, pp. 1–68.
—— and Hara Akira (1972) 'Keizai shintaisei' (The New Economic Order), *Nihon seiji gakkai nenpō*, Tōkyō: Iwanami Shoten, pp. 71–133.
Nihon Hyōron-sha (1991) *Shin hōgaku jiten* (New dictionary of legal terms), Tōkyō: Nihon Hyōron-sha.
NKK (Noda Keizai Kenkyū-jo) (1940) *Senji-ka no kokusaku-gaisha* (The wartime National Policy Companies), Tōkyō: Noda Keizai Kenkyū-jo Shuppan-bu.
Obama Toshie (1940) 'Kokusaku-gaisha to kanryō' (National Policy Companies and bureaucrats), *Bungei shunjū* 18, 9: 66–72.
Ōhara Tadashi (1939) 'Kokusaku-gaisha wa hanran-suru' (The flood of National Policy Companies), *Kaizō* 4: 93–9.
Okazaki Tetsuji (1987) 'Senji keikaku keizai to kakaku tōsei' (The wartime planned economy and price controls), *Nenpō kindai Nihon kenkyū* 9: 175–98.
—— (1988) 'Dai-niji sekai taisen-ki no Nihon ni okeru senji keikaku keizai no kōzō to unkō' (The structure and working of the wartime planned economy in Japan during the Second World War), *Shakai kagaku kenkyū* 40, 4: 1–132.
—— (1994) 'The Japanese firm under the wartime planned economy', in M. Aoki and R. Dore (eds) *The Japanese Firm: The Sources of Competitive Strength*, Oxford: Oxford University Press, pp. 350–78.
Rōyama Masamichi (1939) *Kōeki kigyō – kokusaku kigyō* (Public service companies and National Policy Companies), Tōkyō: Hyōron-sha.
—— (1981) *Kokusaku kigyō – kō-kigyō ron* (On National Policy Companies and public companies), Tōkyō: Kokudo-sha.
Seki Hiroharu (1984) 'The Manchurian Incident, 1931', in J. W. Moreley (ed.) *Japan erupts: The London naval conference and the Manchurian Incident, 1928–1932*, New York: Columbia University Press, pp. 139–230.
Shimizu Toshiyoshi (1984) 'Unternehmensformen', in Horst Hammitzsch (ed.) *Japan-Handbuch* (2nd edn), Wiesbaden: Steiner (first published 1981), column 2282–309.
Takahashi Kamekichi (1930) *Kabushiki-gaisha bōkoku ron* (On the stock corporation as a cause of national decay), Tōkyō: Banrikaku Shobō.
Takata Gensei (1942) *Eidan to tōsei-kai* (Public corporations and control associations), Tōkyō: Tōyō Shokan.
—— (1943) *Kō-kigyō no kokka-sei* (National character of public companies), Tōkyō: Tōyō Shokan.
Takenaka Tatsuo (1942) *Kō-kigyō kōwa* (Discourse on public companies), Tōkyō: Chikuma Shobō.

8

WARTIME FINANCIAL REFORMS AND THE TRANSFORMATION OF THE JAPANESE FINANCIAL SYSTEM

Okazaki Tetsuji

INTRODUCTION

In recent years it has been proposed that the Second World War brought about irreversible changes in Japan's economic system. The government carried out various institutional reforms in order to manage the war economy. Those reforms substantially influenced the economy's evolutionary path, allowing the contemporary system to emerge.

Our conceptual framework is provided by 'comparative institutional analysis', an approach developed by several economists at Stanford University and at the University of Tōkyō (Aoki 1988, Aoki *et al.*, 1996). This approach conceptualizes an institution as an equilibrium in a game among economic players. Studying changes in the rules of the game (the composition of the players, the pay-off matrix, etc.) is essential to understand how the institution has evolved. The wartime reforms in Japan's financial system can be seen as influencing these rules.

Much research has been done on the reforms. Hara (1966), Itō (1983), Yamazaki (1991a, 1991b) and Teranishi (1993) have explained the system of financial control and the contents of the New Financial Order (*Kinyū shintaisei*).

Based on these works, this chapter provides some new perspectives. First, it analyzes the financial control based on the Temporary Fund Control Law (*Rinji shikin chōsei-hō*). Second, it scrutinizes the mediation of loan consortia by the National Financial Control Association (*Zenkoku kinyū tōsei-kai*), which was a key part of the New Financial System. Teranishi (1993) focused on the loan consortia which developed during the war and regarded them as a prototype of the main bank system (the banking system currently used in Japan, see Aoki and Patrick 1995). However, he analyzed loan consortia that emerged spontaneously, before the National Financial Control Association was set up. This chapter extends Yamazaki's (1991b) analysis and reinforces Teranishi's proposition. It demonstrates the government's role in the evolution of the financial system and discusses reforms in both the Bank of Japan (BOJ) and the private banks. Third, the chapter investigates the activities of the government and private banks in the final stages of the war.

CHANGES IN FLOW OF FUNDS

The influence of the Second World War on the financial system is reflected in the balance between investment and savings. In the early 1930s, investment and savings were almost equal in both the corporate sector and overseas (Figure 5). The government's deficit of 5–10 per cent of GNP was financed by almost the same level of excess private-sector savings. But from the late 1930s on, the government deficit rose rapidly, as did investments in the corporate sector. This large deficit was financed by the private sector. The government deficit was caused by military expenditures, while that of the corporate sector was due to the expansion in production capacity (*seisan-ryoku kakujū*) promoted by the government. Extraordinarily large inter-sectoral flows of funds took place during the war, in turn influencing the financial system carrying these flows.

Personal savings were very large, and most were held in financial institutions. In the early 1940s, deposits accounted for 70 per cent of these private savings (Figure 6), increasing the role of indirect finance. In the

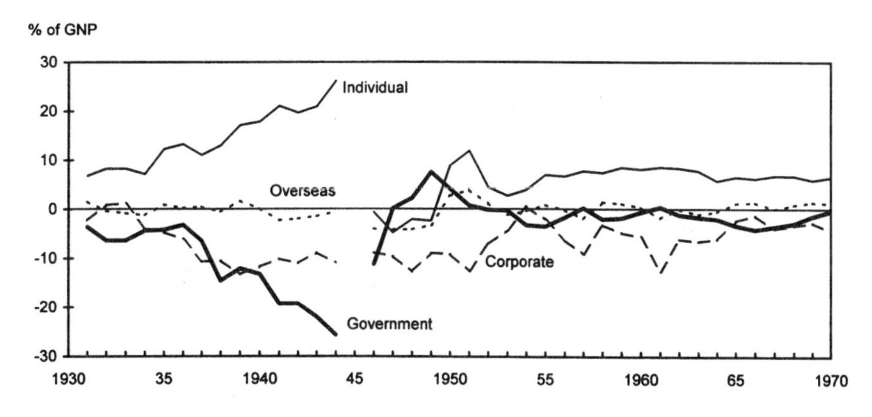

Figure 5 Investment–savings balance by sector

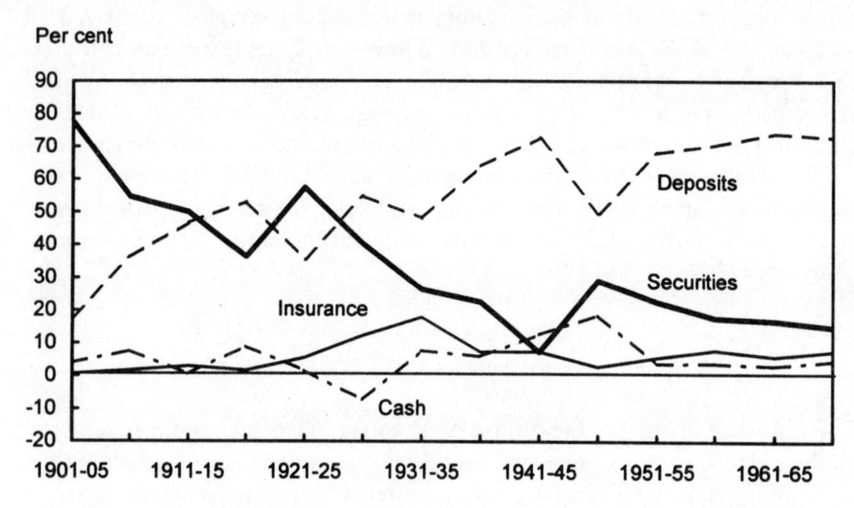

Figure 6 Composition of private savings in Japan (*Source:* Emi *et al.* 1988).

same period, government liabilities consisted mainly of bonds, and corporate-sector liabilities were mainly borrowings (Table 4). During the war most private investment took place in heavy munitions industries, concentrating those funds flowing to the corporate sector into these industries. The next section focusses on the mechanisms used to allocate these funds.

Table 4 Government and corporate liabilities (million yen)

		1931–5	*1936–40*	*1941–5*
Government	Government bonds	3,898	19,994	110,964
	Treasury bills	255	593	2,113
	Borrowings	(471)	(109)	55,374
	Total	3,682	20,478	168,452
Corporate	Stocks	2,629	10,538	16,794
	Debentures	69	1,641	6,378
	Borrowings	(571)	12,169	75,169
	Others	83	128	2,032
	Total	2,210	24,476	100,373

Source: Tōyō Keizai Shinpō-sha (1991)

THE TEMPORARY FUND CONTROL LAW AND FINANCIAL CONTROLS IN THE EARLY WAR

In April 1938, the Cabinet set a savings target for the 1938 financial year (FY) of ¥8 billion. Of this, ¥5 billion was for government bonds and ¥3 billion for expanding production capacity (Ōkura-shō, Zaisei-shi shitsu 1957: 173). The government aimed to promote personal savings to balance rising government and corporate-sector deficits due to the Sino–Japanese War.

The plan for financial allocations became more systematic after 1939 FY. A Fund Control Plan (*Shikin tōsei keikaku*) was drawn up each year, along with plans for materials mobilization (*busshi dōin keikaku*), foreign trade (*bōeki keikaku*), labour mobilization (*rōmu dōin keikaku*) and other activities. The fund control plan aimed to allocate personal savings to the government, munitions and export industries, and investment in Japan's colonies and occupied territories.

The Temporary Fund Control Law played a central role in implementing this plan (Hara 1966). Its essential role was to place all capital funds (*setsubi shikin*) for each company under government control. Government approval was required for any loan for investment in equipment, security underwriting, company establishment, company capital increase, debenture issue, or similar purposes.

The Temporary Fund Control Law gave the government wide-ranging authority to control financial flows. However, substantial limits remained. Working funds stayed outside the government's control. And the law could only prevent funds from flowing to industries seen as non-essential to the war; it did not directly promote financial allocations to the munitions industry or the government. As discussed later, these limits caused serious problems after 1939 FY. Tamura (1941) describes the authorities' recognition of such problems.

The Temporary Fund Control Law was implemented in the following way. The government designated associations of private financial institutions as 'organizations for self-control' (*jichi-teki chōsei kikan*) and gave them a substantial degree of authority over the allocation of funds. These organizations screened and approved each loan and underwriting in accordance with the Industrial Fund Control Criteria (*Jigyō shikin chōsei hyōjun*). These criteria were determined by the Temporary Fund Control Committee (*Rinji shikin chōsei iinkai*), chaired by the Prime Minister, which was the supreme decision maker on applying the fund control law.

The criteria classified industries by priority into six categories (Aa, Ab, Ba, Bb, Bc, C). The self-control organizations were allowed to approve loans up to a certain limit for the Aa, Ab and Ba industries. If a loan item exceeded this limit, the organization had to consult with the Bank of Japan. For loans to Bb industries, the organizations were also required to consult the BOJ. Loans to Bc and C industries were prohibited in principle, but if such loans were thought to be necessary, the relevant self-control organization could consult the BOJ.

The BOJ forwarded only the most important loan requests it received to the Temporary Fund Examination Committee (*Rinji shikin shinsa iinkai*), which had the authority to approve loans. This committee was chaired by the governor of the BOJ and included the BOJ's vice-governor and directors, and bureau chiefs from the ministries of Finance, Industry and Commerce, and Agriculture and Forestry.

The classification of the industries in the criteria was based on their relationship to the Production Capacity Expansion Plan (*Seisan-ryoku kakuju keikaku*) and their importance for munitions and exports (Nihon Ginkō

Table 5 Number of industries in each category of the Industrial Fund Control Criteria

Industry sector	*Category and score*						*Average score*
	Aa 5	*Ab* 4	*Ba* 3	*Bb* 2	*Bc* 1	*C* 0	
Munitions	1						5.00
Mining	22	8	4	5		4	3.81
Electricity and gas	1		2				3.67
Gravel extraction	5	4	2	2		4	3.00
Telecommunications			1				3.00
Trade	1				1		3.00
Metal	23	4	23	5	5	13	2.95
Agriculture and forestry	3		8	10			2.81
Fisheries		1	5	7	3		2.25
Chemicals	16	10	28	6	24	25	2.20
Machinery	13	8	20	6	12	24	2.18
Transportation		4	2		4	3	2.00
Ceramics		5	6	4		9	1.92
Others			5	19	6	29	1.00
Warehousing					4		1.00
Lumber				1	1	2	0.75
Textiles			3	3		17	0.65
Food			2	4	2	19	0.59
Commerce					1	1	0.50
Finance						5	0.00
Insurance						1	0.00
Printing						1	0.00
Real estate						1	0.00

Source: Ōkura-shō, Zaisei-shi shitsu 1957

1986). Table 5 summarizes the criteria used in September 1937. It shows the number of industries in each of the six priority categories, along with scores given to each category for this analysis: an industry in category Aa receives a score of 5, Ab a score of 4, and so forth. The average scores of the various industry sectors are shown in the right-hand column. Munitions, mining, electricity and gas, telecommunications, trade, metal industries and agriculture and forestry have high scores, while finance, insurance, printing and real estate have low scores.

In September 1937, at about the same time as the temporary fund control legislation, the BOJ set up the Bureau of Fund Control (*Shikin chōsei kyoku*) (Nihon Ginkō 1962: 68). In the same month, the Ministry of Finance announced guidelines for self-control by financial institutions and securities underwriters (*Kinyū kikan oyobi shōken hikiuke gyōsha no jichi-teki chōsei taikō*). In many cases, existing associations of financial institutions and security companies were authorized to act as self-control organizations. For ordinary banks, however, new Regional Financial Self-Control Organizations (*Chiho shikin jichi chōsei-dan*) were established within each BOJ branch office's area of jurisdiction (Nihon Ginkō 1962: 74–80).

The Temporary Fund Control Law is thought to have been effective since Aa and Ab industries indeed took a large share of the total supply of funds (Ōkura-shō, Zaisei-shi shitsu 1957, Hara 1966, Yamazaki 1991a). But exactly how effective was it? To discover this, it is necessary to look at financial allocations before and after the law took effect.

Because loan statistics by industry were compiled only after the law took effect, it is necessary to aggregate data from individual companies to build up a picture of an industry sector as a whole. Suitable data on 186 major non-financial companies are provided by various issues of *Honpō jigyō seiseki bunseki* (Analysis of business performance) published by the *Mitsubishi Keizai Kenkyū-sho* (Mitsubishi Institute of Economic Research). Table 6 shows indices for the aggregated amounts borrowed by each industry sector in 1937 to 1942 FY.

Table 7 shows regressions for these indices against the scores in Table 5 for each fiscal year. In 1937 FY there was no significant relationship between the indices and the scores, which is natural because the law was enacted only in October 1937. In 1938 FY a significant positive relationship emerged. That is, borrowings rose more rapidly in industries given higher priority in the fund control criteria. This means that the law functioned effectively to direct financial allocations. This was echoed at the Round Table Conference of the Banks and Trust Companies (*Ginkō shintaku-gaisha kondan-kai*) in November 1938, when the president of Dai-ichi Bank, Akashi Teruo, stated, 'the Fund has been supplied smoothly so far, and there is no need for compulsion'. The governor of the BOJ, Yuki Toyotarō, also said, 'the financial society is self-controlled better than any other sectors. Legal compulsion is not necessary' (Nihon Ginkō, Chōsa-kyoku 1970b: 339).

Table 6 Index of borrowings by industry

	IFCC score*	Index of borrowing (end of 1936 FY = 100)					
		1937	1938	1939	1940	1941	1942
Mining	3.81	80	330	483	1024	1755	1616
Electricity and gas	3.67	151	180	127	187	218	305
Trade	3.00	155	122	152	244	153	128
Metal	2.95	143	170	216	405	235	253
Agriculture	2.81	218	221	160	102	96	23
Fisheries	2.25	65	100	69	121	185	300
Chemicals	2.20	103	121	147	239	313	418
Machinery	2.18	255	420	812	754	972	865
Transportation	2.00	111	123	132	144	162	155
Ceramics	1.92	197	412	525	721	940	1346
Warehousing	1.00	81	50	37	26	10	9
Lumber	0.75	194	189	316	293	164	39
Textiles	0.65	145	127	150	280	354	361
Food	0.59	108	136	148	161	137	173
Commerce	0.50	118	72	154	135	140	153
Printing	0.00	102	118	137	169	158	155
Real estate	0.00	64	11	4	158	74	56

* Industrial Fund Control Criteria average scores (from Table 5)
Source: Mitsubishi Keizai Kenkyō-sho (various issues)

Table 7 Effects of the Temporary Fund Control Law

	Coefficient of score	*t-value*	*R-squared*
1937	9.8	0.88	0.049
1938	42.5	1.97	0.207
1939	46.7	1.14	0.082
1940	90.6	1.76	0.171
1941	157.1	1.86	0.188
1942	157.1	1.79	0.177

However, in 1939 FY the significant positive relationship disappeared, suggesting a declining effectiveness of the controls. Although a positive relationship emerged again in 1940 FY, another problem occurred: the increase in loans by banks slowed, and simultaneously stock prices fell (Figure 7). In other words, in 1940 FY funds were allocated according to the priorities, but the total amount loaned rose more slowly.

These problems reflected the limitations of the financial control system. The Temporary Fund Control Law was confined to funds for capital equipment. At the meeting of banks and trust companies in November 1939, the chief of the Ministry of Finance's Banking Bureau said:

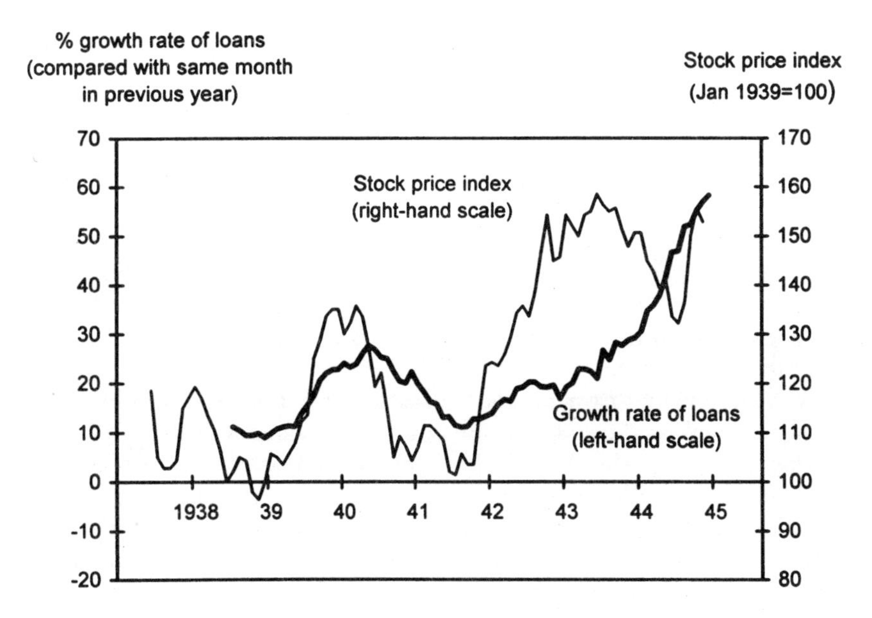

Figure 7 Average stock prices and growth of bank loans

> This year it seems that substantial amounts of working fund loans have been applied to the fund for equipment. For example, there were cases in which companies raised funds for equipment through overdrafts. Therefore, it is said that an institutional reform is necessary to carry out financial control completely.
>
> (Nihon Ginkō, Chōsa kyoku 1970b)

According to a Ministry of Finance survey of 60 major banks, in June 1937 loans consisted of ¥2.4 billion for equipment funds and ¥5 billion for working funds. In December 1939 the equipment fund loans had increased only slightly to ¥3 billion, while working fund loans had risen sharply to ¥9 billion (Nihon Ginkō 1986: 297–8). Most of the increase occurred in working funds, which were outside the control of the Temporary Fund Control Law. These loans were used for speculation as well as investment in equipment (Nihon Ginkō 1962: 341–3).

On the other hand, the basic reason for the fall in stock prices was the government's move towards the New Economic Order (*Keizai shintaisei*). The government resisted raising official prices based on the ideology that eliminating the profit motive was necessary. It also intended to reduce the power of shareholders in corporate governance (Okazaki 1987, 1993a, 1993b). Faced with lower profits and fewer rights, investors naturally hesitated to invest in stocks. Similarly, banks hesitated to loan money for projects yielding low returns, and because reduced shareholders' power would weaken monitoring by fund suppliers in general (Teranishi 1993: 76–7).

Three reasons specific to the financial market also made banks negative towards loans. First, both the size of individual loans and the amounts loaned to each company rose substantially from 1938 to 1940 (Teranishi 1993: 76–7). Some of the banks' reconstruction plans provided to General Headquarters after the war include lists of firms they had lent more than ¥10 million to during the war. Tables 8 and 9 are based on these lists; they show the ten major borrowers each year from the Mitsubishi and Sumitomo banks. (Mitsui Bank and Dai-ichi Bank were merged to form Teikoku Ginkō [Imperial Bank] in 1943; its reconstruction plan contains only data from 1943).

Twelve companies each received loans of more than ¥10 million from Mitsubishi Bank at the end of 1940. Seven were affiliates of the Mitsubishi *zaibatsu*, including the Mitsubishi holding company itself (Ōkura-shō, Zaisei-shi shitsu 1981: Appendix, pp. 21–30). Four of the other five companies were in the textile industry, the largest industry in prewar Japan. The top ten borrowers accounted for 26.3 per cent of the bank's total loans, with the Mitsubishi companies accounting for two-thirds of the money made available to the top ten (Table 8).

Sumitomo Bank also loaned amounts higher than ¥10 million to twelve companies at the end of 1940. Seven were Sumitomo affiliates, while another three were textile firms. The top ten borrowers took 16.2 per cent of the bank's total loans, with Sumitomo affiliates accounting for nearly 80 per cent of this (Table 9). (Asajima (1987: 211) also found that Sumitomo Bank's loans to Sumitomo *zaibatsu* affiliates rose continuously from 1936 to 1942.)

For both banks, the percentage of total loans going to the top ten borrowers rose from 1940 to 1941, as did the importance of the *zaibatsu* affiliates within the top ten. The loans of both banks thus became more concentrated on a few large borrowers.

The second problem causing banks to reduce their lending was a growing mismatch in the term structure of deposits and loans, which was recognized as a serious problem in financial circles at the time. A report by the Research Section of Tōkyō Bank Club (*Tōkyō ginkō shūkai-jo*) regarded the 1941 slowdown in bank loans as a symptom of the difficulty in supplying funds to expand productive capacity. This reflected a 'contradiction between the characteristics of the Japanese financial system and the nature of the industrial fund demand' (Nihon Ginkō, Chōsa-kyoku 1971: 466). While the banks usually used funds for short-term commercial finance because most of their deposits were short-term and liquid, the emergent industries demanded long-term, stable funds to raise production capacity. The Research Section concluded that this mismatch was a fundamental reason for the difficulties facing industrial finance, and that to resolve it, financial institutions would have to shift from commercial to industrial finance.

Table 8 Sums borrowed by the ten largest borrowers from Mitsubishi Bank (1,000 yen)

	Dec 1940	*Dec 1941*	*Dec 1942*	*Mar 1944*	*Mar 1945*
Mitsubishi & Co.*	42,216			40,582	
Mitsubishi Mining*	40,460	94,350	61,577	75,386	191,277
Kanegafushi Cotton Spinning	32,250	30,105			
Asahi Glass*	28,821	36,945	53,295	78,735	
Mitsubishi Headquarters*	28,000	35,400	48,200	100,200	154,500
Nihon Light Metal	17,750	26,250	25,458		
Toyo Cotton Spinning	17,250		20,172	51,296	74,400
Mitsubishi Steel*	13,830	16,431	33,984	50,477	83,300
Nihon Chemical*	13,168	15,177	28,925		
Fuji Gas Cotton Spinning	12,171				
Mitsubishi Heavy Industry*		32,463			1,235,000
Mitsubishi Electric*		22,804	33,984	130,214	278,053
Cotton Cloth Export Association		15,592			
Important Materials Control Co.			30,236		
Cotton Spinning Association			23,756		
International Trade Co.				121,314	124,795
Industrial Equipment Co.				83,359	200,232
Kanegafuchi Manufacturing				48,309	
Mitsubishi Chemical*					244,173
Tokyo Marine Insurance*					93,033
Top 10 total	245,916	325,517	359,587	779,872	2,678,763
Total loans	935,791	1,147,888	1,308,753	3,229,127	6,843,530
Top 10 as % of all loans	26.3	28.4	27.5	24.2	39.1
Mitsubishi affiliates as % of top 10	67.7	77.9	72.3	61.0	85.1

* Direct affiliates of Mitsubishi *zaibatsu*

Source: GHQ/SCAP records, RG331, box no. 7715

Table 9 Sums borrowed by the ten largest borrowers from Sumitomo Bank, 1940–5 (1,000 yen)

	Dec 1940	*Dec 1941*	*Dec 1942*	*Mar 1944*	*Mar 1945*
Sumitomo Headquarters*	82,100	94,955	104,675	151,631	191,638
Sumitomo Metal*	39,000	82,100	63,600	178,500	535,500
Mitsui & Co	30,120	31,587	39,661	67,530	
Sumitomo Mining*	25,200	34,045	31,230	46,154	123,545
Sumitomo Telecommunication*	17,989	26,368	33,313	63,668	77,328
Sumitomo Electric*	15,985	20,020	28,696	63,065	156,846
Sumitomo Aluminium*	13,920				
Manchuria Sumitomo Metal**	12,750				
Kanegafuchi Manufacturing	12,500	26,106	27,100	36,448	
Kyushu Aircraft	11,621	18,231			
Sanko*		25,167	32,174	47,104	
Sumitomo Chemical*		17,030	17,200		115,480
Nihon Electricity Generation & Supply			16,297		
International Trade Co.				63,626	
Industrial Equipment Co.				52,290	122,777
Mitsui Headquarters					94,042
Osaka Sumitomo Marine Insurance*					92,045
Daiken Industry*					77,126
Top 10 total	261,185	375,609	393,946	770,016	1,586,327
Total loans	1,612,317	1,912,417	2,147,325	3,326,115	5,761,715
Top 10 as % of all loans	16.2	19.6	18.3	23.2	27.5
Sumitomo affiliates as % of top 10	79.2	79.8	78.9	71.4	86.3

* Direct affiliate of Sumitomo *zaibatsu*.

** Quasi-directly affiliated with Sumitomo *zaibatsu*.

Source: GHQ/SCAP records, RG331, box no. 7715

Itō (1983) showed that for banks as a whole, the ratio of time deposits to total deposits fell over time, as did that of discount bills to total loans. (The amount of discount bills is a proxy for the amount of short-term loans). Figure 8 shows that while this was true in both city and regional banks, the ratio of discount bills decreased more rapidly in the city banks. Therefore the mismatch of the term structure was more serious in the city banks, which had closer relationships to munitions companies.

The third factor reducing the availability of loans was a maldistribution of funds between the city and regional banks. Around 1939, government funds and investments by companies expanding their production capacity flowed to rural areas, rapidly increasing the deposits of the regional banks. However, most of these banks' customers were consumer goods firms, loans to which were decreasing because of the financial and material controls (Nihon Ginkō, Chōsa-kyoku 1941a: 250–3). Furthermore, it was difficult for the regional banks to lend to munitions companies because these required very large sums and the regional banks had little experience in industrial finance. Therefore, the regional banks had little alternative but to buy low-yielding bonds. Some made loans without appropriate credit analysis (Yamazaki 1986: 30). The city banks, on the other hand, suffered from a shortage of funds (Nihon Ginkō, Chōsa-kyoku 1941b: 468–70).

In order to cope with these problems, in 1938 and 1939 banks began to organize loan consortia (Yamazaki 1986: 29; Teranishi 1995: 66–70). This approach had several advantages. It diversified the risks to each bank (which had risen because of the two problems described above). A consortium could delegate the monitoring of loans to its lead bank. This was especially valuable for the regional banks, which could use the city bank's ability to monitor munitions companies. A consortium approach was necessary for the

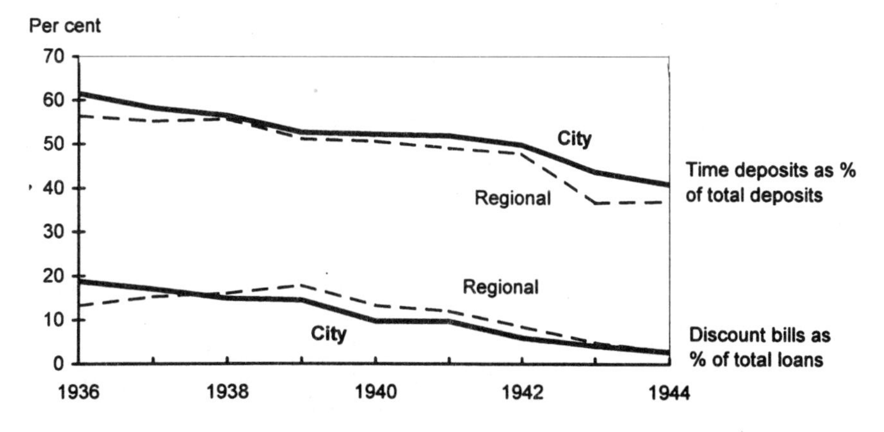

Figure 8 The maturity structure of loan deposits of city and regional banks (*Source:* Goto 1971).

regional banks to lend to the central industrial companies (Nihon Ginkō, Chōsa-kyoku 1941a).

According to a survey by the Tōkyō Bank Club, in June 1941 there were 130 bank consortia serving 113 companies (Teranishi 1995). The publicly owned Industrial Bank of Japan (IBJ) managed consortia serving 71 of these companies.

However, this measure could not overcome the problems described above. Nor could the Temporary Fund Control Law, since it did not actively promote the flow of funds to specific sectors. As a consequence, in 1940 and 1941 it was difficult to manage the flow of funds using this financial control system.

THE 'NEW FINANCIAL ORDER'

The government took a series of measures to cope with the flaws in the early controls. In September 1939, the Chief of the Ministry of Finance's Banking Bureau (*Ginkō kyoku*) warned banks against making loans for speculative purposes. From December 1939 on, financial institutions were obliged to submit monthly reports on their working fund loans; from September 1940 they also had to provide quarterly reports on outstanding loans (Nihon Ginkō 1962: 341–3; Yamazaki 1991a: 211–2).

The BOJ passed these reports on to the Banking Bureau with its comments. In examining the reports, the BOJ aimed to eliminate practices such as equipment loans disguised as working fund loans, and loans for speculation or hoarding raw materials. The BOJ directed financial institutions not to provide loans if a borrower had unused funds, or if a regional bank or trust company had a disproportionately large loan compared with the government bonds it held (Nihon Ginkō 1962: 374–8). Instructions to this effect were issued by the chief of the Banking Bureau on 17 January 1940 and by the BOJ's Fund Adjustment Bureau on 19 January.

In October 1940, the Banks and Other Financial Institutions Fund Application Act (*Ginkō to shikin unyo-rei*) was passed. This enabled the government to regulate the fund application plans of financial institutions, and placed all loans above a certain level under government control. The government also became able to order financial institutions to make loans to certain companies.

The last provision meant extending loan orders (*yushi meirei*) to all financial institutions. Under the Company Profit Dividends and Fund Loan Act (*Kaisha rieki haitō oyobi shikin yūzū-rei*) of April 1939, the IBJ could already be required to provide loans. In fact, however, the government rarely ordered other financial institutions to do so. The essential point of the Banks and Other Financial Institutions Fund Application Act was therefore to place working as well as equipment funds under government control. The approval procedure was usually carried out by the BOJ, which sent only especially important items for consideration by the Temporary Fund Examination Committee (Yamazaki 1991a: 212–13).

The BOJ stated that 'it seems that the Act was not so effective, compared to the amount of effort needed to implement the controls' (Nihon Ginkō 1986: 299). Contrary to this assertion, Table 7 shows that after 1940, the level of loans to each industry was more closely related to the government's priority index for that industry (Tables 5 and 6). This implies that the Banks and Other Financial Institutions Fund Application Act did indeed contribute to concentrating funds into the priority industries.

However, other measures were needed to prevent the total amount of funds from stagnating. It is not too much to say that the total fund supply stagnated in 1940 and 1941 because the Act effectively restricted the amount of money flowing to 'unnecessary' industries. In order to solve this problem at its root, in 1940 the government (including the Ministry of Army, Planning Board, Ministry of Finance and BOJ) drew up plans for a 'New Financial Order' (*Kinyū shintaisei*).

Itō (1983) and Yamazaki (1991b) explain these plans and how they were compiled. According to the original draft of the Planning Board (*Kikaku-in*), financial institution policies that stressed the soundness of investments were to be changed in order to alter companies' behaviour (Yamazaki 1991b: 451). This view was related to the Planning Board's policy on corporate governance (Okazaki 1993a, 1993b) and the New Economic System.

However, opposition by the BOJ and private financial institutions led to this radical approach being modified (Yamazaki 1991b: 454–61). Instead, in July 1941 the Cabinet adopted an Outline of the Basic Fiscal and Financial Policies (*Zaisei kinyū kihon hōsaku yōkō*). This promoted the idea of loan consortia, stressing the need for intimate relationships between industries and financial institutions (Nihon Ginkō, Chōsa-kyoku 1973: 151–4). This modification was natural because giving up soundness as a principle and intervening heavily in financial institutions might have undermined depositors' confidence and brought about the collapse of the whole financial system.

In a speech to bankers in August 1941, the Minister of Finance, Ogura Masatsune, said:

> So far, loan procedures by ordinary banks can be described as oriented to commercial finance. But as circumstances change, the greatest demand for funds will be industrial rather than commercial in nature. In such a situation, banks should change their procedures and make loans using methods most appropriate to industrial finance.
>
> (Tōkyō Ginkō Shukai-jo 1941: 188)

As a concrete measure, he asked that loan consortia be extended: 'It is necessary to examine a method of cooperation in monitoring the borrowers, and the government is ready to support the monitoring' (Tōkyō Ginkō Shukaijo 1941: 188).

In response, the IBJ and ten city banks organized the Emergency Cooperative Loan Syndicate (*Jikyoku kyōdō yūshi-dan*) in October 1941. A firm seeking a loan could apply to the syndicate's office at the IBJ. The IBJ and the 'main correspondent bank' (*shutaru torihiki ginkō*) examined the applicant firm and passed loan and reference materials to a liaison committee (*renraku iinkai*) composed of branch heads of the member banks. The syndicate's 'representative committee' (*daihyōsha iinkai*) determined the loan suitability and conditions, apportioned the loan among member banks, and determined the management of collateral. The IBJ and the main correspondent bank were delegated to monitor the loan. These roles of the main correspondent bank were thus prototypes of the main banking system that has played a central role in Japan's postwar financial system (Teranishi 1993).

The IBJ played a substantial role in this system. It took part in all of the loans and was manager (*kanji*) of the liaison and representative committees. At the end of June 1941, 61.9 per cent of the loan consortia were managed by the IBJ (Teranishi 1993). This suggests that the other banks had little capability to monitor borrowers and organize consortia. With its experience in long-term finance since before the war, the IBJ made up for the other banks' lack of monitoring and organizing capabilities.

The National Financial Control Association (NFCA), established in 1942, took over the IBJ's role in supporting loan consortia. The president of the NFCA was the president of the BOJ, and the BOJ *de facto* managed the association. The controlling rules for the association (*Zenkoku kinyū tōsei-kai tōsei kitei*), issued by the Ministry of Finance in July 1942, include a provision for the president of the NFCA to mediate loan consortia of member financial institutions. In accordance with this, the president was consulted beforehand about all loan consortia and mediated such issues as the consortium's membership, amounts, interest rates and loan shares (Ōkura-shō 1957: 295–6).

Yamazaki (1991b) used original BOJ materials to show that distribution (i.e., rationing) organizations accounted for the largest amount of loans mediated by the NFCA; they were followed by the textile industry. The IBJ managed by far the most consortia, followed by the five major city banks (Teikoku, Mitsubishi, Sumitomo, Yasuda, and Sanwa). Most financial institutions took part in the consortia as members rather than managers.

Further analysis of the data used by Yamazaki (1991b) shows that loans mediated by the NFCA rose rapidly, reaching about 20 per cent of total bank loans by the end of 1943 (Table 10). The overwhelming majority of consortia were managed by a single bank (Table 11). A total of 537 firms borrowed from consortia, many receiving loans from several (Table 12). But

Table 10 Estimated cooperative loans mediated by the NFCA

		Loans mediated through NFCA (¥1000)	*% of total loans of all banks*
1942	Sept	332,130	1.4
	Dec	2,068,296	8.2
1943	Mar	3,527,671	13.2
	Jun	4,838,286	17.3
	Sept	5,834,204	19.4
	Dec	6,773,440	20.7

Source: BOJ materials

Note: The NFCA loan data (column 1) were converted from flows to stocks by assuming they were not repaid until their due dates. This was necessary to make them comparable to the total loans data (column 2).

Table 11 Number of manager banks in each consortium

Manager banks	*No. of consortia*	*%*
0	125	7.9
1	1,358	86.2
2	88	5.6
3	4	0.3
Total	1,575	100.0

Source: BOJ materials

Note: The NFCA loan data (column 1) were converted from flows to stocks by assuming they were not repaid until their due dates. This was necessary to make them comparable to the total loans data (column 2).

Table 12 The relationship between firms and banks in loan consortia

		No. of firms	*%*
A	One consortium, one manager bank	192	35.8
B	Several consortia with same manager bank	237	44.1
C	Several consortia, each with different manager banks	39	7.3
D	Consortia with more than one manager bank	34	6.3
E	No manager bank in consortium	35	6.5
	Total	537	100.0

Source: BOJ materials

Note: The NFCA loan data (column 1) were converted from flows to stocks by assuming they were not repaid until their due dates. This was necessary to make them comparable to the total loans data (column 2).

some 429 firms, about 80 per cent of the 537 firms, dealt with a single manager bank (rows A and B in Table 12). Only 35 firms (6.5 per cent) received loans from consortia with no manager bank. The remainder dealt with more than one manager bank, either because they received loans from a consortium with more than one manager, or because they borrowed from two or more consortia with different managers.

Table 12 also shows the stability of the bank–firm relationship. Among the 310 firms for which more than one loan consortia was organized (rows B, C and D), 76.4 per cent stayed with the same manager bank (row B). If we exclude firms whose consortium had multiple managers (row D), the proportion rises to 85.9 per cent. During this (relatively short) period of 17 months, therefore, firms tended to depend on the same manager bank.

Table 13 shows the relationships among the banks in the various consortia. As Yamazaki (1991b) points out, the IBJ managed the largest number of consortia: nearly one-quarter of the total. Of the 429 firms dealing with a single consortium manager, the IBJ managed 107 (Table 14). But the IBJ's share was much smaller than the 61.9 per cent of loans it managed at the end of June 1941 (see above). We can conclude that the NFCA resulted in other banks taking on a larger role in managing consortia.

Table 13 also shows the number of consortia each bank was a member of. Teikoku Bank, for example, participated in 303 (79 per cent) of the 382 consortia led by the IBJ. Table 15 summarizes these data as participation ratios. The top row shows that the major five city banks took part in around 70 per cent of the loan consortia organized by the IBJ. The rest of the table shows that they also were frequently members of consortia led by another major city bank: except for consortia organized by Mitsubishi Bank, the participation ratios range from 40 to 60 per cent.

This mutual participation meant that the tasks of monitoring were distributed among the banks. The NFCA's mediation helped form a network of reciprocal, delegated monitoring to take advantage of the monitoring and organizing capabilities of the major city banks. In the postwar main bank system, such reciprocity has ensured effective monitoring (Sheard 1994: 16–18). The NFCA's mediating role was similar to the BOJ's loan mediation activities (*yūshi assen*) in the latter half of the 1940s (Okazaki 1996).

Tables 13–19 show the major borrowers of the cooperative loans mediated by the NFCA. Rationing organizations were the main borrowers, as Yamazaki (1991a) pointed out. But it is also notable that major firms affiliated to *zaibatsu* also borrowed large amounts: Mitsui Mining, Tōkyō Shibaura and Mitsui and Company (from consortia led by Teikoku Bank); Nippon Aluminium, Nihon Chemical and Mitsubishi Mining (Mitsubishi Bank); Sumitomo Telecommunication and Sumitomo Chemical (Sumitomo Bank). At the same time, however, some *zaibatsu*-affiliated companies did not take consortia loans. These companies, along with almost all major

Table 13 Bank–bank relationships in loan consortia

Manager	*No. of consortia managed*	*Av. no. of members per consortium*	*No. of consortia of which bank was a member*							*Total*
			IBJ	*Teiko-ku*	*Mitsu-bishi*	*Sumi-tomo*	*Yasu-da*	*Sanwa*	*All others*	
IBJ	382	9.2	382	303	269	256	262	275	1,785	3,532
Teikoku	270	4.6	49	270	149	124	131	110	417	1,250
Mitsubishi	111	3.1	8	59	111	21	25	21	98	343
Sumitomo	125	5.6	14	76	64	125	86	75	254	694
Yasuda	61	5.5	6	37	27	27	61	25	150	333
Sanwa	67	4.7	1	33	25	38	37	67	112	313
Others	530	4.9	17	128	76	97	227	84	1,950	2,579
Total	1,546	5.8	477	906	721	688	829	657	4,766	9,044

Consortia with more than one manager are repeated in more than one row

Source: BOJ materials

Note: The NFCA loan data (column 1) were converted from flows to stocks by assuming they were not repaid until their due dates. This was necessary to make them comparable to the total loans data (column 2).

Table 14 Number of firms served by consortia managed by major banks*

Manager bank	*No. of firms*	*%*
IBJ	107	24.9
Teikoku	57	13.3
Mitsubishi	14	3.3
Sumitomo	32	7.5
Yasuda	24	5.6
Sanwa	21	4.9
Others	174	40.6
Total	429	100.00

* Firms served by consortia led by only one bank (rows A + B in Table 12)

Source: BOJ materials

Note: The NFCA loan data (column 1) were converted from flows to stocks by assuming they were not repaid until their due dates. This was necessary to make them comparable to the total loans data (column 2).

Table 15 Cross-participation of banks in loan consortia

	Member banks (%)					
Manager bank	*IBJ*	*Teikoku*	*Mitsubishi*	*Sumitomo*	*Yasuda*	*Sanwa*
IBJ	100	79	70	67	69	72
Teikoku	18	100	55	46	49	41
Mitsubishi	7	53	100	19	23	19
Sumitomo	11	61	51	100	69	60
Yasuda	10	61	44	44	100	41
Sanwa	2	49	37	57	55	100

Source: Table 13

Table 16 Major borrowers from loan consortia managed by the IBJ

Borrower	*Total of cooperative loans (million yen)*
Industrial Equipment Co.	540
Important Materials Control Co.	393
Metal Collection Control	320
Iron and Steel Raw Materials Control	297
Ship Management Association	220
Tachikawa Aircraft	193
Nihon Coal	158
Tokyo Shibaura Electric	154
Wartime Finance Bank	154
Nihon Light Metal	140

Source: BOJ materials

Note: The NFCA loan data (column 1) were converted from flows to stocks by assuming they were not repaid until their due dates. This was necessary to make them comparable to the total loans data (column 2).

Table 17 Major borrowers from loan consortia managed by Teikoku Bank

Borrower	*Total of cooperative loans (million yen)*
International Trade Co.	398
Central Food Co.	350
Important Materials Control Co.	329
Tachikawa Aircraft	180
Mitsui Mining	163
Tokyo Shibaura Electric	154
Mitsui & Co.	150
Nihon Starch	134
Kanegafuchi Cotton Spinning	106
Teikoku Fat Control	93

Source: BOJ materials

Note: The NFCA loan data (column 1) were converted from flows to stocks by assuming they were not repaid until their due dates. This was necessary to make them comparable to the total loans data (column 2).

Table 18 Major borrowers from loan consortia managed by Mitsubishi Bank

Borrower	*Total of cooperative loans (million yen)*
International Trade Co.	398
Nihon Automobile Distribution	105
Important Materials Control Co.	99
Nihon Aluminium	59
Nihon Chemical	58
Mitsubishi Mining	30
Iron and Steel Sales Control	22
Cement Syndicate	20
Osaka Lumber	18
Nihon Starch	14

Source: BOJ materials

Note: The NFCA loan data (column 1) were converted from flows to stocks by assuming they were not repaid until their due dates. This was necessary to make them comparable to the total loans data (column 2).

firms, were provided consortia loans through the BOJ's mediation after the war (Okazaki 1996).

The expansion of loan consortia checked the tendency of concentration of loans observed up to 1941 FY. From the end of 1941 to the end of 1942, the proportion of loans given to the top ten borrowers and the *zaibatsu* affiliates declined for both the Mitsubishi and Sumitomo banks (Tables 8 and 9).

Each of the major banks strengthened its internal organization for monitoring as the delegated monitoring system emerged. Before the war, only

Table 19 Major borrowers from loan consortia managed by Sumitomo Bank

Borrower	*Total of cooperative loans (million yen)*
Cotton Products Central Distribution Control	105
Fujikoshi Steel	70
Kansai Electricity Distribution	52
Sumitomo Telecommunication	38
Wakayama Prefecture Lumber	30
Sumitomo Chemical	22
Nihon Cotton Weavings Wholesale Association	19
Nihon Synthetic Chemicals	14
Nishi Nihon Railways	13
Nihon Telecommunication & Telephone	12

Source: BOJ materials

Note: The NFCA loan data (column 1) were converted from flows to stocks by assuming they were not repaid until their due dates. This was necessary to make them comparable to the total loans data (column 2).

Table 20 The establishment of monitoring systems in major city banks

Date		*Bank*	*Action*
1941	Jul	Mitsubishi	Domestic Section divided into Dept. of Credit Analysis and Dept. of Business
1942	Aug	Yasuda	Section of Credit Analysis separated from First Section of Business
1943	Jan	Sumitomo	Dept. of Credit Analysis established
	Apr	Mitsui and Daiichi	On merger to form Teikoku Bank, First and Second Depts of Credit Analysis set up
1944	Jan	Yasuda	Section of Munitions Loans separated from the Section of Loans
	Feb	Mitsubishi	Sixth Section of Dept. of Credit Analysis in charge of munitions loans established
		Yasuda	Section of Inspection incorporated into Section of Credit Analysis
	Mar	Teikoku	Dept. of Munitions Loans established
	Apr	Mitsubishi	Sixth Section of Dept. of Credit Analysis renamed Section of Munitions Loans
	Aug	Sumitomo	Dept. of Munitions Loans established
1945	Apr	Mitsubishi	Dept. of Munitions Loans separated from Dept. of Credit Analysis
	May	Teikoku	First and Second Depts of Credit Analysis merged to form Dept. of Ordinary Loans

Source: Corporate history of each bank

one (Sanwa) of the six major city banks had credit analysis units independent from their loan departments. In July 1941, Mitsubishi Bank made its Department of Credit Analysis (*Shinsa-bu*) independent from its Domestic Section (*Naikoku-ka*). Yasuda, Sumitomo and Teikoku (Mitsui and Dai-ichi) followed suit (Table 20) (Okazaki 1994: 28). By April 1943, all of the major city banks had independent credit analysis units.

The BOJ also underwent reform. Under the existing Bank of Japan Act (*Nippon ginkō jōrei*), it was prohibited from providing industrial finance, including using stocks as collateral – though in fact it did so under another name. In 1942 the Bank of Japan Law (*Nippon ginkō-hō*) formally allowed it to issue finance with stocks and debentures as collateral. The BOJ's Bureau of Research (*Chōsa-kyoku*) described this reform as:

> Although the statement of the law was simple, its significance was extremely large in the sense that it modified the commercial banking principle, to which the BOJ had stuck, and that it made clear that the role of the central bank included adjustment of industrial finance.
>
> (Nihon Ginkō, Chōsa-kyoku 1970b: 266)

The BOJ also expanded its Department of Inspection (*Kōsa-bu*) to form the Bureau of Inspection (*Kōsa-kyoku*) so as to manage the NFCA (Nihon Ginkō, Chōsa-kyoku 1952: 70). The bureau's chief acted as the informal secretary general of the NFCA (Nihon Ginkō 1986: 332). The BOJ's ability to monitor commercial banks was thus reinforced.

We can summarize the process in the few years after 1940 as follows. The banks did not perform well in their role as a capital market substitute because they lacked the institutional basis for indirect finance. The slowdown in bank loans in 1940 and 1941 reflected this. The New Financial System helped the banks prepare the institutional base for this type of finance.

FINANCES FOR THE MUNITIONS INDUSTRY

The resulting system of indirect finance was influenced by the 'designated financial institution' system, introduced in January 1944 through the Munitions Corporation Law (*Gunju-gaisha-hō*). The Ministry of Finance designated one financial institution for each munitions corporation, directing it to provide loans quickly to the munitions firm. This resulted in most of the loan consortia being dissolved, and a situation where 'the designated financial institutions cannot help but supply the funds requested by the munitions corporations' (Nihon Ginkō, Chōsa-kyoku 1970a: 244). The level of monitoring by banks declined as a result (Itō 1983, Okazaki 1993a, 1993b, Teranishi 1993). Mitsubishi and Sumitomo banks both rapidly increased their loaning up to the end of 1944 FY and concentrated on large borrowers, indicating lower bank management discipline (Tables 8 and 9).

However, some qualifications are necessary to the above statement (Okazaki 1994: 34–5). Early on, the financial authorities regarded the decline in financial discipline and the soft budget constraints on munitions corporations as a serious problem. For example, at a meeting of BOJ bureau and branch chiefs (*Bu-kyoku-chō shiten-chō kaigi*) in April 1944, cases were reported that some munitions corporations had bought restaurants at extravagant prices using loans from their designated financial institutions. The Fukuoka branch chief stated that:

> It is irrational that the munitions corporations have *de facto* taken charge of their designated financial institutions. On the contrary, we should devise a mechanism through which bank clerks take part in the accounting and management of the corporations.
>
> (Nihon Ginkō 1986: 308–9)

In July 1944 the guidelines for designated financing were revised. The designated financial institutions were to receive from the munitions corporations plans for monthly fund receipts and quarterly payments in advance, and pass them to the Ministry of Finance through the BOJ (Nihon Ginkō, Chōsa-kyoku 1970b: 421–3).

The move to reconstruct financial monitoring was accelerated by the January 1945 Munitions Finance Special Treatment Law (*Gunju kinyū to tokubetsu sochi-hō*), which prepared the legal basis of the designated financial institution system. This law stressed the 'effective use of funds' as well as 'smooth and proper financing' (Article 1) (Nihon Ginkō, Chōsa-kyoku 1967: 739). It obliged designated financial institutions to ensure the munitions corporations used funds effectively (Article 4). The designated financial institutions were to appoint 'persons in charge of munitions finance' (*gunju kinyū tantō-sha*) to each munitions corporation to maintain continuous contact with it (Article 7). The government could require the BOJ, designated financial institutions or control associations to inspect the accounts of the munitions corporations (Article 22). Furthermore, the corporation's deposits were concentrated in its designated financial institution (Article 12 of the Detailed Regulation for Enforcement), enabling the financial institution to monitor all its payments and receipts (Nihon Ginkō, Chōsa-kyoku 1967: 752).

These measures made the designated financial institutions monitor the munitions corporations in the effective use of funds. The government ensured the banks had incentives to act as monitors. It deliberately avoided guaranteeing loans of the designated financial institutions on the grounds that if it did so, 'the bank clerks would feel their responsibility is so light that they would not take sufficient care in loaning'. In case banks thought they could not bear a risk, they could apply to the government (Nihon Ginkō, Chōsa-kyoku 1967: 759).

Along the same lines, the Ministry of Finance instructed banks to examine a corporation's liquidity carefully and guide it to avoid wasting funds. Accordingly, Teikoku Bank attempted to limit payments by examining each corporation's raw material availability before deciding on the size of a loan. It also divided loans according to the corporation's actual needs so as to prevent spending on other purposes and to guarantee the money was used effectively (Dai-ichi Ginkō, date unknown, pp. 391–4).

Mitsubishi Bank gave the following instructions to its branches for complying with the Munitions Finance Special Treatment Law:

> You should change your perception of the designated corporations as your customers and should deal with them as their financial consultant and supervisor. . . . You should make efforts to keep continuous contact with the corporations' staff and monitor the actual financial state of the corporations. . . . Monitoring the payments and receipts of corporations is an effective way of knowing their financial state . . . you should make them maintain their checking accounts with our bank and monitor daily receipts and payments of their checking accounts.
>
> (Mitsubishi Ginkō 1954: 351–2)

These were the same as the standard practices used by the main banks with their customers after the war. There were, of course, substantial limits to financial discipline because the government guaranteed the munitions corporation's management through its price policy. However, the resulting institutions and practices provided an opportunity for learning and influenced the evolution of intimate bank–firm relationships.

THE EFFECT OF REFORMS ON THE FINANCIAL SYSTEM

The mobilization of resources for the war made it necessary to shift huge amounts of money from the personal sector to the government and corporate sectors. Centered on direct finance, the prewar financial system could not cope, and indirect finance lacked an institutional basis. The early financial control system based on the Temporary Fund Control Law faced problems, and a fundamental reform to establish the New Financial System was carried out.

The core of the reform was to extend loan consortia through mediation by the IBJ, NFCA or BOJ. Especially after the NFCA was formed, loan consortia were extended substantially and a network of reciprocal, delegated monitoring among the banks was formed. This became an essential part of the postwar main bank system. The mediation strengthened the major city banks' capabilities in monitoring firms and organizing loan consortia, since they had previously had little experience in industrial finance.

Each major city bank set up an independent credit analysis organization, and the BOJ strengthened its inspection capabilities. The loan consortia, the network of delegated monitoring, banks' capability for monitoring firms, and the BOJ's ability to monitor banks, can be seen as institutional bases for indirect finance. The New Financial System of indirect finance replaced the prewar direct finance system. When the designated financial institution system reduced monitoring, a series of reforms in the last part of the war corrected this by institutionalizing the bank's role as a monitor. Based on these experiences, the BOJ again mediated loan consortia organized by the main banks in the early postwar period to support Japan's economic recovery (Okazaki 1996).

REFERENCES

Unpublished material

GHQ/SCAP (General Headquarter/Supreme Commander of the Allied Powers) records, Record Group RG 331, box no. 7715.

Books and articles

Aoki Masahiko (1988) *Information, Incentives, and Bargaining in the Japanese Economy*, New York: Cambridge University Press.

Aoki Masahiko and Hugh Patrick (eds) (1995) *The Japanese Main Bank System: Its Relevance for Developing and Transforming Economies*, New York: Oxford University Press.

Aoki Masahiko, Okuno-Fujiwara Masahiro and Kim Hyung-ki (eds) (1996) *The Role of Government in East Asian Development: Comparative Institutional Analysis*, New York: Oxford University Press.

Aoki Masahiko and Okuno-Fujiwara Masahiro (eds) (1996) *Keizai shisutemu no hikaku seido bunseki* (Comparative institutional analysis of economic systems), Tōkyō: University of Tōkyō Press.

Asajima Shōichi (1987) 'Sumitomo zaibatsu,' in Asajima Shōichi (ed.) *Zaibatsu kinyū kōzō no shiteki kenkyū* (A historical study of the financial structure of *zaibatsu*), Tōkyō: Ochanomizu Shobō.

Dai-ichi Ginkō (Dai-ichi Bank) (date unknown) *Dai-ichi ginkō 80 nen-shi kōhon* (Draft of the 80-year history of Dai-ichi Bank), vol. 3, Tōkyō: Dai-ichi Ginkō.

Emi Koichi, Itō Masakichi and Efuchi Eichi (1988) *Chochiku to tsūka* (Savings and currency), Tōkyō: Tōyō Keizai Shinpō-sha.

Gotō Shinichi (1971) *Nihon no kinyū tōkei* (Financial statistics of Japan), Tōkyō: Tōyō Keizai Shinpō-sha.

Hara Akira (1966) 'Shikin tōsei to sangyō kinyū' (Financial control and industrial finance), *Tochi seido shigaku* (The Journal of Political Economy and Economic History), vol. 34, pp. 52–74.

Itō Osamu (1983) 'Senji kinyū saihensei' (Reorganization of the financial system during the war), *Kinyū kenkyū*, vol. 203, pp. 59–86 and vol. 204, pp. 57–71.

Mitsubishi Ginkō (Mitsubishi Bank) (1954) *Mitsubishi ginkō shi* (History of Mitsubishi Bank), Tōkyō: Mitsubishi Ginkō (Mitsubishi Bank).

Mitsubishi Keizai kenkyū-sho (Mitsubishi Institute of Economic Research), *Honpō jigyō seiseki bunseki* (Analysis of business performance), various issues, Tōkyō: Mitsubishi Keizai kenkyū-sho.

Nihon Ginkō (Bank of Japan) (1962) *Nihon Ginkō enkaku shi* (History of the Bank of Japan), series 3, vol. 17, Tōkyō: Nihon Ginkō (Bank of Japan).

Nihon Ginkō (Bank of Japan) (1986) *Nihon Ginkō hyaku-nen shi* (100 years history of the Bank of Japan), Tōkyō: Nihon Ginkō (Bank of Japan).

Nihon Ginkō, Chōsa-kyoku (Bank of Japan, Bureau of Research) (1941a) '*Chihō futsū ginkō no seikaku*' (The characteristics of the regional ordinary banks), in Nihon Ginkō, Chōsa-kyoku (Bank of Japan, Bureau of Research) (1971) *Nihon kinyū shi shiryō* (Materials on the financial history of Japan), Shōwa series, vol. 30, Tōkyō: Ōkura-shō (Ministry of Finance).

Nihon Ginkō, Chōsa-kyoku (Bank of Japan, Bureau of Research) (1941b) '*Saikin no ginkō gōdō mondai*', in Nihon Ginkō, Chōsa-kyoku (Bank of Japan, Bureau of Research) (1972) *Nihon kinyū shi shiryō* (Materials on the financial history of Japan), Shōwa series, vol. 32, Tōkyō: Ōkura-shō (Ministry of Finance).

Nihon Ginkō, Chōsa-kyoku (Bank of Japan, Bureau of Research) (1952) *Nihon Ginkō no enkaku to genjo gaisetsu* (Overview of the past and present of the Bank of Japan), Tōkyō: Nihon Ginkō (Bank of Japan).

Nihon Ginkō, Chōsa-kyoku (Bank of Japan, Bureau of Research) (1967) *Nihon kinyū shi shiryō* (Materials on the financial history of Japan), Shōwa series, vol. 19, Tōkyō: Ōkura-shō (Ministry of Finance).

Nihon Ginkō, Chōsa-kyoku (Bank of Japan, Bureau of Research) (1970a) *Nihon kinyū shi shiryō* (Materials on the financial history of Japan), Shōwa series, vol. 27, Tōkyō: Ōkura-shō (Ministry of Finance).

Nihon Ginkō, Chōsa-kyoku (Bank of Japan, Bureau of Research) (1970b) *Nihon kinyū shi shiryō* (Materials on the financial history of Japan), Shōwa series, vol. 29, Tōkyō: Ōkura-shō (Ministry of Finance).

Nihon Ginkō, Chōsa-kyoku (Bank of Japan, Bureau of Research) (1971) *Nihon kinyū shi shiryō* (Materials on the financial history of Japan), Shōwa series, vol. 31, Tōkyō: Ōkura-shō (Ministry of Finance).

Nihon Ginkō, Chōsa-kyoku (Bank of Japan, Bureau of Research) (1973) *Nihon kinyū shi shiryō* (Materials on the financial history of Japan), Shōwa series, vol. 34, Tōkyō: Ōkura-shō (Ministry of Finance).

Okazaki Tetsuji (1987) 'Senji keikaku keizai to kakaku tōsei' (Wartime planned economy and price control), in Kindai Nihon Kenkyū-kai *Nenpō kindai Nihon kenkyū*, vol. 9, Tōkyō: Yamakawa Shuppan-sha.

Okazaki Tetsuji (1993a) 'Kigyō shisutemu' (Corporate governance), in Okazaki Tetsuji and Okuno-Fujiwara Masahiro (eds) *Gendai Nihon keizai shisutemu no genryū* (Historical origins of the contemporary Japanese economic system), Tōkyō: Nihon Keizai Shinbun-sha.

Okazaki Tetsuji (1993b) 'The Japanese firm under the wartime planned economy', *Journal of the Japanese and International Economies*, vol. 7: 175–203.

Okazaki Tetsuji (1994) 'Nihon: Seido kaikaku to keizai shisutemu no tenkan' (Japan: Institutional reforms and transformation of the economic system), *Shakai keizai shigaku* (The Socio-Economic History), vol. 60(1), pp. 10–40.

Okazaki Tetsuji (1996) 'Sengo fukkōki no kinyū shisutemu to Nihon Ginkō yūshi assen' (The Japanese financial system in the period of economic recovery and loan mediation by the Bank of Japan), *Keizai-gaku ronshū*, vol. 60(4).

Okazaki Tetsuji and Okuno-Fujiwara Masahiro (1993) 'Gendai Nihon no keizai shisutemu to sono rekishi-teki genryū' (The contemporary Japanese economic system and its historical origins), in Okazaki Tetsuji and Okuno-Fujiwara Masahiro (eds) *Gendai Nihon keizai shisutemu no genryu* (Historical origins of the contemporary Japanese economic system), Tōkyō: Nihon Keizai Shinbun-sha.

Ōkura-shō, Zaisei-shi shitsu (Ministry of Finance, Financial History Section) (1957) *Shōwa zaisei-shi* (Financial history of the Shōwa era), vol. 11, Tōkyō: Tōyō Keizai Shinpō-sha.

Ōkura-shō, Zaisei-shi shitsu (Ministry of Finance, Financial History Section) (1981) *Shōwa zaisei-shi – Shūsen kara kōwa made* (History of public finance in the Shōwa era: From the end of the war to the peace treaty), vol. 2, Tōkyō: Tōyō Keizai Shinpō-sha.

Sheard, P. (1994) 'Reciprocal delegated monitoring in the Japanese main bank system', *Journal of the Japanese and International Economies*, vol. 8, pp. 1–21.

Tamura Tsuyoshi (1941) '*Seisan-ryoku kakujū to kaisei kokka sōdōin-hō*' (Production capacity expansion and revised state mobilization law), in Nihon Ginkō, Chōsa-kyoku (Bank of Japan, Bureau of Research) (1972) *Nihon kinyū shi shiryō* (Materials on the financial history of Japan), Shōwa series, vol. 32, Tōkyō: Ōkura-shō (Ministry of Finance).

Teranishi Jūrō (1993) 'Mein banku shisutemu' (Main bank system), in Okazaki Tetsuji and Okuno-Fujiwara Masahiro (eds) *Gendai Nihon keizai shisutemu no genryū* (Historical origins of the contemporary Japanese economic system), Tōkyō: Nihon Keizai Shinbun-sha.

Teranishi Jūrō (1995) 'Emergence of loan syndication in wartime Japan', in Aoki Masahiko and Hugh Patrick (eds) *The Japanese Main Bank System and its Relevance for Developing and Transforming Economies*, New York: Oxford University Press.

Tōkyō ginkō shukai-jo (Tōkyō Bank Club) (1941) *Ginkō tsūshin-roku* (Bank information), 20 September 1941: 188.

Tōyō Keizai Shinpō-sha (1991) *Kanketsu Shōwa kokusei sōran* (Final version of the historical statistics of the Shōwa era), Tōkyō: Tōyō Keizai Shinpō-sha.

Yamazaki Shirō (1986) 'Senji kinyū tōsei to kinyū shijo' (Wartime financial control and financial market), *Tochi seido shigaku* (The Journal of Political Economy and Economic History), vol. 112, pp. 18–36.

Yamazaki Shirō (1991a) 'Nihon Ginkō to kinyū tōsei' (The Bank of Japan and financial control) in Imuta Toshimitsu (ed.) *Senji taisei-ka no kinyū kōzō* (The financial structure under the war economy), Tōkyō: Nihon Keizai Hyōron-sha.

Yamazaki Shirō (1991b) 'Kyōchō kinyū taisei no tenkai' (Development of cooperative finance) in Imuta Toshimitsu (ed.) *Senji taisei-ka no kinyū kōzō* (The financial structure under the war economy), Tōkyō: Nihon Keizai Hyōron-sha.

9

THE TRANSFORMATION OF THE JAPANESE ECONOMY

Itō Osamu

INTRODUCTION

The term 'Japanese-type economic system' is often used to indicate the distinctive characteristics of Japan's economy. But Japan's economic system after the Second World War differed considerably from that before it. In Japanese economic history, the wartime period (1937–45) was as important as the period of reforms after the war (1945–54).

This chapter surveys the main changes during the wartime period, their causes and results. It will focus mainly on domestic factors and microeconomic systems in Japan's economy. However, these factors are closely related to the international environment and macroeconomic conditions. The most important developments around the Second World War were:

- The war was a turning point in the world political system. Instead of the anarchic power games played by each major country in the prewar period, a system of cooperation was formed to avoid universal ruin from competitive power relationships. At the same time, the colonial system began to collapse. Japan lost all of its colonies, and its military was abolished.
- Japan's economy became a closed system, and despite gradual liberalization, remained essentially closed until the 1970s. This enabled a rapid catch-up process under conditions of unusual tension.
- Beginning in the second half of the 1930s, Japan's economy entered a phase of high investment (Figure 9). The percentage of GNP devoted to fixed-capital formation jumped, and continued at high levels throughout the postwar period. During the war, the main deficit sectors were the government and firms; after the war, firms became the main deficit sector. The basic conditions of the Japanese-type economic system were high investment, expansionist firm behaviour, high growth, and a tight financial market (capital shortage) (Itō 1995).

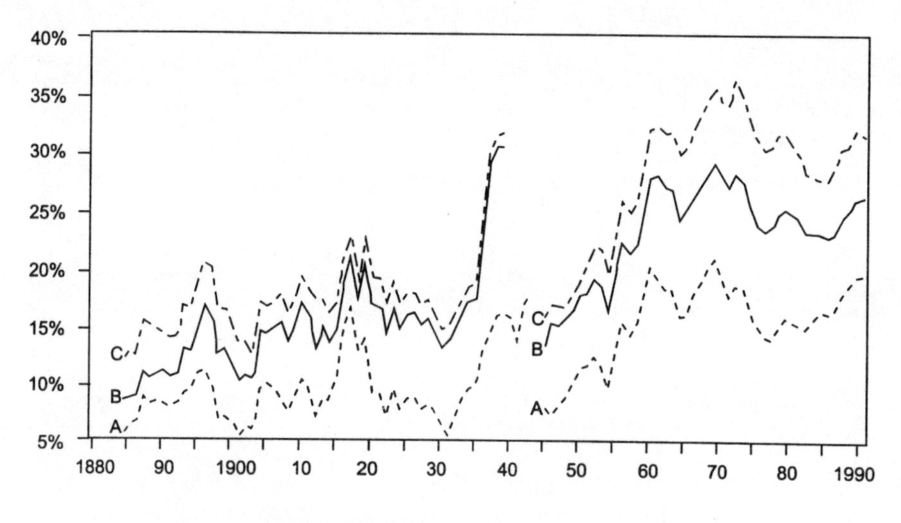

Figure 9 Fixed capital formation as a percentage of GNP (current prices). (*Source:* before 1940 – Ōkawa *et al.* 1974; after 1941 – Keizai Kikaku-chō [Economic Planning Agency], various years).

The main factors that changed during the war include: corporate ownership, governance and financing; the financial system; relations among firms; the market structure; relations between the government and firms; and the social structure. This chapter examines each in turn.

CORPORATE OWNERSHIP, GOVERNANCE AND FINANCING

The structure of Japanese firms changed markedly between the prewar and postwar periods. Before the war, most firms were owned privately by individual investors or their families. Some were owned by joint investors and were governed exclusively by their owners. The *zaibatsu*[1] were family conglomerates typical of privately run businesses. Most big firms were administered by professional managers, but the final right to make decisions belonged to the owners. Most *zaibatsu* tried to provide all their own financing internally, and avoided borrowing or selling stocks – though some newly rising *zaibatsu* (the so-called *shinkō zaibatsu* such as Nissan) developed by selling stocks.

From the end of the 1930s, nevertheless, firms began to depend on outside capital because their ability to finance themselves did not match their increasing need for funds (Table 21). At the same time, wartime economic controls restricted the owners' decision-making rights. In this way the exclusive, private nature of corporate ownership, finance and governance was relaxed during the course of the war (Okazaki and Okuno-Fujiwara 1993). After the war, the US occupation forces' policy of dissolving the *zaibatsu* finally destroyed the prewar structure.

THE FINANCIAL SYSTEM

The shift to tight financial regulation

The features of the financial system are closely related to corporate ownership, governance and financing. At the beginning of the twentieth century, the financial system was essentially unregulated. After a series of difficulties and panics in the banking system (Itō 1995), a new regulatory scheme was introduced in the 1920s. New government policies encouraged mergers of banks and other financial institutions, and restricted competition among them. Regulations were introduced, and private ownership and governance declined, in finance earlier than in other sectors. During the war, mergers of financial institutions proceeded at a rapid pace. The highly concentrated structure of financial institutions and the protected financial system of postwar Japan are direct results of wartime changes. For example, there were over 2,000 banks in 1920, but only 69 in 1945.

Table 21 Capital composition of large corporations (%), 1935–50

	1935 (2nd half)	*1940 (2nd half)*	*1945 (1st half)*	*1950 (1st half)*
Liabilities	38.5	47.5	72.2	77.3
Notes, bills and accounts payable	10.6	16.4	23.4	23.1
Corporate bonds	16.5	10.6	8.7	3.8
Borrowings	4.1	7.1	12.0	27.1
Others	7.3	13.0	28.1	23.3
Own capital	61.5	52.8	27.8	22.7
Paid-in capital	46.7	37.1	20.9	11.0
Reserve	14.8	15.7	6.9	11.7
Total capital	100.0	100.0	100.0	100.0
Current liabilities	17.9	29.4	51.5	61.5
Own capital and fixed liabilities	82.1	70.6	48.5	38.5

Source: Mitsubishi Keizai Kenkyū-sho (Mitsubishi Institute of Economic Research) (various years)

Another important wartime policy was the control of loan allocations. The purpose was to concentrate loans in 'important' industries – i.e., munitions. This policy was realized by making financial institutions ignore risks, organizing competition to expand loans to munitions industries, and forming close client-customer relationships between manufacturers and banks (see the chapter by Okazaki in this volume). Patterns of expansionist behaviour among financial institutions developed as a result. Controls related to loan allocations continued for nearly ten years after the war, then declined during the postwar high-growth era. The main objectives of government controls then shifted towards protecting the stability of the financial system.

The 'main-bank system'

As mentioned above, in the wartime era the main deficit sectors were the government and firms. The securities market was allotted the function of absorbing national debt, and corporate finances depended on bank loans. As a whole, the share of bank deposits and loans in financial transactions increased during the war (first three rows of Table 22).

At the same time, in order to make loans efficiently, the government introduced the 'joint loan' (syndicated loan) and 'appointed bank' systems. In the latter system, the government appointed (usually) one bank to each munitions corporation; this bank responded to loan requests as far as it could and as efficiently as possible. Some experts argue that this practice was the beginning of the 'main-bank system', as the 'delegated monitoring system' became known (Okazaki and Okuno-Fujiwara 1993, Noguchi 1995). During the war, however, the appointed banks neither functioned

Table 22 Market shares (%) of volume of funds, by type of financial institution, 1935–90

	1935	*1940*	*1945*	*1950*	*1970*	*1990*
City banks	23.0	23.5	30.0	39.8	25.5	20.0
Local banks	19.8	21.5	17.9	19.8	15.1	13.0
Long-term credit banks	11.8	12.2	10.8	9.2	5.7	4.9
Trust accounts	7.5	4.7	2.7	1.2	7.6	8.3
Mutual loan and credit banks	1.3	1.3	1.0	3.2	6.6	5.2
Credit associations	0.9	1.2	1.4	3.2	8.1	7.1
Agricultural co-op.	5.9	7.5	10.7	8.8	6.5	4.9
Insurance companies	12.9	10.5	6.6	3.6	7.0	12.3
Postal savings	20.9	20.1	26.3	18.1	14.3	21.5

Note: columns do not add up to 100 per cent because of overlapping accounts and the presence of other financial institutions not included in the table.

Source: Nihon Ginkō, Tōkei-kyoku (Bank of Japan, Statistics Bureau) (various years)

as monitors, nor produced information on borrower firms; they also disbursed loans without sufficient scrutiny (Itō 1984).

The insurance function of the main-bank system was especially important in the postwar period. Main banks provided insurance to their customer corporations by acting as lenders of last resort; the government protected the main banks almost completely. This means that business risks were borne by the main banks, and were effectively managed almost exclusively by the main banks and government. Firms and investors became accustomed to disregarding risks. This is an important reason underlying Japanese firms' aggressive expansion (Itō 1995).

Banks also played a leading role in financial markets in the postwar period. One reason was that the real value of financial assets decreased sharply, and these assets were distributed far more equally because of hyperinflation and social reforms after the war (see Figure 10). This led people to keep the major part of their assets in safe investments such as bank accounts (Teranishi 1982).

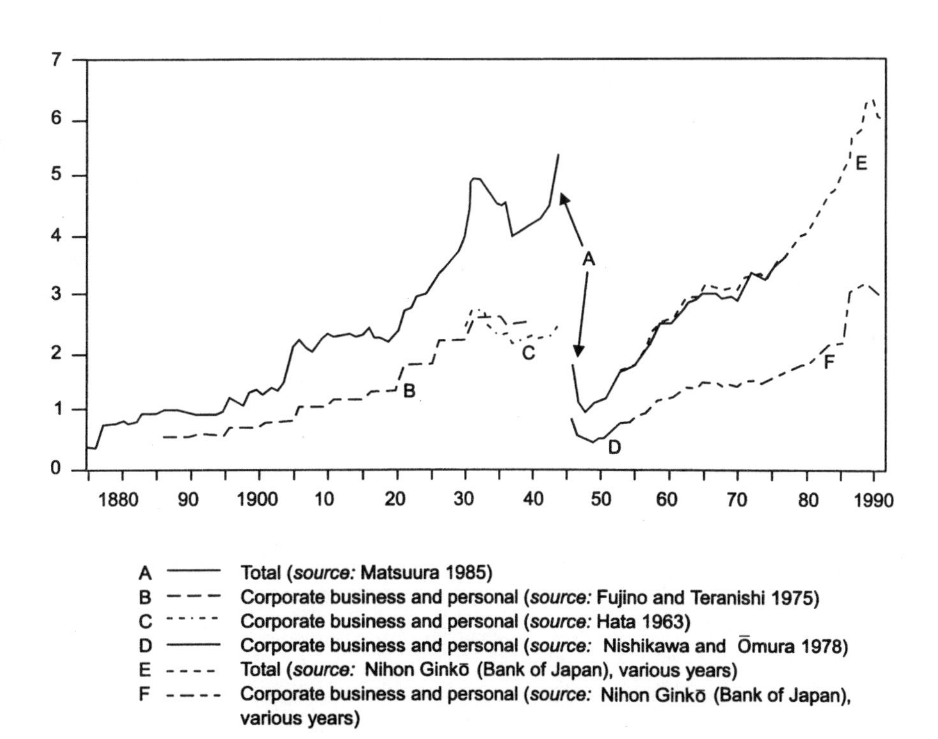

Figure 10 Financial assets as a proportion of GNP

RELATIONS AMONG FIRMS

Relaxation of *zaibatsu* control

Vertical ties among firms weakened as the exclusive nature of the *zaibatsu* was relaxed during the war, and were destroyed by the dissolution of the *zaibatsu* afterwards. As a result, firms and their managers became more independent (Itō 1988).

Business associations

During the war, the government organized business associations such as control associations (*tōsei-kai*) in each industry to organize and control economic activities (Okazaki and Okuno-Fujiwara 1993; see also Okazaki in this volume). They were dissolved by the US occupation forces after the war because they were regarded as private monopolies. But the development of horizontal connections in each industry had an important influence on postwar firms.

Business groups and 'keiretsu'

The exclusive, private structures of ownership in big business were destroyed by the dissolution of *zaibatsu* after Japan's surrender. But beginning about 1950, the newly independent firms again began to organize into corporate groups. The new business groups (*kigyō shūdan*) were different from the vertically organized *zaibatsu*: instead they were organized horizontally through multilateral cross-stockholdings among large firms (Table 23).

The 'big six' business groups are examples of horizontal combination (Okumura 1976). Among these six, Mitsubishi, Sumitomo, Mitsui and Fuyo (Yasuda) groups are successors of four large *zaibatsu*. The other two, Sanwa and Dai-ichi-Kangin (short for Dai-ichi Kangyō Ginkō, the First Industrial

Table 23 Percentage of stocks by holder, 1945–90

	1945	*1949*	*1955*	*1970*	*1990*
Government	8.3	2.8	0.4	0.2	0.6
Financial institutions	11.2	9.9	23.6	31.0	45.2
Security companies	2.8	12.6	7.9	1.2	1.7
Non-financial corporations	24.7	5.6	14.6	23.1	25.2
Individuals, etc.	53.1	69.1	53.4	39.9	23.1

Note: columns do not add up to 100 per cent because other types of stock holders are omitted from the table

Source: Zenkoku Shōken Torihiki-sho Kyōgi-kai (National Conference of Stock Exchanges) (various years)

Bank) are organizations of some former medium-sized *zaibatsu*. Each of these six groups is composed of leading companies in most major industries, and they are centered around major city banks (the 'main banks' of each group) and major trading companies (*sōgō shōsha*). Most firms (except for the four big *zaibatsu*, which already had such ties) began building long-term customer relationships with their main banks during the war. So we can say that the origins of such combinations as business groups are to be found in the wartime era.

There are also independent groups such as Toyota, Panasonic (Matsushita) and Nippon Steel. These have pyramid-like structures of several layers of firms under giant corporations at the apex. Such a structure is common in the big six, too, and it is a factor in 'vertical' combination. Its origin is the subcontracting system, which had expanded during the war.

MARKET STRUCTURE

Competition between oligopolistic firms

Before the war, most industries had a 'Gulliver': a dominant company much larger than the others. But during the war, there were important changes in market structures, including a general decline in concentration ratios (Table 24) and a tendency towards equalization of scale among the several major firms in each industry (Table 25). The result in the postwar era was intense competition among similarly sized firms – a competitive oligopoly. This framework was one of the sources of the rapid economic growth after the war (Itō 1988). One cause of the changes in market structure was that demand for munitions industries such as metals and machinery grew rapidly from the mid-1930s on, leading to waves of new business entries and rapid growth of medium-sized firms. Another important factor following the war was the break-up of large businesses by the anti-trust policy under the US occupation.

Table 24 Number of industries becoming more and less concentrated, 1937–49

	No. of industries			
Concentration toward	*Increased concentration*	*Decreased concentration*	*Other*	*Total*
Largest firm in industry	12	32	3	47
Top 3 firms	12	27	8	47
Top 5 firms	11	23	13	47
Top 10 firms	11	17	19	47

Sources: Kōsei Torihiki Iin-kai (Fair Trade Commission), 1951, 1957.

Table 25 Market shares (%) of the top five firms in ten industries, 1937 and 1949

Industry	*Year*	*No. of firms in industry*	*Size of firm* *Largest*	*2nd*	*3rd*	*4th*	*5th*
Iron	1937	20	83.9	10.1	3.8	–	–
	1949	53	40.7	25.2	22.6	1.3	0.8
Steel	1937	30	41.0	8.0	7.2	5.4	4.8
	1949	72	26.7	14.6	10.9	6.8	6.2
Electric motors	1937	7	36.1	24.4	12.2	10.3	8.2
	1949	39	23.5	19.0	10.0	8.5	6.8
Steel ships	1937	24	35.4	16.9	15.3	12.0	7.2
	1949	49	14.6	13.7	10.6	9.8	7.7
Paper	1937	17	71.7	6.0	5.4	3.8	3.1
	1949	85	27.0	25.0	10.4	6.9	4.8
Cement	1937	28	23.1	8.6	8.4	7.6	6.6
	1949	15	22.2	16.2	13.9	9.7	8.7
Beer	1937	4	63.6	28.9	7.0	0.6	–
	1949	3	38.5	35.8	25.7	–	–
Butter	1937	53	80.5	9.2	1.2	1.0	0.8
	1949	110	67.8	13.6	3.9	2.8	0.9
Cotton spinning	1937	82	15.4	10.0	8.5	5.0	3.9
	1949	34	14.4	12.7	11.4	10.0	8.7
Cotton weaving	1937	45,000	7.3	5.1	4.1	3.6	2.7
	1949	5,000	7.3	6.9	5.9	5.8	5.1

Source: Kōsei Torihiki Iin-kai (Fair Trade Commission), 1951

Expansion of medium-sized and small firms

As described above, medium-sized and small firms in the munitions and heavy industries multiplied and grew rapidly, forming thick lower layers of the industrial pyramid in these sectors. In consumer industries such as food, textiles and commerce, on the other hand, concentration levels increased as firms disappeared. But after the war, there were waves of new entries as demand grew, and a great mass of small firms re-emerged. This became one of the distinctive characteristics of Japan's economy (Tables 26 and 27).

The subcontracting system

During the war, the subcontracting system (*shita-uke*) spread in the rapidly developing heavy and chemical industries. Subcontracting was particularly important in assembly industries (such as machinery), which were to become

Table 26 Number of corporations, 1920–55

	Total	*Manufacturing**	*Commerce*
1920	42,488	14,058	18,578
1930	63,545	16,148	34,854
1935	94,592	23,992	54,740
1940	91,028	29,204	47,003
1944	102,316	49,527	41,211
1945	95,773	48,307	36,801
1950	235,515	116,663	85,628
1955	411,997	162,595	170,424

* Includes construction

Sources: Ōkura-shō, Kokuzei-chō (Ministry of Finance, National Tax Administration Agency) (various years): Tōyō Keizai Shinpō-sha (1980).

Table 27 Number of factories* in various industries, 1935–44

	Food	*Textiles*	*Metals*	*Machinery*	*Chemicals*	*All manufacturing*
1935	13,684	29,378	7,351	10,250	4,629	84,625
1939	22,793	38,272	11,717	22,972	8,766	137,079
1942	21,194	28,251	11,190	24,910	8,493	125,680
1946	9,927	11,860	9,260	19,688	6,807	84,393
1950	26,243	31,923	12,804	20,961	13,380	156,173
1955	33,911	39,016	16,925	23,937	13,366	187,101

* Factories employing 5 or more workers

Source: Tsūshō sangyō-shō (Ministry of International Trade and Industry) (1961)

the leading sector of the postwar economy. This was a major change from the prewar style of relations between big and small businesses, where small firms were ruled by wholesale merchants (*tonya*). These wholesalers were greatly weakened by the wartime controls on the distribution system.

RELATIONS BETWEEN THE GOVERNMENT AND FIRMS

Wartime economic controls

During the war, there was widespread advocacy of economic controls or planning, supported by an ideological belief denying the legitimacy of profit maximizing and owners' control. This ideology was, directly or indirectly, based on Marxism. The economic systems of the Soviet Union and Hitler's Germany were thought of as concrete models (Nakamura 1989, 1993; see also the chapters by Nakamura and Kerde in this volume).

Inevitably, such ideas brought about ideological and political conflicts. As a result, the principle of profit maximization was not – or could not be – denied. Economic controls were more-or-less effective, precisely because government demands to expand munitions production were compatible with the firms' own incentives. At the time, expansion seemed the best choice for maximizing gains. But on the other hand, this compatibility existed only under the wartime conditions when firms' freedom of decision making was restricted. This was an important precedent in that companies became accustomed to being guided by the government.

Postwar relations

Economic controls remained in place until the end of the 1940s and stayed essentially the same as in the wartime period. After 1949, when the policy for stabilization (anti-inflation) and deregulation led by Joseph M. Dodge was implemented, economic controls were rapidly abolished. So-called 'industrial policies' (*sangyō seisaku*) were still implemented in the 1950s, including controls over foreign trade and international capital transactions, and instruments aimed at developing specific industries; but after that, government intervention decreased year by year. The high-growth era was basically led by the private sector; to use a term such as 'government-led growth' is inaccurate (Tsuruta 1982).

Important regulations protecting the interests of existing corporations still remain. In addition, the government has often employed administrative guidances or discretionary regulations (*gyōsei shidō*) without any direct legal foundation. But these were not directly related to the wartime economic controls. These methods worked effectively only insofar as they accorded with the economically rational calculations and selections of each firm. That is, firms obeyed government guidance only because some relative gains could be expected. A firm ignoring such guidance risked lower long-term profits because of official penalties and retaliation from rivals (Shindō 1992, Itō 1995).

Therefore, relations between the government and firms after the war were not the result of a direct inheritance of wartime economic controls contradictory to economic rationality. Both wartime economic controls and postwar regulations were effective only when their systems were compatible with economic rationality. Firms made choices in wartime under strong constraints. Their wartime experiences only indirectly contributed to their decisions and behaviour after the war.

Public interventions after the war were oriented towards eliminating 'market failures' in a wide range of economic sectors, for example, by improving their 'dynamic efficiency' or protecting financial systems to avoid panics.

SOCIAL STRUCTURE

Social classes and income distribution

Prewar Japanese society could be characterized as 'unhindered private capitalism'. Inequalities between social classes were wide (Table 28). During the war, the private character of capitalism with such features as exclusive ownership declined, and inequalities seemed to decrease. Postwar changes such as hyper-inflation, the dissolution of the *zaibatsu*, land reform and labour reform thoroughly transformed Japanese society (Teranishi 1982, Mizoguchi 1986).

Public finance

The features of public finance were closely related to the social structure. First, government expenditures expanded during the war, led by huge increases in military procurements (Figure 11). But government expenditures decreased again after the war, and Japan has since had a relatively small government. The 'displacement effect' (the tendency for governments to expand during wartime but not to shrink afterwards) (Peacock and Wiseman 1961) cannot be observed in Japan.

Second, the tax base shifted to personal and corporate incomes (Figure 12). In the nineteenth century, most tax revenues were collected as land taxes; in the period 1900–40, indirect taxes and customs duties were predominant; after the 1940 tax reforms, personal income taxes and corporation taxes accounted for an increasing share (Jinno 1993). At the same time, the

Table 28 Gini coefficients* of income distribution, 1890–1986

	A	*B*	*C*	*D*
1890	0.311			
1900	0.417			
1910	0.357	0.420		
1920	0.417	0.463		
1930	0.431	0.451		
1940	0.467	0.641		
1956			0.313	
1962			0.382	0.361
1973				0.350
1986				0.356

* Gini coefficients can range from 0 (perfect equality) to 1 (perfect inequality)

A: Ono and Watanabe (1976)
B: Ōtsuki and Takamatsu (1978)
C: Wada (1975)
D: Terasaki (1990)

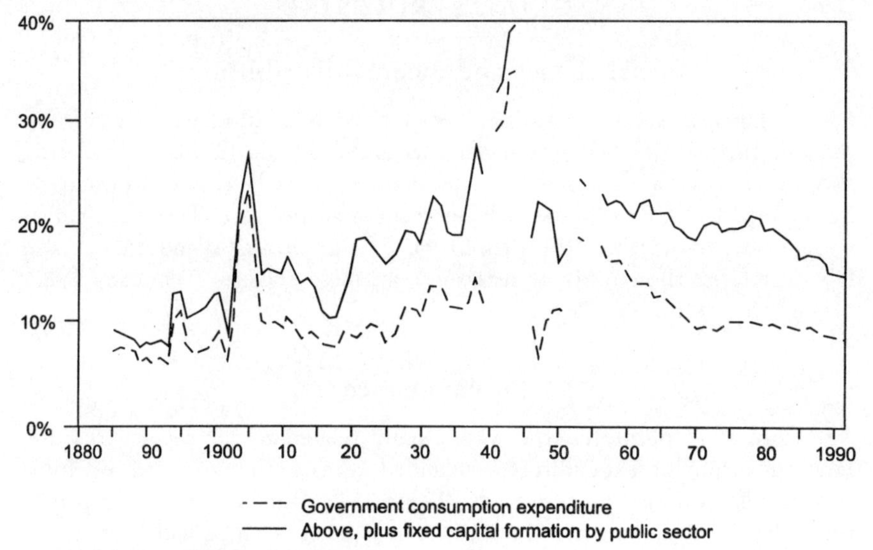

Figure 11 Government expenditure as a percentage of GNP (real prices). (*Sources:* before 1940 – Ōkawa *et al.*, 1974; after 1941 – Keizai Kikaku-chō [Economic Planning Agency], various years).

burden of direct (income) taxation shifted to the wider population. These trends were strengthened by the Shoup Tax Reform under the US occupation.

Third, as Table 29 shows, government expenditures shifted away from the military towards industrial infrastructure (in the high-growth period) and later to social security and welfare.

CONCLUSIONS

When we survey the long-term development of Japan's economy, the period from the Second World War to the end of the high-growth era in the 1970s can be regarded as one phase. Common features included high levels of investment under the closed system, patterns of expansionist economic behaviour, and a rapid catch-up process under unusual economic tensions. The wartime period was the first part of this phase.

Prototypes or fundamental structures of some features of the postwar economic system were formed during the war. The exclusive, private character of

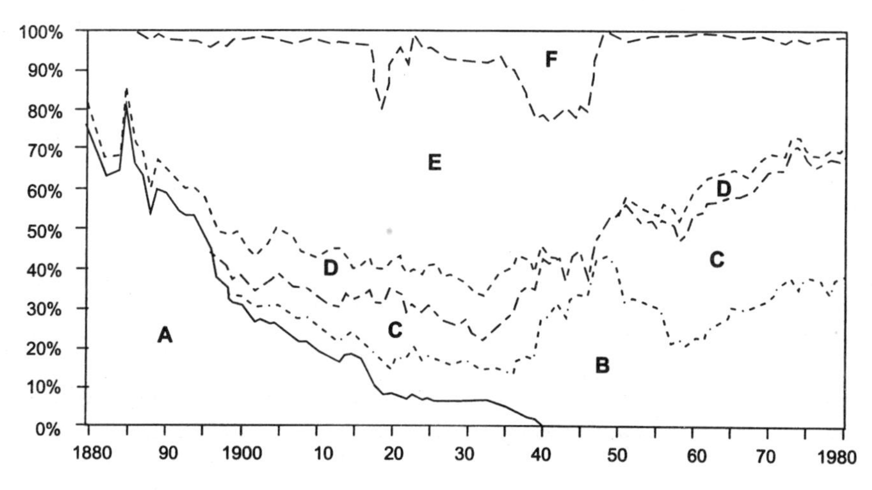

A: Land tax
B: Personal income tax
C: Corporation texes (corporation tax, first category (corporation) income tax, business profit tax, business tax)
D: Customs duties
E: Other indirect income taxes (except D)
F: Others

Figure 12 Structure of national tax by principal items (%). (*Sources:* Ōkura-shō [Ministry of Finance], 1969; Ōkura-shō, Kokuzei-chō [Ministry of Finance, National Tax Administration Agency], various years).

Table 29 Structure of government expenditure (general account of central government) (%)

	1930	*1935*	*1940*	*1960*	*1980*
Defence	28.6	46.3	50.3	7.8	5.2
Transfers to local govt.	0.1	0.0	5.2	19.1	18.1
Development of resources	5.9	5.8	3.1	16.9	13.8
Industry & economy	15.7	2.4	9.0	9.4	9.2
Education & culture	9.0	6.8	3.5	12.1	10.7
Welfare	1.1	1.4	1.6	13.3	21.3
Government debt	17.7	17.6	15.5	1.5	12.7
Others	21.9	19.7	11.8	19.9	9.0
Total	100	100	100	100	100

Source: Ōkura-shō (Ministry of Finance) (1969)

corporate structures weakened. Distinctive characteristics of Japan's industrial organization began to emerge: competition between oligopolistic firms of similar size, the large numbers of small businesses, the spread of the subcontracting system, and firms accustomed to being organized within industries. The strongly protected financial system emerged, the core of which was long-term customer relationships between banks and firms. The government regulated firms within business associations, creating a precedent for the postwar use of administrative guidance and other unofficial controls. The socio-political structure changed from 'private capitalism' to a more equalized and 'corporate-centred' mass society.

On the other hand, many factors changed after the war. The determining factor for changes in the corporate structure was political: the postwar dissolution of the *zaibatsu*. The government shrank quickly after the war, particularly because the military was abolished. Controls over resources and fund allocation, which had been the core of the wartime economic system, declined with the beginning of the postwar high-growth era. Shocks resulting from inflation and social reforms after the war strongly influenced the features of postwar economy and society. Although the framework of the main-bank system as a form was established in wartime, it no longer successfully served the function of producing information and monitoring corporations.

To conclude: it is not correct to say that the succession from wartime to postwar periods was direct and straightforward. More precisely, one can say that the prototypes, frameworks and fundamental structures formed in the wartime period began to function in an optimal manner during more propitious conditions of the high-growth era.

NOTE

1 The term *zaibatsu* (lit. financial clique) refers to big company conglomerates organized on a pyramidal basis, with a holding company acting as a central focus. The *zaibatsu* dominated the Japanese economy before 1945. Japanese economists often referred to them using the German word *Konzern*, thereby neglecting fundamental differences between the German *Konzern* and the Japanese *zaibatsu*.

REFERENCES

Fujino Shōzaburō and Teranishi Jūrō (1975) 'Shikin junkan no chōki dōtai' (Long-run dynamics of the flow of funds), *Keizai kenkyū* (Economic Review, Hitotsubashi University), 29, 4: 334–58.

Hata Ikuhiko (1963) *Kinyū shisan fusai zandaka-hyō 1930–1945* (Money, assets and liabilities balance sheet 1930–1945), Tōkyō: Keizai Kikaku-chō, Keizai Kenkyū-sho.

Itō Osamu (1984) 'Senji kinyū saihensei – sono sōten to tenkai (2)' (Reorganization of the financial system in wartime Japan: Issues and processes (2)), *Kinyū keizai* (Journal of Financial Economics) 204: 57–71.

Itō Osamu (1988) 'Nihon no sangyō soshiki to kigyō – Senzen sengo no hikaku bunseki' (Industrial organization and the firm in Japan: A comparative analysis of pre- and post-Second World War periods), *Shōkei Ronsō* (Review of Economics and Commerce, Kanagawa University) 24, 1: 1–41.

Itō Osamu (1995) *Nihon-gata kinyū no rekishi-teki kōzō* (The historical structure of Japan's financial system), Tōkyō: Tōkyō Daigaku Shuppan-kai (University of Tōkyō Press).

Jinno Naohiko (1993) 'Nihon-gata zei zaisei shisutemu' (The Japanese-type tax and fiscal system), in Okazaki Tetsuji and Okuno-Fujiwara Masahiro (eds) *Gendai Nihon keizai shisutemu no genryū* (Historical origins of the contemporary Japanese economic system), Tōkyō: Nihon Keizai Shinbun-sha.

Keizai Kikaku-chō (Economic Planning Agency) (various years) *Kokumin keizai keisan nenpō* (Annual report on national accounts), Tōkyō: Keizai Kikaku-chō (Economic Planning Agency).

Kōsei Torihiki Iin-kai, (Fair Trade Commission) (1951) *Nihon ni okeru keizai-ryoku shūchū no jittai* (Concentration of economic power in Japan), Tōkyō: Jitsugyō-no-Nippon-sha.

Kōsei Torihiki Iin-kai (Fair Trade Commission) (1957) *Nihon sangyō shūchū no jittai* (Industrial concentration in Japan), Tōkyō: Tōyō Keizai Shinpō-sha.

Matsumoto Kazuo (1986) *Kigyō shūeki to kigyō kinyū* (Profits and finances of Japanese corporations), Tōkyō: Tōyō Keizai Shinpō-sha.

Matsuura Hiroshi (1985) 'Meiji-ikō money flow no tokushoku' (Characteristics of money flow since the Meiji Era), *Statistical Data Bank* (Tsukuba University) 3, 1: 1–32.

Mitsubishi Keizai Kenkyū-sho (Mitsubishi Institute of Economic Research) (various years) *Honpō jigyō seiseki bunseki* (Analysis of business results of Japanese enterprises), Tōkyō: Mitsubishi Keizai Kenkyū-sho.

Mizoguchi Toshiyuki (1986) 'Nihon no shotoku bunpai no chōki hendō' (The long-run changes of income distribution in Japan), *Keizai kenkyū* (Economic review, Hitotsubashi University) 32, 2: 152–8.

Nakamura Takafusa (ed.) (1989) *Keikaku-ka to minshū-ka* (Planning and democratisation), Tōkyō: Iwanami Shoten.

Nakamura Takafusa (1993) *Nihon keizai: Sono seichō to kōzō* (The Japanese economy: Its growth and structure), 3rd edn, Tōkyō: Tōkyō Daigaku Shuppan-kai (University of Tōkyō Press).

Nihon Ginkō (Bank of Japan) (various years) *Shikin junkan kanjō* (Flow of funds account), Tōkyō: Nihon Ginkō.

Nihon Ginkō, Tōkei-kyoku, (Bank of Japan, Statistics Bureau) (various years) *Keizai tōkei nenpō* (Economic statistics annual), Tōkyō: Nihon Ginkō, Tōkei-kyoku.

Nishikawa Shunsaku and Ōmura Keiichi (1978) 'Kinyū shisan fusai zandaka-hyō' (Money, assets, and liabilities balance sheet), in Ōkura-shō, Zaisei-shi shitsu (Ministry of Finance, Tax History Section) (1978) *Shōwa zaisei-shi – Shūsen kara kōwa made: Dai 19 kan – Tōkei* (History of public finance in the Shōwa era – From the end of the war to the peace treaty, vol. 19 – Statistics), Tōkyō: Tōyō Keizai Shinpō-sha.

Noguchi Yukio (1995) *1940nen taisei* (The 1940 system), Tōkyō: Tōyō Keizai Shinpō-sha.

Ōkawa Kazushi, Takamatsu Nobukiyo and Yamamoto Yūzō (eds) (1974) *Chōki keizai tōkei* 1 (Long-term economic statistics 1), Tōkyō: Tōyō Keizai Shinpō-sha.

Okazaki Tetsuji and Okuno-Fujiwara Masahiro (1993) 'Gendai Nihon no keizai shisutemu to sono rekishi-teki genryū' (The contemporary Japanese economic system and its historical origins), in Okazaki Tetsuji and Okuno-Fujiwara Masahiro (eds) *Gendai Nihon keizai shisutemu no genryū* (Historical origins of the contemporary Japanese economic system), Tōkyō: Nihon Keizai Shinbun-sha.

Okumura Hiroshi (1976) *Nihon no roku-dai kigyō shūdan* (The big-six business groups in Japan), Tōkyō: Daiyamondo-sha.

Ōkura-shō (Ministry of Finance) (1969) *Ōkura-shō 100nen-shi* (100-year history of the Ministry of Finance), Tōkyō: Ōkura-shō Insatsu-kyoku.

Ōkura-shō (Ministry of Finance) (various years) *Zaisei tokei* (Budgetary statistics), Tōkyō: Ōkura-shō (Ministry of Finance).

Ōkura-shō, Kokuzei-chō (Ministry of Finance, National Tax Administration Agency) (various years) *Kaisha-hyō* (Table of corporations), Tōkyō: Ōkura-shō, Kokuzei-chō.

Ōkura-shō, Kokuzei-chō (Ministry of Finance, National Tax Administration Agency) (various years) *Kokuzei-chō tōkei nenpō* (Annual statistical report of NTAA), Tōkyō: Ōkura-shō, Kokuzei-chō.

Ōkura-shō, Zaisei-shi shitsu (Finance Ministry Tax History Section) (1978) *Shōwa zaisei-shi – Shūsen kara kōwa made: Dai 19 kan – Tōkei* (History of public finance in the Shōwa period – From the end of the war to the peace treaty – vol. 19 – Statistics), Tōkyō: Tōyō Keizai Shinpō-sha.

Ono Akira and Watanabe Tsunehiko (1976) 'Changes in income inequality in Japanese economy', in Hugh Patrick (ed.) *Japanese Industrialization and its Social Consequences*, Berkeley: University of California Press, pp. 363–89.

Ōtsuki Toshiyuki and Takamatsu Nobukiyo (1978) 'An aspect of the size distribution of income in prewar Japan', in International Development Center of Japan *Papers and Proceedings of Conference on Japan's Historical Experience and the Contemporary Developing Countries: Issues for Comparative Analysis*, Tōkyō: IDEJ.

Peacock, A.T. and J. Wiseman (1961) *The Growth of Public Expenditure in the United Kingdom*, Princeton: Princeton University Press.

Shindō Muneyuki (1992) *Gyōsei shidō* (Administrative guidance), Tōkyō: Iwanami Shoten.

Teranishi Jūro (1982) *Nihon no keizai hatten to kinyū* (Japanese economic development and finance), Tōkyō: Iwanami Shoten.

Terasaki Yasuhiro (1990) 'Sekai no shotoku kakusa' (Income inequalities of the world), *Nihon keizai kenkyū* (Japan Economic Research Center economic journal) 20: 121–9.

Tōyō Keizai Shinpō-sha (1980) *Shōwa kokusei sōran* (General survey of the state of the nation in the Shōwa period), Tōkyō: Tōyō Keizai Shinpō-sha.

Tsuruta Toshimasa (1982) *Sengo Nihon no sangyō seisaku* (Industrial policies in postwar Japan), Tōkyō: Nihon Keizai Shinbun-sha.

Tsūshō Sangyo-shō (Ministry of International Trade and Industry) (1961) *Kōgyō tōkei 50nen-shi* (History of the census of manufactures: 1909–58), Tōkyō: Ryūkei Shosha.

Wada, Richard O. (1975) 'Impact of economic growth on the size distribution of income', in JERC and CAMS *Income Distribution, Employment and Economic Development in Southeast and East Asia*, Tōkyō: Japan Economic Research Center and Council for Asian Manpower Studies, pp. 516–61.

Zenkoku Shōken Torihiki-sho Kyōgi-kai (National Conference of Stock Exchanges) (various years) *Kabushiki bunpu jōkyō chōsa* (Number of stocks by holder), Tōkyō.

A SHORT BIBLIOGRAPHICAL NOTE

On studies concerning Japan's war economy

Erich Pauer

Investigation into the history of economic, industrial and technological development in Japan during the Second World War started shortly after the beginning of the Allied occupation of the country. The sections responsible in the GHQ/SCAP included among other sections the Military Intelligence Section, the Natural Resources Section and the Economic and Scientific Section. There was also a US Naval Technical Mission to Japan, which was in charge of compiling several technical reports. The findings of these investigations have been published in various multi-volume (mostly typescript) series by the US and/or British government in the postwar period (e.g., CIOS, BIOS Reports and others).

The United States Strategic Bombing Survey (USSBS), an investigation into the results of the strategic bombing efforts in Germany as well as in Japan (where the strategic air war had started on 15 June 1944), was based on on-the-scene investigation, assessment of damage, and interrogation of the people responsible, as well as an analysis of captured Japanese documents. The investigation began in early September 1945. In addition to military studies, economic studies covered most of the important manufacturing sectors, i.e., aircraft, oil and chemicals, military supplies, capital equipment and construction, urban areas, manpower, food and civilian supplies, ship and rail transportation and electric power. The investigation was even extended to the civilian sector, which included public morale, medical supply and civil defence (for the conduct of the survey see MacIsaac 1969). In the course of the survey a large amount of historical materials, statistics and various industrial documents were collected and analyzed. Consequently the 108 published reports provide interesting insights into Japan's economic and industrial activities during the war (for a guide to the documents see Daniels 1981). However, although the survey was done by academically trained people using scientific methods, the reports differ widely in terms of value.

BIBLIOGRAPHICAL NOTE

The first scientific research into Japan's war economy was done by Thomas A. Bisson (1945) and was published only a few weeks after Japan's surrender. Having monitored developments in the Japanese economy since 1941 as an analyst who also wrote several articles on the topic, he singles out the *zaibatsu's* negative role during the war. According to Bisson, the *zaibatsu* were the most powerful driving force during the war and the real centre of power in Japan. The key focus of his research is on the complex relationship between the *zaibatsu* and the military (see also Bisson 1954). However, fifty years have passed since this book was published, and today the role of the *zaibatsu* is assessed rather differently from the way in which Bisson saw it.

A more comprehensive view on Japan's war economy was delivered by Jerome B. Cohen (1949) in his study of the economic development of Japan from 1937 up to 1949, which is based on the findings of the GHQ/SCAP and USSBS research sections, the interrogations prepared by the US Navy and Japanese sources from the wartime period. This careful analysis of the planning, controlling, financing and the development of Japan's war industries shows clearly how Japan overestimated its economic capacity. Misleading assumptions and the lack of foresight led Japan to fight the war until it was defeated. From among the research on Japan's war economy that was done during the occupation period, Cohen's book survived and is still regarded as a highly useful source, especially by scientists who are not able to deal with Japanese sources directly.

The same can be said of the research done by Bruce F. Johnston (1953) on Japan's agriculture and wartime management of food. Thanks to his Japanese collaborators he was not solely dependent on the facts to be found in the reports of the USSBS, SCAP and other occupation agencies, but could also draw on Japanese sources. His research broadly covers the whole range from food production, food imports, food consumption before and during the war, food control during the phase of the economic mobilization, distribution problems, etc. The book also contains a chapter on the food shortage after the war.

The research done by mostly American scientists in the decade after Japan's surrender was to some degree hampered by their inability to use Japanese language material. Research into Japan's war economy by non-Japanese in the following years faced the same problems. Since most English language materials had already been used by the above-mentioned researchers, the following studies (few as they were) did not extend beyond the scope of the earlier studies.

Foreign researchers' activities as well as their Japanese colleagues' research on topics from the wartime period in Japan were mostly hampered by inadequate sources. Starting from the outbreak of the Sino–Japanese War the publication of statistical data gradually became more and more difficult. During the 1941–5 period hardly any figures were officially published which were adequate and useful for academic research. Shortly after the war a three-volume series on Japan's industrial development in the Shōwa period (Tōyō Keizai Shinpō-sha 1950) provided the first useful statistics for at least a certain part of the Japanese economic development from the 1920s to the early postwar years. Covering the various manufacturing industries, it starts with the mining industry, followed by the heavy industry, the former military (i.e., army and navy) industries, the chemical industry, textile, food and other industries. Most of the authors come from the respective industries, firms or industrial federations or from the former military. The publisher and compiler was able therefore to draw on sources and figures often collected for agencies like the various *tōsei-kai* (control associations) during the war by the respective companies or federations. Other official institutions like the various ministries also collected data not available to the public during the war which became accessible in the postwar years. Several ministries and other official agencies also started to compile and publish wartime plans and figures during the 1950s.

Although the publications on Japan's war economy convey the impression that this topic was not the main focus of economists or economic historians in the two decades after the end of the Second World War, there have been some researchers who devoted almost their entire lives to the study of the various aspects of Japan's war economy. Starting with an article on Japan's controlled economy, Andō Yoshio (then lecturer at the University of Tōkyō, later professor there) published regularly on Japan's war economy until his death in 1985. To him, the period of Japan's war economy was one facet of Japan's state monopoly capitalism. A collection of the research on Japan's war economy which he had conducted during the postwar period, his 'lifework' (already compiled in 1961), was published posthumously in 1987 (Andō 1987).

Nevertheless the lack of adequately compiled and edited sources stimulated researchers in the early postwar period to collect and prepare relevant materials on the economy of the first half of the twentieth century and especially the wartime economy. Take as an example the *Ōhara shakai mondai kenkyū-sho* (Ōhara Institute for Social Research), which had been publishing its *Nihon rōdō nenkan* (Japan Labour Yearbook) since 1920, and which was banned from publishing from 1940 to 1945. In the early sixties the institute's staff started to compile materials on the change of labour conditions during the war, on controlled labour, mobilization of the labour force and its distribution, wages and controlled wages, prices, food rationing and the living conditions of the labourers, the situation in rural areas (especially the control of farm labour), etc., and published these valuable sources in 1964 (see Ōhara 1964).

Starting in the 1960s a 45-volume series entitled *Gendai-shi shiryō* (Sources of contemporary history) was published by Misuzu Shobō. Besides valuable sources on Manchuria, Korea, Taiwan, the nationalist and the socialist movements in interwar Japan, the Second World War itself, mass media, the Sorge incident, etc., there are two volumes especially dedicated to the topic of mobilization, although other volumes also contain sources related to the war economy. The volume on economic mobilization (vol. 43) was compiled by Nakamura Takafusa and Hara Akira (Nakamura and Hara 1970). Both had already started their research and publications on economic and financial topics from the war period earlier in the 1960s. These two authors also heavily influenced academic thinking and the perception of the planned or controlled economy of the Second World War in the following years. Nakamura's book *Nihon no keizai tōsei* (The controlled economy of Japan) (Nakamura 1974), published as a pocket book for the general public, gave an overview of the development of Japan's controlled economy from the very beginning of the world depression at the end of the 1920s until the Dodge Line in 1949, when controls were abolished. Shortly afterwards Nakamura and Hara also contributed to the Iwanami series on Japanese history (Nakamura 1977 and Hara 1976), two volumes of which cover the political and economic developments of the 1930s and 1940s. These authors as well as their colleagues were able to refer to a great many valuable study series and sources and a number of monographs published before and after 1970.

Sources on the various aspects of military mobilization, planning and manufacturing can be found in some volumes of the multi-volume war history series as early as the 1960s. They were compiled by the War History Room of the Defence Research Institute. The four volumes on the mobilization of the armies and navy (Bōei-chō 1967, 1969, 1979, 1975) are especially valuable. Other volumes of the series also contain related materials. Concerning a quite different aspect of the wartime economy, the series on public finance during the Shōwa period (Ōkura-shō 1955–65), which was published from the mid-1950s to the mid-1960s and covers the years up to 1945, should be mentioned. The early postwar years are treated in the follow-up series published from the mid-1970s to the mid-1980s (Ōkura-shō 1976–84). The series on sources for Japanese financial history published by the Research Department of the Bank of Japan (Nihon Ginkō, Chōsa Kyoku 1961–74) is also valuable, especially volumes 27 and 29 which deal with wartime sources of finance. Since Japan planned to rely on a range of resources from Manchuria in the late 1930s, programmes and plans concerning the economic relations between Japan and the puppet state of Manchukuo are of interest for economic historians as well. An Association for Studies of Modern Japanese History at Tōkyō University published a three-volume series which indicates sources for Japanese–Manchurian financial and economic relations (Nihon kindai shiryō kenkyū-kai 1970). It also contains sources from the late 1930s, obtained privately from a former member of a Japanese-Manchurian study group after the war. For various aspects of mobilization in other fields like politics, health and welfare, science and technology, transportation, education and culture, as well as aspects concerning the colonies, the series *Kokka sōdōin-shi* (History of national mobilization) (Ishikawa 1975) can by no means be ignored.

The ideological background for economic measures implemented during the war is a topic rarely discussed in academic circles. Nevertheless, several chapters of a volume on modern Japanese economic ideas compiled by Chō Yukio and Sumiya Kazuhiko (1971) deal with the economic concepts underlying the Japanese form of Fascism as well as with the ideology of the Industrial Patriotic Movement (*Sangyō hōkoku-kai*) and the ideas of the New Zaibatsu about an industrialized rural area (*nōson kōgyō*) and scientific manufacturing (*kagaku-shugi kōgyō*).

The everyday aspects of the war economy that affected the daily life of the ordinary people are well depicted in some series whose titles at first glance do not reveal a connection to the subject in question. In the 1960s and the 1970s study groups of citizens in various locations throughout Japan began to collect materials on their own and their ancestors' lives and the hardships suffered especially during and after the air raids. Much of this material has already been published. These sources contain more than the personal memoirs of people who survived the bombings. They show not only how difficult times were during the war, they also offer an insight into the political and economic structures which affected people's lives in the cities. They describe the problems of distributing food and commodities in the big cities, the difficulties of commuting to school or work, life at home or within the neighbourhood and block associations, political indoctrination and the mass media and many other aspects. One of the earliest and most interesting is the series on the effects of the air raids on Tōkyō, which is well compiled and full of sources (Tōkyō kūshū o kiroku suru kai 1975). Similar series have since been published in many other cities. Besides series explicitly dealing with the wartime experience, there are also several histories of big cities, towns and villages, published every year in Japan, which contain one or two volumes dedicated to the suffering of the people during the war or which at least refer to the wartime in one or two chapters. In many cases interesting insights into the daily lives of all kinds of people are thereby provided. Most publications dealing with local aspects of Japan's war economy have been published in (local) journals, sometimes only privately, but they are too numerous to be listed here. Not many foreign researchers were aware of the various sources published in Japan in the past. One who took up the topic of the people's experiences in wartime Japan and also included the various aspects of daily economic life was Thomas R.H. Havens in his *Valley of Darkness* (1978). Slightly later Ben-Ami Shillony (1981) gave some valuable insights into wartime economic aspects, although his main interest was in the political and cultural sphere.

A much broader look at the period in question was taken by the Institute of Social Science/University of Tōkyō in a series on Fascism, which considered not only Japan but also countries like Germany and Italy. The results of a joint research project on Japan's war economy were published in 1979 (Shakai kagaku kenkyū-sho 1979). Individual chapters concentrate on the collapse of Japan's war economy, the ideological background of the army in connection with a controlled economy, the economic policy of Takahashi Korekiyo, the public financing of Fascism, the industrial structure during the war, the 'New Order', and the controlled agriculture during the war.

There are not many monographs on individual aspects of the wartime economy. Some authors who were involved in the implementation of wartime economic policies and/or certain mobilization plans reveal interesting details about their work during the wartime and are often able to provide reliable figures as well. The 'Secret history of Japan's war economy' by Tanaka Hobuichi (1975) is a very good example of such works based on the author's own experience.

In the 1970s the broader aspects of Japan's war economy also came into focus. The most comprehensive work on these aspects was written by Kobayashi Hideo (1975). In it, he discusses the role of the colonies (Taiwan, Korea), Manchuria, Northern China and the occupied territories in the manufacturing of arms, as well as the provision of food, raw materials and labour for the Japanese arms industry. A broad database makes this book an invaluable source even today.

Those looking for a reference book about the wartime bureaucratic system and the people employed at the various governmental agencies should not miss the huge volume prepared by a study group on the prewar bureaucratic system (Senzen-ki kanryō-sei kenkyū-kai 1981).

As we have seen, studies on Japan's war economy were not the main focus of scholarly attention in the 1960s and 1970s. The situation changed at the beginning of the 1980s. Scholars dealing with the subject up to then had usually experienced the war at first hand. Some of the authors had been employed by the government during the war and/or had been involved in the wartime planning process or other aspects of the arms industry. Scholars whose works have been published from the 1980s onwards usually are not troubled by such a burden. They can look on the wartime economy as on any other subject of study. Their studies relied heavily on the enormous work the former generation had done by excavating, compiling and publishing the many series and monographs containing sources on the wartime period as has been mentioned. Thereby a good basis for further studies had been provided, and a more differentiated look into the various aspects of the war economy was rendered possible.

Not only were specialized studies on manufacturing industries during the period of the controlled economy made possible (e.g., Nagashima 1986), but also the concentration on one industrial group (e.g., Saitō 1987, which contains a good bibliography on several of the 'New *zaibatsu*') gave deeper insights into the wartime economy. Nagashima, for instance, considers how a controlled economy could gain ground in a capitalist environment, how such a development was possible under the guidance of bureaucrats who in one form or another represented the state. He thus focuses on the relation, or rather, the tension between the state (bureaucracy) and private capital. Saitō on the other hand, experienced in writing corporate histories, concentrates on one industrial leader (Ōkōchi Kazuo) and his ideas on industry, technology and management and his relation to the industrial group Riken, which had the Institute of Physical and Chemical Research (*Ri-kagaku kenkyū-sho*) as its core. Shimotani Masahiro (1990) offers a broader view on several industry sectors (including the heavy industry, iron and steel, chemicals, textiles, coal and electric power) of Japan's war economy. Other specialized studies concentrate on specific aspects of the war economy, like Furukawa's 1992 publication, which addresses the 'New Order' and especially the role of the Planning Board during the war.

Despite this trend towards specialized studies highlighting one or the other aspect of the wartime economy or industry, recent research has gone in two directions. One direction questions the character of Japanese capitalism and tries to re-define economic and industrial development by including the developments in prewar Japan as well as changes during the war. The other trend, which at first glance looks very similar but reflects a different paradigm, concentrates on the question of continuity and discontinuity in economic development.

The representative work for the first of these trends was written by Kobayashi Hideo (1995a). By taking up the slogan of 'Japan Inc.' (a catchphrase already established by the American Ministry of Commerce in 1972) he puts the reformist bureaucrats in the center of his study. He shows how their experiences in Manchuria (e.g., Kishi Nobusuke, who became vice minister of the Ministry of Munitions in 1943 and Prime Minister after the war) were used to form a specific economic and industrial system during the war. Kobayashi, besides doing research on Southeast Asia following his studies on the Great East Asian Co-Prosperity Sphere, did research on Manchuria and the bureaucrats themselves. Based on such research he published a most valuable biography of one of the most influential planners and bureaucrats of the 1930s and 1940s, Miyazaki Masayoshi (Kobayashi 1995b).

The other trend is best represented by a publication by Okazaki Tetsuji and Okuno Masahiro (1993) on the historical origins of the contemporary Japanese economic system, which includes several articles on various aspects of the wartime economy and its relevance for the postwar period. Another representative book was written by Noguchi Yukio (1995). The book's title, *1940nen taisei* (The 1940 system) soon became a catchphrase. A collection of articles published by Amemiya Shōichi in 1997 also reflects the above trend.

Apart from these trends a lot of other publications depicting Japan's war economy as a whole or concentrating on specific aspects have recently been published. Among them Hara Akira's volume on Japan's wartime economy

(Hara 1995), which is a balanced collection of articles on industrial mobilization, the reform of the financial system, problems of foreign economic relations, the subcontracting system, labour mobilization and food control should be mentioned. Other aspects relating to economic development during the war can be found in more general publications by a study group on wartime social problems (Senji-ka Nihon shakai kenkyū-kai 1992) and by Yamanouchi *et al.* (1995).

The books mentioned by no means cover the whole range of publications concerning aspects of Japan's war economy which have been published since the end of the Second World War; however, they can indicate some further reading. Most of the books mentioned have bibliographical notes. Apart from these books many articles on the subject have been published during the last decade, but these are too numerous to be referred to in detail here.

However, there is one surprising point for those interested in the subject, and this is the gap between the state of the research in Japan on the one side and in Europe and the USA on the other. Hardly anything published outside Japan deals extensively with the war economy. Nakamura's *Lectures on Modern Japanese Economic History, 1926–1994* (Nakamura 1994; originally publ. in 1986 as *Shōwa keizai-shi* [Economic history of the Shōwa period]) includes chapters on 'Guns and Butter' and 'The Claw Marks of War'. He examines the emergence of wartime economic control, arguing that the economic institutions which developed in the prewar and wartime period prepared the ground for Japan's successful development after the war. This view represents one of the recent trends in the study of Japan's wartime economy as mentioned above. In the context of prewar and wartime economic policy, one should not overlook the relevant chapters in Chalmers Johnsons important book on the MITI (Johnson 1982) 'The Rise of Industrial Policy', the 'Economic General Staff' and 'From the Ministry of Munitions to MITI'. Johnson, too, depicts a certain continuity from prewar to postwar times.

Japan's technological development during the war – a field almost entirely neglected by non-Japanese writers – has only recently come into focus. Tessa Morris-Suzuki (1994) and Richard J. Samuels (1994) both deal briefly with questions of wartime technology. In a short chapter Morris-Suzuki concentrates on science and technology between 1937 and 1945 in a broader sense, thereby criticizing the hitherto dichotomous perspective of a 'militarised, imperialistic and semi-modern Japan' versus the 're-constructed Japan of the high-growth era', with the Second World War as the dividing-point (Morris-Suzuki 1994: 143). Samuels also shows clearly that earlier analysts' views were wrong when they entirely ignored developments made in the Japanese industry during the war. Although technical knowledge often remained shallow and disjointed, Japan had been able to achieve Western technological standards (Samuels 1994: 128). Thereby the foundations essential for technological progress in the postwar era had been laid.

These recent publications show clearly that representative writers from both sides, the Japanese and the Western, agree in rejecting the former view of a wartime Japan being neither part of the prewar nor the postwar era, but something like an 'unlucky incident' which had lead Japan into a dead-end road. A view of continuities and change within the economic development of Japan which includes the wartime period like any other period of Japan's development promises a much more accurate view. This also applies to a famous economist who contributed to industrial policy in Japan in the prewar as well as the postwar period. Bai Gao (1994) – by taking up the example of Arisawa Hiromi (1896–1988) – shows how the theory of 'managed economy' and its influence on practical policy contributed to the continuity of Japanese capitalism before and after the war. His article is one of the rare examples explaining economic developments by also taking into account that an influential person's views are shaped by the intellectual environment of the time. Thus the author offers a deeper insight into the mental shaping forces which usually cannot be traced so easily.

A big task still remains for the Western scholar despite the numerous books published on Japan's war economy by Japanese authors. Questions asked by Western scholars concerning their countries' respective war economies have often not been taken up and applied to the Japanese example and vice versa. Thus a continuous exchange on the topic could further deepen researchers' insights into a period that had a major influence on both economic and political and social change in the twentieth century.

REFERENCES

Andō Yoshio (1987) *Taiheiyō sensō no keizai-shiteki kenkyū – Nihon shihon-shugi no tenkai katei* (A study of the Pacific war from the standpoint of economic history – the process of development of Japanese capitalism), Tōkyō: Tōkyō Daigaku Shuppan-kai.

Amemiya Shōichi (1997) *Senji sengo taisei-ron* (Studies on the wartime and postwar system), Tōkyō: Iwanami Shoten.

Bai Gao (1994) 'Arisawa Hiromi and his theory of a managed economy', *The Journal of Japanese Studies*, vol. 20, no. 9: 115–53 (Winter 1994).

Bisson, Thomas A. (1945) *Japan's War Economy*, New York: Institute of Pacific Relations.

—— (1954) *Zaibatsu Dissolution in Japan*, Berkeley: University of California Press.

Bōei-chō, Bōei-kenshū-sho, Senshi-shitsu (Defence Agency, Defence Research Institute, War History Room) (1967) *Rikugun gunju dōin (1) Keikaku-hen* (The army's mobilization (1) – Planning), (Senshi sōsho), Tōkyō: Asagumo Shinbun-sha.

Bōei-chō, Bōei-kenshū-sho, Senshi-shitsu (Defence Agency, Defence Research Institute, War History Room) (1969) *Kaigun gunju dōin (1)* (The navy's mobilization [1]), (Senshi sōsho), Tōkyō: Asagumo Shinbun-sha.

Bōei-chō, Bōei-kenshū-sho, Senshi-shitsu (Defence Agency, Defence Research Institute, War History Room) (1970) *Rikugun gunju dōin (2) Jisshi-hen* (The army's mobilization [2] – Execution), (Senshi sōsho), Tōkyō: Asagumo Shinbun-sha.

Bōei-chō, Bōei-kenshū-sho, Senshi-shitsu (Defence Agency, Defence Research Institute, War History Room) (1975) *Kaigun gunju dōin (2)* (The navy's mobilization (2)), (Senshi sōsho), Tōkyō: Asagumo Shinbun-sha.

Chō Yukio and Sumiya Kazuhiko (eds) (1971) *Kindai Nihon keizai shisō-shi II* (History of modern Japanese economic thought, part 2) (Kindai Nihon shisō-shi taikei, vol. 6), Tōkyō: Yuhikaku.

Cohen, Jerome B. (1949) *Japan's Economy in War and Reconstruction*, Minneapolis: University of Minnesota Press.

Daniels, Gordon (ed.) (1981) *A Guide to the Reports of the United States Strategic Bombing Survey*, Royal Historical Society Guides & Handbooks 12, London: Offices of the Royal Historical Society.

Furukawa Takahisa (1992) *Shōwa senchū-ki no sōgō kokusaku kikan* (Comprehensive national policy bodies during the Shōwa period war), Tōkyō: Yoshikawa Kōbun-kan.

Hara Akira (1976) 'Senji tōsei keizai no kaishi' (The introduction of wartime controlled economy), in *Iwanami kōza Nihon rekishi* vol. 20 – Kindai 7 (Iwanami series on Japanese history vol. 20 – Modern Japan part 7), Tōkyō: Iwanami Shoten, pp. 217–68.

—— (ed.) (1995) *Nihon no senji keizai – keikaku to shijō* (Japan's wartime economy – planning and markets), Tōkyō: Tōkyō Daigaku Shuppan-kai.

Havens, Thomas R.H. (1978) *Valley of Darkness*, New York: Norton (reprint: Lanham/New York/London: University Press of America 1986).

Ishikawa Junkichi (1975) *Kokka sōdōin-shi* (History of national mobilization), 11 vols, Tōkyō: Kokka Sōdōin-shi Kankō-kai (reprint: 1982).

Johnson, Chalmers (1982) *MITI and the Japanese Miracle. The Growth of Industrial Policy, 1925–1975*, Stanford, Cal.: Stanford University Press.

Johnston, Bruce F. (1953) *Japanese Food Management in World War II*, Stanford, Cal.: Stanford University Press.

Kobayashi Hideo (1975) *'Dai-Tō-A kyōei-ken' no keisei to hōkai* (Formation and collapse of the Great East Asian Co-Prosperity Sphere), Tōkyō: Ochanomizu Shobo.

—— (1995a) *'Nihon kabushiki kaisha' no Shōwa-shi* (The History of 'Japan Inc.' during the Shōwa period), Tōkyō: Sōgen-sha.

—— (1995b) *'Nihon kabushiki kaisha' o tsukutta otoko – Miyazaki Masayoshi no shōgai* (The man who built 'Japan Inc.' – The life of Miyazaki Masayoshi), Tōkyō: Shogakkan.

MacIsaac, David (1969) 'The United States Strategic Bombing Survey, 1944–1947', unpublished PhD thesis, Duke University.

Morris-Suzuki, Tessa (1994) *The Technological Transformation of Japan. From the Seventeenth to the Twenty-first Century*, Cambridge: Cambridge University Press.

Nagashima Osamu (1986) *Nihon senji tekkō tōsei seiritsu-shi* (History of the establishment of a controlled iron and steel industry during Japan's wartime), Kyōto: Hōritusu Bunka-sha.

Nakamura Takafusa (1974) *Nihon no keizai tōsei – Zenji-zengo no keiken to kyōkun* (The controlled economy of Japan – Experience and lessons from wartime and after the war), Nikkei shinsho no. 208, Tōkyō: Nihon Keizai Shinbun-sha.

—— (1977) 'Sensō keizai to sono hōkai' (War economy and its collapse), in *Iwanami kōza Nihon rekishi,* vol. 21 – Kindai 8 (Iwanami series on Japanese history vol. 21 – Modern Japan part 8), Tōkyō: Iwanami Shoten, pp. 109–60.

—— (1994) *Lectures on Modern Japanese Economic History, 1926–1994*, Tōkyō: LTCB International Library Foundation.

—— and Hara Akira (1970) *Kokka sōdōin (1) Keizai* (National mobilization part 1 – Economy), Gendai-shi shiryō, vol. 43, Tōkyō: Misuzu Shobō.

Nihon Ginkō, Chōsa Kyoku (Bank of Japan, Research Department) (1961–74) *Nihon kinyū-shi shiryō – Shōwa hen* (Sources of Japanese Financial History, Shōwa period), 35 vols, Tōkyō: Ōkura-shō Insatsu-kyoku.

Nihon kindai shiryō kenkyū-kai (Association for Studies of Modern Japanese History) (1970) *Nichi-Man zaisei keizai kenkyū-kai shiryū* (Sources of the Japan-Manchuria Finance and Economics Society), 3 vols, Tōkyō: Tōkyō Daigaku Kyōyō-gakubu, Shakaikagaku.

Noguchi Yukio (1995) *1940nen taisei – saraba 'Senji keizai'* (The 1940 system: Farewell to the 'war economy'), Tōkyō: Tōyō Keizai Shinpō-sha.

Ōhara shakai mondai kenkyū-sho) (Ōhara Institute for Social Research) (1964) *Taiheiyō sensō-ka no rōdō-sha jōtai* (Labour conditions during World War II), Tōkyō: Tōyō Keizai Shinpō-sha.

Okazaki Tetsuji and Okuno Masahiro (eds) (1993) *Gendai Nihon keizai shisutemu no genryū* (Historical origins of the contemporary Japanese economic system), Tōkyō: Nihon Keizai Shinbun-sha.

Ōkura-shō (1955–65) *Shōwa zaisei-shi* (History of public finance during the Shōwa period), 18 vols, Tōkyō: Tōyō Keizai Shinpō-sha.

—— (1976–84) *Shōwa zaisei-shi* (History of public finance during the Shōwa period), 20 vols, Tōkyō: Tōyō Keizai Shinpō-sha.

Saitō Satoshi (1987) *Shinkō kontserun Riken no kenkyū* (Studies on the new konzern Riken), Tōkyō: Taihei-sha.

Samuels, Richard J. (1994) *'Rich Nation, Strong Army': National Security and the Technological Transformation of Japan*, Ithaca and London: Cornell University Press.

Senji-ka Nihon shakai kenkyū-kai (1992) *Senji-ka no Nihon* (Japan in wartime), Kyōto: Kōro-sha.

Senzen-ki kanryō-sei kenkyō-kai (1981) *Senzen-ki Nihon kanryō-sei no seido – soshiki – jinji* (The system, structure and people of the prewar Japanese bureaucracy), Tōkyō: Tōkyō Daigaku Shuppan-kai.

Shakai kagaku kenkyū-sho (Institute of Social Science, University of Tōkyō) (1979) *Senji Nihon keizai* (Japan's economy in wartime), (Fashizumu-ki no kokka to shakai 2), Tōkyō: Tōkyō Daigaku Shuppan-kai.

Shillony, Ben-Ami (1981) *Politics and Culture in Wartime Japan*, Oxford: Clarendon Press.

Shimotani Masahiro (ed.) (1990) *Senji keizai to Nihon kigyō* (Japanese firms and the war economy), Kyōto: Shōwa-dō.

Tanaka Hobuichi (1975) *Nihon sensō keizai hisshi* (Secret history of Japan's war economy), Tōkyō: Konpyuuta eeji-sha.

Tōkyō kūshū o kiroku suru kai (Study group for recording the air raids on Tōkyō) (1975) *Tōkyō kūshū – sensai shi* (Tōkyō air raid – war damage records), 5 vols, Tōkyō: Kōdan-sha.

Tōyō Keizai Shinpō-sha (1950) *Shōwa sangyō-shi* (History of the industry during the Shōwa period), 3 vols, Tōkyō: Tōyō Keizai Shinpō-sha.

Yamanouchi Yasushi, J. Victor Koschmann and Narita Ryūichi (eds) (1995) *Sōryoku-sen to gendai-ka* (Total war and modernization), Tōkyō: Kashiwa Shobō.

INDEX

Note: Page numbers relating to figures and tables are shown in *italics*